MEMOIRS OF THE REIGN

OF

KING GEORGE THE THIRD

IN FOUR VOLUMES

VOL. III.

Sir J. Reynolds, Pinxt.

Edmund Burke.

HORACE WALPOLE

MEMOIRS OF THE REIGN OF KING GEORGE THE THIRD

FIRST PUBLISHED BY SIR
DENIS LE MARCHANT BART.
AND NOW RE-EDITED BY

G. F. RUSSELL BARKER

WITH SIXTEEN PORTRAITS

VOLUME III

BOOKS FOR LIBRARIES PRESS
FREEPORT, NEW YORK

First Published 1894

Reprinted 1970

STANDARD BOOK NUMBER:
8369-5489-0

LIBRARY OF CONGRESS CATALOG CARD NUMBER:
70-126262

PRINTED IN THE UNITED STATES OF AMERICA

CONTENTS

OF

THE THIRD VOLUME

CHAPTER I

CHAPTER II

CHAPTER III

CHAPTER IV

CHAPTER V

CHAPTER VI

CHAPTER VII

CHAPTER VIII

CHAPTER IX

CHAPTER X

CHAPTER XI

CHAPTER XII

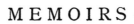

MEMOIRS

MEMOIRS

OF THE REIGN OF

KING GEORGE THE THIRD

CHAPTER I

Debates on East Indian Affairs.—Wilkes and the Duke of Grafton.—
Expulsion of the Jesuits from Spain.—Parliamentary Discussions.—
Attempts to construct a new Administration in Prospective.—The Court
of Proprietors vote themselves a Dividend in spite of the Ministry.—
Extraordinary Conduct of Townshend in the House of Commons.

1767

I HAVE said that the Opposition, perceiving how much
the tide ran against them, determined to attempt putting
an end to the East Indian business the moment the
examination was closed ; a weak and silly plan, that
betrayed a jealousy of their own cause. Sir William
Meredith fixed on the 14th for making that attempt.
Lord Bute had been seriously alarmed, and he and the
Duke of Grafton exerted themselves to defeat the Opposition. Beckford observed that the evidence had proved
all he had asserted, and said he intended to make some
motions in consequence, but the examination had been so
voluminous, he had not had time to digest his matter.
Sir William Meredith said, he doubted whether it was fit
to proceed at all further or not : that it had been Beckford's
own fault if the examination had been voluminous. His
questions to the evidences had been unjust, and would
not have been admitted in a court of justice. It were
better to stop, if violence alone was to be the consequence.

The Ministers in the Treasury ought to make the motions, if any were proper ; but *they* did not seem to be trusted in this question. The Company would not make proposals while a doubt subsisted of their having any property in the territorial acquisitions. He did not know what motion to make ; he thought that the Speaker should leave the chair. Townshend and Conway spoke for allowing more time ; Grenville for going into the Committee to see if any one had any proposal to make. Beckford declared he would never propose any question of forfeiture. Norton, in a very indefinite speech, said, if the Company had exceeded their charter, the Crown could call them to account. That the acquisitions were not conquest, because the King was not at war with the Mogul : they seemed to be only plunder. It seemed to be difficult to know judicially what to do with those acquisitions. They ought to be restored, but nobody wished to see that. The Attorney-General[1] desired Norton to give his opinion how to try the case. He refused, saying, 'It will be alleged that a prerogative lawyer has pointed out to the Crown a way of getting possession.' The Attorney-General showed that, by the nature of a process in the courts of law, it was impossible for the King to recover his right by law, supposing the territory were his by his prerogative, or by the forfeiture of the Company. There must be an information of intrusion : a jury must be chosen where the lands lie, and yet where there is no sheriff. The sheriff must deliver the profits ; must appoint a receiver for the three provinces, who must give security for two years in a court of law to examine the necessary witnesses. The court would not order possession to be delivered. Then there must be a sequestration of the Company's effects. Having thus exposed with much humour the fruitlessness of a legal suit, he said if nobody else would, he would move for a bill to prevent the Company from making a dividend beyond such a sum without consent of Parliament. It

[1] Sir William de Grey.—E.

was necessary to frighten them : he would not violate their charter, but as he thought they had no right to their territorial revenues, *he would take the half of them.* Wedderburn replied, that an action might lie against the Company as a corporation : all he desired was to ascertain the right ; the Legislature would settle the rest. Grenville declaimed against any violence, and said with passion, *the view was not to vest money in the public, but in the Crown ;* and a profuse Minister had been found who wanted to give four millions to the King, a year before the general election. He should advise to take this money by taxation. Conway said boldly, he should insist on *security* that this money, if taken, should be vested in the public, not in the Crown. Taxation was like Mr. Grenville's Morocco politics. Burke pleaded that in the last charter the Crown had granted the Company privileges as indemnification : what could that mean but territory, revenue, and commerce? Yet he owned there was a political reserve in the charters.

The debate lasted till one in the morning, when the Opposition were beaten by 213 to 157. After the division I told the Duke of Richmond that, notwithstanding our victory, I was as ready as ever to unite Conway and his Grace's friends on the American affairs. The King was informed of Grenville's apprehensions that the money to be taken from the Company was designed for his Majesty, and highly resented the insinuation—perhaps resented Grenville's dislike of such a disposition. There wanted no new aggravation of Grenville's offences. His tediousness in the closet had left a lasting impression ; and an ill-judged obstinacy of economy in an article of no great moment, but which was ever before the King's eyes, could not be forgotten. When his Majesty took in a portion of the Green Park to form a new garden for Buckingham House, the fields on the opposite side of the road were to be sold ; the price twenty thousand pounds. This sum Grenville refused to issue from the Treasury. The ground was sold to builders, and a new row of houses, each of which overlooked the King in his private walks, was erected, to his great annoyance.

Wilkes had come over the last year, during the recess of Parliament, to try to obtain his pardon, and by the Duke of Grafton's desire wrote a very submissive letter to his Grace, to be shown to the King. The Duke then told him his pardon could not be obtained without the concurrence of Lord Chatham, and wished him to write to the latter too. Wilkes, who had been abandoned and stigmatized by Lord Chatham, though formerly intimate with and flattered by him, had too much spirit to throw himself at Chatham's feet, and refused : but, irritated at his disappointment, he published an exaggerated account of that transaction, with unjust severity on the Duke,[1]— and returned to Paris. His Grace, Lord Rockingham, and others of that connexion, had yearly contributed the sum of £1000 or £1100 to his support. Mr. Fitzherbert [2] collected their donations. It was now the season of collection. In defiance of the Duke, Wilkes sent over a new abusive pamphlet against the Administration.[3]

March 16th.—The Houses adjourned for the holidays.

At this period happened the sudden and total expulsion

---

[1] The pamphlet alluded to was intituled 'A Letter to his Grace the Duke of Grafton, First Commissioner of his Majesty's Treasury.' Editions were printed at London, Paris, and Berlin. It bears with less severity on the Duke than on Lord Chatham, who is held up to public ridicule and scorn as an apostate to the cause of liberty, and 'the abject crouching deputy of the proud Scot,' whom he is represented as having previously persecuted and insulted. This virulent and tedious invective concludes thus :—' But I have done with Lord Chatham ; I leave him to the poor consolation of a place, a pension, and a peerage, for which he has sold the confidence of a great nation. Pity shall find and weep over him.' It is altogether a poor performance. The only part now of any interest is the narrative it contains of Wilkes's arrest and examination for the publication of the *North Briton*, in 1763.—(Almon's *Correspondence of Wilkes*, 1805, vol. iii. pp. 178-220.—Almon's *Biographical Anecdotes*, vol. i. p. 6.)—L. M.

[2] William Fitzherbert, M.P. for Bramber, 1761-2 ; for Derby from 1762 until his death on 2nd January 1772. He was appointed a Commissioner of the Board of Trade in 1765. His youngest son was created Baron St. Helens in 1791.—E.

[3] *A Complete Collection of the Genuine Papers, Letters, etc., in the Case of John Wilkes, Esq.*, Paris, 1767. 12mo.

of the Jesuits from Spain,—a measure so unexpected by
them, that they were made prisoners in their convents
throughout the kingdom, without having had the
least intimation of their intended ruin ; a moment of
history that will ever be remarkable. The order, renowned for their subtlety and art, dreaded for the empire
they had obtained over the consciences of princes and
private persons, and seated in the most bigoted country
upon earth, had neither sagacity to surmise their impend-
ing destruction, nor one penitent so weak and devout as
to give them intelligence of what, for a whole year, was in
agitation against them. That fabric of human policy and
wickedness fell to the ground in an instant. Not a murmur was heard against the rigour of the sentence, though
they were conducted to the sea-coasts like exiled male-
factors, thrust into ships, and sent like cargoes of damaged
goods to their proprietor, the Pope. Clement XIII., though
an enthusiast, could not receive them. They were at
last despatched to Corsica, one and all, after being
tossed about at sea for *some months,* stowed in the
narrow compass of a few vessels,—a fate so severe, that
the greatest enemy of Catholic imposition must com-
miserate the sufferers.[1] However detestable the maxims
of the society, however criminal some of the order might
have been, the greater part were undoubtedly innocent—
many, perhaps, conscientious men ; who, trusting to the
establishment and laws of the country, and believing the
doctrines they had been taught, had entered into religion.
Let the impartial mind weigh the weight of the calamity
that fell like thunder on those poor men ! Torn from the
tranquillity of their convents ; too old or too ignorant to
turn to new professions ; delivered up to an element they
were totally unaccustomed to, sickening with the natural
effect of the waves, and with want of room and air ;

---

[1] Their number was nearly 6000. Lorenzo Ricci, the General of the Order,
was equally responsible with the Pope for repelling them from Civita
Vecchia. His object seemed to have been to arouse public sympathy. The
King of Spain ultimately allowed the survivors a pension of 2 paoli a day.—
Coxe's *Memoirs of the Kings of Spain,* etc. (1813), vol. iii. pp. 328-330.—E.

banished for ever from their country, relations, and friends ;
uncertain to what clime they were driven ; finding with
difficulty one that would receive them, and that one in a
state of war, and the most unwholesome spot in Europe ;
—what a state of lamentation and hopeless misery !
What, too, must the parents and friends of those unhappy
men have felt ?   Could no middle term be found ?   What
a horrible post is that of a minister, when the benefit or
policy of the State calls for such sacrifices !   No doubt
was entertained but that the Court of Madrid had discovered that the Jesuits had been the incendiaries of the
late insurrection there ; [1] and its ministers seemed to have
learnt and imbibed the deep secrecy and resolute vigour of
the Count D'Oyeras, the prime minister of Portugal, the
profoundest and most desperate politician of the age.
From M. de Mello, the Portuguese minister in England,[2]
I received this account of the springs that first gave birth
to that revolution.   When D'Oyeras became all-powerful
at Lisbon, he found the Portuguese settlements in America,
that bordered on the French, extremely neglected.   Apprehending a rupture with France from that quarter, he
sent his own brother to examine the Portuguese possessions.
At the same period Ferdinand's Queen, who held the reins
of the Spanish monarchy during the incapacity of her
husband, had made a treaty with Portugal for an exchange
of lands, in which Spain would have been gainer ; intending to involve the Court of Lisbon in a quarrel with the
Jesuits of Paraguay, part of which country was to be
ceded to the Portuguese.   The event happened as she had
foreseen ; the Jesuits refused the exchange ; and, imputing

---

[1] This insurrection had been directed against the Marquis de Squillaci, the
Italian Minister of Charles III., who had issued an unpopular edict forbidding
the use of flapped hats and long cloaks.—E.

[2] M. de Mello afterwards became Minister of Marine in Portugal, under
the Marquis of Pombal, and held that post several years with great reputation.
His ability and experience in business obliged the Court to retain him in
the Government after the disgrace of Pombal, notwithstanding his connexions
with that statesman, and the known liberality of his opinions.—(Despatch
from Mr. Walpole, minister at Lisbon, in John Smith's *Memoirs of the
Marquis of Pombal* (1843), vol. ii. pp. 303-5.—L. M.

the machination to D'Oyeras, endeavoured to excite the confessors of both Kings and Queens to attempt the ruin of that minister.[1] This step drew upon them the wrath of

[1] The exchange to which Walpole refers was not accomplished without serious difficulty, the Indian Militia raised by the Jesuits having long successfully resisted the Spanish and Portuguese forces employed to carry the treaty into effect. The transaction has generally been ascribed to the intrigues of the Dominicans, the ancient enemies of the Jesuits, and their competitors for spiritual dominion in the New World. The conspiracy of Tavora quickly followed, and furnished Pombal with the ostensible pretext he so ardently desired, for the expulsion of the order from Portugal (in 1759), and it also shook their influence throughout Europe. They lingered on in France, proscribed by the Parliaments, and odious to the great majority of the people, until 1764, when the edict against them was wrung from Louis xv. by the importunities of Choiseul. The same minister has been supposed to have determined the Court of Spain to pursue a similiar course ; and no doubt his influence and that of his master were used for that purpose. But the real author of the bold and statesmanlike measure described in the text, was Don Pedro D'Aranda, the Captain-General, and President of the Council of Castile. During a lengthened absence from Spain, he had formed in the society of Montesquieu, D'Alembert, and Diderot, as well as of Frederic the Great, plans of national reform, which he knew to be incompatible with the existence of the Jesuits ; and from the moment of his accession to power he seems to have been bent on their destruction. His manly and persuasive eloquence, a mind full of resources, and a character indomitably resolute, gained him an extraordinary sway over the divided counsels of an ignorant and imbecile Court. The Jesuits had irritated Charles by their intrigues, both at Rome and Madrid, during the reign of his predecessor. Their interference with the various departments of the State had gradually identified them, in the opinion of the people, with the grievous abuses under which the country suffered, and all the rising talent of Spain was secretly opposed to them. D'Aranda boldly arraigned them as the instigators of the insurrection against Squillaci, which, for some hours, had placed the royal family and the capital at the mercy of the mob. He availed himself of the influence he had acquired by quelling that insurrection to press the charge with his characteristic impetuosity. The alarm of the King, and the confidence of the accuser, supplied the deficiency of conclusive proofs, and D'Aranda prevailed.

No sooner was the edict obtained, than it appeared that the most minute arrangements had been made throughout Spain for its immediate execution by Campomanes, then a young man, and lately appointed to the ministry ; and the skill with which this was accomplished is still cited by the native historians as the masterpiece of that statesman, high as his reputation deservedly stands in his own country as an economist, a writer, and a minister. See the Supplementary Chapter by Muriel to the French translation of Coxe's *History of the Spanish Bourbons* (1827), vol. v. pp. 31-67, one of the most valuable of that work.—L. M.

that vindictive man, who, possessing all the spirit of intrigue which seemed to have deserted the fathers, never stopped till he had accomplished the destruction of the order. Had D'Oyeras [1] been a Jesuit instead of a statesman, the Jesuits might have subsisted till the Roman Church itself shall fall like other structures of human invention. So true it is, what I have more than once remarked in these pages, that great benefits are seldom conferred on mankind by good men. It is when the interests and passions of ambition, villainy, and desperation clash, that some general advantage is struck out.

On the 28th, when the Houses re-assembled, nothing was ready for their discussion. The Duke of Grafton had passed the holidays at Newmarket, and when he returned, could not obtain admission to Lord Chatham. The Directors of the East India Company, alarmed at the strength of the evidence against them, had determined to make a compromise or bargain with the Government; and, fearing Lord Chatham would reject their proposal, had sent severally round to the members of the Cabinet, to desire to treat. At a Council held the evening before the meeting of the Parliament, Conway brought them all over to his opinion for a treaty; and he, with the Duke of Grafton, and Charles Townshend, were commissioned by the rest to negotiate. The last was grown a great advocate for the Company, and said, that now, on the death of his wife's mother,[2] the Duchess of Argyle, he himself was become a considerable proprietor of India

---

[1] Sebastian Joseph de Carvalho a Mello Count D'Oyeras, and Marquis of Pombal, was born in 1699, and died in 1782, in his 83rd year. He had been Minister and master of Portugal from 1750 to 1777—a period rendered interesting by his vigorous efforts for the regeneration of his country. This was an undertaking, however, beyond the power of any individual, however eminent or able, to accomplish; and the harsh and often unprincipled means he employed to attain his ends made his reforms odious to a large portion of the community, and precipitated their decline from the moment that he had fallen into disgrace.—L. M.

[2] Jane Warburton, widow of John, Duke of Argyle, and mother of Caroline, Countess Dowager of Dalkeith, who had married for her second husband Charles Townshend, and inherited a great fortune on her mother's death.

stock—all the truth was, that he intended to be so; the Duchess had not a shilling in that fund. He had acted with the same lightness when, as Chancellor of the Exchequer, he had been to open the Budget before the holidays: he had caused Onslow to make his excuse on pretence of illness, and then appeared there walking about the House. Two days after he did open it—but of that more hereafter, when I come to speak of his proposed taxes.

March 29th was the day appointed at the desire of the Opposition for the call of the House,[1] and Conway had proposed they should go on the India business on that day, but Grenville had said he would insist on the House being called over. They now would have put off the call for a week to keep the members of their party in town, but Conway fixed them to their first proposal, and on a division carried it by a majority of fifty. Rigby then said, 'We will put it off for a fortnight;' 'No,' said Conway, '*I* will do that, for the Indian business is in a more promising way than ever.' Grenville was thunderstruck: Conway's spirit showed how much he was pleased with his triumph—Grenville being the only man who had ever inspired him with animosity.

The next morning he came to me early, and said, the Duke of Grafton had told him things could not go on as they were; that Lord Chatham must either come forth, or quit; and he thought would do the latter. Conway therefore desired I would go to the Duke of Richmond, and say that I had persuaded him to let me come to his Grace and tell him that if he and his friends would not join Grenville, he (Conway) would assist them in a new Administration, but would take no civil place under any; should like to be Secretary at War, and Minister of the House of Commons, if Townshend had his wish and was created a peer. His idea was, that he might be Minister

---

[1] A call of the House was last enforced on 19th April 1836. (*Parliamentary Debates*, Third Series, vol. xxxii. 1195-6. See May's *Treatise on the Law, Privileges, Proceedings, and Usage of Parliament* (1883), pp. 230-2.—E.

for the Military Department, if Lord Granby[1] could be removed.

I said, all this was idle ; that neither the King nor the House of Commons would come into it. That if he would not be First Minister, Grenville must. That he (Conway) must take the Treasury, or nothing would last; Lord Rockingham's Administration had not lasted a year, though with the assistance of the Duke of Grafton and his friends, and with the hopes of acquiring Lord Chatham ; now would have neither of them. He could not be Minister of the House of Commons without power ; had Lord Rockingham imparted any to him before? He confessed he should like some share of power, and I thought would not be sorry to have the whole if Lord Rockingham could be brought to waive it. I told him I would carry no such message as he proposed, for should it afterwards prove necessary to place him at the head of the Treasury, the Duke of Richmond and Lord Rockingham might say I had given them false hopes and deceived them. Conway replied, all he meant was to keep them from Grenville, whom he feared they would join. I saw no occasion, I said, for any message : Rockingham and his friends would be rejoiced to have him whenever he would go to them ; but I would propose nothing so ridiculous as Rockingham and Dowdeswell over again. He said, I only refused because I wished him Minister in some other system, but he would *never more be of any but with his old friends.* It was all, I replied, that I desired too ; our only difference was, that I chose they should act under him, not he under them, which would never do. In the meantime I would positively carry no message. A few days after I gave him my reasons in writing, and convinced him. He then proposed to be Secretary of State for America,[2] which I approved.

---

[1] John Manners, Marquis of Granby, the eldest son of John, third Duke of Rutland, was Commander-in-Chief from August 1766 to January 1770.—E.

[2] A Secretary of State for the American or Colonial Department was appointed in 1768, but the office was abolished in 1782 on the loss of the American Colonies, by 22 Geo. III. c. 82.—E.

It was the sphere in which he might make the greatest figure. His application was indefatigable ; his temper, moderation, attention to the business of others when applied to, and the popularity he had already gained with the Colonies, adapted him peculiarly to that province. We agreed to adjust this plan with Lord Rockingham— but that project, like a thousand others of that season, was disappointed.

The King asked Lord Hertford by what means any composition with the East India Company had been obtained ? He replied, that sensible of his Majesty's difficulties, and fearing that, notwithstanding the right of the Company had been weakened by the examination, the House would never be induced to vote it away ; he and his brother had prevailed on the rest of his Majesty's servants to take the gentler method of treaty. The King owned that he was inclined to keep Lord Chatham, if capable of remaining in place, *having seen how much his Government had been weakened by frequent changes.* He wished that things might remain as they were, at least till the end of the Session, when he might have time to make any necessary alterations. At his levée his Majesty asked James Grenville aloud, how Lord Chatham did ? he replied, 'Better.' The King said, ' If he has lost his fever, I desire to be his physician, and that he would not admit Dr. Addington any more into his house. He shall go into the country for four months ; not so far as Bath, but to Tunbridge.' He repeated the same words publicly to Lord Bristol ; everybody understanding that his Majesty's wish was to retain Lord Chatham.[1]

On the 1st of May Beckford was to have proposed his resolutions; but Crabb Boulton,[2] an India Director,

---

[1] See Lord Bristol's letter to Lord Chatham of the 5th of April, conveying the King's kind message and the King's own letter to Lord Chatham of the 30th of April, to the same effect.—*Chatham Correspondence*, vol. iii. pp. 240, 252. His Majesty appears to have acted most considerately and handsomely towards Lord Chatham throughout his illness.—L. M.

[2] Henry Crabb Boulton, M.P. for Worcester, see *supra*, vol. ii. p. 289. —E.

informing the House that there was now a prospect of accommodation with the Ministry, and that a general court to ratify the terms could not be held till the next week, when he did not doubt but they would approve the plan, which was only temporary, Beckford consented to postpone his motions. Sir W. Meredith called on him to read his questions. Rigby with much roughness said, he believed Beckford had no questions to propose; yet he should have some hopes of the accommodation succeeding, if Mr. Townshend (who was the fittest to be at the head of *that* Administration) would, as Chancellor of the Exchequer, say *he* had hopes. Townshend, with great decency, declared he had. Grenville, who had early in the session declared for a temporary accommodation, was much hampered and hurt: and having nothing to object, reverted to the former wrangle on Morocco politics, and said, that to take by violence was squeezing laws, as Mahometan governments do; but anything might be taken by legal taxation. Conway took this up with infinite humour, ridiculing *legal tyranny*; and as Grenville had asked if Lord Chatham would come into this agreement, said, he hoped it would be no mortification to hear that the Council would be unanimous. He laughed too at Rigby, who had been on the point of saying that Charles Townshend was the fittest man to be at the head of *any* administration; but he had turned round in time and seen his friend Mr. Grenville, or it might have made a fatal difference! Grenville replied angrily, he did not envy any junction between Lord Chatham and Conway: he knew what attempts had been made to disunite him and the Bedfords. Rigby in a greater rage said, nothing should disunite them; (he might have said, *but interest*, which made Rigby leave Grenville in less than two years;) himself had always stuck by his friends—he did not abandon his family and friends. As this was levelled at Conway, it either meant his former separation from the Court when Lord Hertford remained with it, or his disunion now with the Rockinghams, amongst whom was not one of his family but the Duke of Richmond, his wife's son-in-law. Rose Fuller said properly, he did not understand such unparliamentary declarations, as of being actuated only by connexions. Conway protested he did not know what Rigby had meant, who called out contemptuously, 'Oh! I meant nothing.' The House was unanimous for waiting till that day sennight.

When I went to the Duke of Richmond the next morning with Conway's plan of being Secretary for America, I found him displeased at Conway's attack on Grenville and Rigby. I urged, as was true, that they had given the provocation, and that Conway had not said half enough in return. His Grace was hurt too, on thinking that Conway had declared an union with Lord Chatham. I said, I was come a proof of the contrary ; that Conway would oppose the American Bill, and was resolved to resign—though I would not be bound that he would ; that he declared he would not take the Treasury from Lord Rockingham. But I was come, I said, to ask, in case Lord Chatham's health should not permit him to go on, and the King should order Conway to form an Administration, whether his Grace and his friends would take on ? The Duke insisted on Conway's resigning before the end of the session. It was true, in his discontent with Lord Chatham, Conway had told them he would quit, though with no definite time marked ; and it was on that rash promise the Rockinghams built all their hopes of breaking up the Administration—a point I was as eager to prevent the accomplishment of. I replied coldly, it had been usual for ministers to send for opponents : it was new to hear an Opposition order a minister to come to them. 'But, my lord,' said I, 'to cut matters short, Mr. Conway will not resign before the end of the session.' The Duke said, Dowdeswell was reserved, and would not speak out while Mr. Conway remained in place. I laughed, and asked, what it signified what Mr. Dowdeswell would do ? My question was, what the party would do ? He said, they would insist on the dismission of two or three of

Lord Bute's friends. I asked, 'Why?' He said, 'To weaken Bute, whose friends would desert him, if they perceived he could not protect them.' 'Then, my lord,' replied I, 'either he will not let you come in, or will soon turn you out again to prevent that defection.' The Duke was desirous that Grenville should be paymaster. I taxed him with leaning to Grenville. He said, neither he nor his party inclined to Grenville, though the Duke of New-castle laboured for it daily. I asked him why his Grace himself, who had acted so long with Lord Bute was now so averse to him? He said, 'Formerly Lord Holland had swayed him, and that Lord Bute had then followed the same measures as had been observed in the late reign.' I cried, 'Good God! my lord, were general warrants the same measures!' He paused, and said it was true, they had been ill-conducted. The Duke added, his party, Conway and Grenville, would be too strong for Bute. I said, the whole nation united would certainly be too strong for him; but that union would never happen, for there were not places enough to content all. The more his Grace and his friends were averse to Bute, the sooner Grenville would court him: the Tories and the Scotch would always adhere to him. I said at last; 'My lord, I will not be unreasonable; offer Grenville to be Pay-master.' Still the Duke reverted to the dismission of some of Bute's friends. I said, 'If your Grace is in this mind, I will advise Mr. Conway to stay where he is, and not return to a weak and inefficient Opposition. All your Grace says, tends to or must end in making Grenville minister.' He was alarmed, and said, if others would acquiesce, he would not be obstinate.

Here lay the misfortune. The Cavendishes, inveterate to Bute for the affront put on their late brother, saw— would see—no other object of fear. Whereas, though Bute had been the prime source of the attacks made on liberty, his pusillanimity had defeated his own purpose. Grenville, still more arbitrary, was intrepid and inflexible; and whether minister in concert with Bute, or independent of him, was a more formidable enemy to liberty, than an ignorant, trembling, exploded favourite.

Conway was hurt at my report of the above conversation, as I intended he should be. My object was to make the Rockinghams submit to him, or prevent his resignation. He would not hear of Grenville. They stickled for the Bedfords, urging that it would prevent Bute from turning them out again ; whereas, it was more likely to advance it, as Grenville would stoop to Bute rather than remain subordinate to Rockingham and Conway. The intractable man of all was, as usual, Lord John Cavendish. The Duke of Portland himself, inveterate as he was to Bute, had the sense to see that if they came into place before the new Parliament, it would secure all their elections. Nobody's fortune suffered like his Grace's at that ensuing period, by yielding to the obstinacy of Lord John, and the ill-conducted ambition of Lord Rockingham.

Mr. Conway having declared in Council against the intended plan for America, it was determined that Charles Townshend should conduct it through the house, and the 5th of May was settled for his opening it : but his strange irresolution and versatility could not conceal itself, even on so public an occasion. That very morning he pretended to have fallen down-stairs and cut his eye dangerously. On this Lord North was deputed to execute the task, and was going to explain it to the House ; when Rigby, to deprive Lord North of the honour, or to embarrass Townshend, who had shuffled with them, or that Grenville had not determined what part to take, moved, with affected compliments on Townshend's absence, to wait till he could appear, and it was agreed to.

The next day, the Opposition, who, so often foiled, were alert in making a hussar-kind of war, moved by surprise in both Houses to know what had been done on the affair of the Massachusets. In the Commons, the motion made by Grenville was rejected without a division. In the Lords, the majority against the motion was but nine, but with a great majority of proxies.

The East India Company had offered, in consideration
of certain new advantages granted to them in their tea-
trade, to pay four hundred thousand pounds a year for
three years to the Government ; and though this sum was
far below Lord Chatham's first sanguine wishes, the impossibility of their affording more, or the impracticability
of persuading Parliament to extort more, had brought the
bargain nigh to a conclusion ;—when, on the 6th of May,
a general court of proprietors, where faction and speech-
making were as rife as in the House of Commons itself,
suddenly determined to treat themselves with the sweets
of a dividend, before their funds should be tied up for the
purposes of the treaty. The directors had foreseen and
secretly insinuated this to the Ministers for prevention ;
but in the intemperance of the assembly, did not dare to
avow the advice they had given. The dividend, so contrary to the faith of the treaty then pending with, and so
contemptuous of, Parliament, was voted ; and, as if themselves were accountable to none, they dismissed, without
a hearing, five of their own servants, against whom there
were grievous charges.

The indecency and insult of this proceeding raised high
resentment in the House of Commons ; and though
Dempster and W. Burke, two of their own members,
ventured to avow their own share of the criminality,
justifying themselves as proprietors, (a character which
surely, as judges, they ought to have avoided,) yet the
moderation of Conway prevented the House from proceeding to rigour and censure, though he said with firmness,
that if the Company should hang out the flag of defiance,
he should be ready to meet it. The directors were ordered
to give an account the next day of what had passed.

On the 8th the directors appeared at the bar of the
House, and owned that they had disapproved of making
a dividend in the present situation of their affairs, and
pending the negotiation with Parliament. Dyson, on this,
moved for leave to bring in a bill for regulating the
making of dividends.

It was on that day, and on that occasion, that Charles Townshend displayed in a latitude beyond belief the amazing powers of his capacity, and the no less amazing incongruities of his character. He had taken on himself, early in the day, the examination of the Company's conduct; and in a very cool sensible speech on that occasion, and with a becoming consciousness of his own levity, had told the House that he hoped he had atoned for the inconsideration of his past life by the care he had taken of that business. He had scarce uttered this speech, but, as if to atone for that (however false) atonement, he left the House and went home to dinner, not concerning himself with Dyson's motion that was to follow. As that motion was, however, of a novel nature, it produced suspicion, objection, and difficulties. Conway being pressed, and not caring to be the sole champion of an invidious measure, that was in reality not only in Townshend's province, but which he had had a principal hand in framing, sent for him back to the House. He returned about eight in the evening, half-drunk with champagne, and more intoxicated with spirits. He rose to speak without giving himself time to learn, and without caring what had been in agitation, except that the motion had given an alarm. The first thing he did, was to call God to witness that he had not been consulted on the motion, —a confession implying that he was not consulted on a business in his own department; and the more marvellous, as the disgrace of which he seemed to complain or boast of, was absolutely false. There were sitting round him twelve persons who had been in consultation with him that very morning, and with his assistance had drawn up the motion on his own table, and who were petrified at his most unparalleled effrontery and causeless want of truth. When he sat down again, Conway asked him softly, how he could affirm so gross a falsehood? He replied carelessly, ' I thought it would be better to say so ;' but before he sat down, he had poured forth a torrent of wit, parts, humour, knowledge, absurdity, vanity, and fiction, heightened by all the graces of comedy, the happiness of allusion and quotation, and the buffoonery of farce. To the purpose of the question he said not a syllable. It was a descant on the times, a picture of parties, of their leaders, of their hopes, and defects. It was an encomium and a satire on himself; and while he painted the pretensions of birth, riches, connexions, favour, titles; while he affected to praise Lord Rockingham, and that faction, and yet insinuated that nothing but parts like his own were qualified to preside ; and while he less covertly arraigned the wild incapacity of Lord Chatham,[1] he excited such murmurs of wonder, admiration, applause, laughter, pity, and scorn, that nothing was so true as the sentence with which he concluded, when speaking of Government ; he said, it was become what he himself had often been called, a weathercock.

Such was the wit, abundance, and impropriety of this speech, that for some days men could talk or inquire of nothing else. 'Did you hear Charles Townshend's champagne speech?' was the universal question. For myself, I protest it was the most singular pleasure of the kind I ever tasted. The bacchanalian enthusiasm of Pindar flowed in torrents less rapid and less eloquent, and inspires less delight than Townshend's imagery, which conveyed meaning in every sentence. It was Garrick writing and acting extempore scenes of Congreve. A light circumstance increased the mirth of the audience.

---

[1] Mr. Townshend had not many months before entertained a very different opinion of this great man, as appears from the following passage in the Duke of Grafton's MS. Memoirs :—'On the night preceding Lord Chatham's first journey to Bath, Mr. Charles Townshend was for the first time summoned to the Cabinet. The business was on a general view and statement of the actual situation and interests of the various powers in Europe. Lord Chatham had taken the lead in this consideration in so masterly a manner, as to raise the admiration and desire of us all to co-operate with him in forwarding his views. Mr. Townshend was particularly astonished, and owned to me, as I was carrying him in my carriage home, that Lord Chatham had just shown to us what inferior animals we were, and that as much as he had seen of him before he did not conceive till that night his superiority to be so very transcendent.'—L. M.

In the fervour of speaking Townshend rubbed off the
patch from his eye, which he had represented as grievously
cut three days before : no mark was discernible, but to
the nearest spectators a scratch so slight, that he might
have made, and perhaps had made it himself with a pin.[1]
To me the entertainment of the day was complete. He
went to supper with us at Mr. Conway's, where, the flood
of his gaiety not being exhausted, he kept the table in a
roar till two in the morning, by various sallies and pictures,
the last of which was a scene in which he mimicked in-
imitably his own wife, and another great lady with whom
he fancied himself in love, and both whose foibles and
manner he counterfeited to the life. Mere lassitude closed
his lips at last, not the want of wit and new ideas.

To solve the contrast of such parts and absurdity in the
same composition, one is almost tempted to have recourse
to that system of fairy manicheism, wherein no sooner
has one benevolent being endowed the hero of the tale
with supernatural excellence, but a spiteful hag of equal
omnipotence dashes the irrevocable gift with some
counter qualification, which serves to render the accomplished prince a monster of contradictions.

It was not less worth reflection, that, while this phenomenon of genius was, perniciously to himself, and uselessly

---

[1] The following more friendly account of this singular scene is transcribed
from Sir George Colebrooke's Memoirs :—

'Mr. Townshend loved good living, but had not a strong stomach. He
committed therefore frequent excesses, considering his constitution, which
would not have been intemperance in another. He was supposed, for
instance, to have made a speech in the heat of wine, when that was really
not the case. It was a speech in which he treated with great levity, but with
wonderful art, the characters of the Duke of Grafton and Lord Shelburne,
whom, though his colleagues in office, he entertained a sovereign contempt
for, and heartily wished to get rid of. He had a black ribbon over one of
his eyes that day, having tumbled out of bed, probably in a fit of epilepsy,
and this added to the impression made on his auditors that he was tipsy,
whereas it was a speech he had meditated a great while upon, and it was only
by accident that it found utterance that day. I write with certainty, because
Sir George Yonge and I were the only persons who dined with him, and we
had but one bottle of champagne after dinner, General Conway having
repeatedly sent messengers to press his return to the House.'—L. M.

to his country, lavishing an unexampled profusion of parts on wanton buffoonery, only to excite transient and barren applause ; the restorer of his country was lurking in darkness and shrouding a haughty sterility of talents from the public eye, under the veil of frenzy or untractable obstinacy.   The simplicity of a great character was wanting both to Lord Chatham and Townshend

CHAPTER II

Proposal to Tax the Colonies.—Debate on American Affairs.—Passing of the Resolutions.—The House comes to an Agreement with the East India Company.—Private Affairs of Lord Chatham.—Motion for Papers relative to Quebec in the House of Lords.—State of Catholicism in England.—Strength of the Opposition in the House of Lords.—Weakness of the Administration.—Attempts made to strengthen it.

1767

ON the 13th of May came on at last the great American questions. Charles Townshend had already hinted, when he opened the budget, at new taxes which he proposed to lay on the Colonies. He now opened them; and very inadequate indeed did they prove, even in calculation, to the loss of a shilling in the pound on land, part of which deficiency they were intended to supply. Being so inconsiderable, and estimated by himself as likely to produce but from £35,000 to £40,000 a year, the House too lightly adopted his plan before it had been well weighed, and the fatal consequences of which did not break out till six years after. A concurrent cause weighed with many, and added weight to the arguments of more, for inflicting a kind of punishment on the refractory Colonies, some of which had stubbornly refused to comply with the late Act enjoining them to make provision for the army, with other parliamentary injunctions. Massachusets Bay had, as I have said, taken upon themselves to execute the Act in their own names, and on their own sole authority. This deed Townshend said the Privy Council had advised his Majesty to annul. That Colony contained a set of men disposed to inflame all the rest. He stated fully, clearly, and with both

authority and moderation, these several topics ; and concluded, he said, that many would think he proposed too
little, others too much.   The Mutiny Bill had been
opposed almost everywhere ; but Pennsylvania and some
few Colonists had executed all our orders.   He wished
he could name any more instances.   New Jersey had
avoided the Act by appointing commissioners, with injunctions to act *according to the custom of the provinces.*
New York was so opulent that he thought they ought to
be kept in dependence.   General Gage,[1] accordingly, was
sending troops thither.   Yet did the New Yorkists com-
mend themselves and boast that they could not remember
the time when they had refused aid to Britain.   They
had resolved, that if they should grant the present
demand, it *might* exceed their abilities.   This was an
extraordinary excuse.   More contemptuously still, they
promised aid on the requisition of the Crown, but said
nothing of Parliament.   Were these, he asked, the descendants of those men who had fled from prerogative
to America ?   Yet even this gracious compliance they
held themselves at liberty to refuse, if not in proportions
to the other provinces : if unreasonable—nay, if inconvenient.   They would insist, too, on his Majesty's repaying what they should furnish to his troops, when he
should think proper.   He would not read, he said, the
letters to their Governor, Sir Henry More,[2] as too inflammatory.   To comply, they alleged, would be very serious ;
yet desired Sir Henry to represent their obedience favourably.   The Massachusets termed our acts *our* ordinances,

---

[1] Major General the Honourable Thomas Gage, Commander-in-Chief
in North America, 1763-72, was Governor of Massachusetts at the outbreak of
the American war, when he was again appointed Commander-in-Chief, but
resigned after holding that post for two months.   He became a full General
in 1782, and died 2nd April 1787.—E.

[2] Henry More had been created a Baronet in January 1764, for his services
as Lieutenant-Governor of Jamaica.   He was Governor of New York from
1765 until his death in September 1769.   Bancroft calls him 'the well-
meaning, indolent Moore.'   The baronetcy became extinct on the death of his
son in January 1780.—E.

and asserted their own rights of taxation. Many they
had discountenanced and frightened from their assembly.
Governor Bernard, he believed, was a little heated against
them;[1] yet the facts which he charged on them were
true. In general, it did not become Parliament to engage
in controversy with its Colonies, but by one act to assert
its sovereignty. He warned the House to beware lest
the provinces engaged in a common cause. Our right of
taxation was indubitable; yet himself had been for repealing the Stamp Act to prevent mischief. Should their
disobedience return, the authority of Parliament had
been weakened, and unless supported with spirit and
dignity, must be destroyed. The salaries of governors
and judges in that part of the world must be made independent of their assemblies; but he advised the House
to confine their resolutions to the offending provinces.
Pennsylvania was an answer to New York. New Jersey
had limited the sum, but had not said it would not comply.
He thought it would be prudent to inflict censure on New
York alone; that some burthen ought to be lightened at
home, and imposed on America. He had hinted at
taxes; he would name some, though not as Chancellor
of the Exchequer. They were duties on wine, oil, and
fruits from Spain and Portugal as they come back; on
china; and to take off the drawback on glass, paper, lead,
and colours. A commissioner of the customs, too, would
be necessary in America. Parliament ought to exercise
its authority; but not contrary to the constitution of the
provinces. He then moved a resolution that New York
had disobeyed the Act, and that, till they should comply,
the Governor should be restrained from passing *any* act
of their Assembly. This, he owned, some had said would

[1] Francis Bernard, Esq. He had been Governor of New Jersey from 1758
to 1760, when he was promoted to Massachusetts. He is praised by the
writers unfavourable to the Americans for his zeal in maintaining the authority
of the mother country.—(Stedman's *History of the American War*, 1794, vol. i.
pp. 65-66.) Unhappily this zeal was not tempered by judgment. He has
been justly censured by Mr. Burke. He was made a Baronet in 1769, and
died in 1779.—L. M.

be confounding the innocent and the guilty, and would dissolve their Assembly. On the contrary, others had advised to block up harbours and quarter soldiers, but himself could bear to hear of nothing military. Some were for a local tax ; but that would be to accept penalty in lieu of obedience.

This speech,[1] so consonant to the character of a man of business, and so unlike the wanton sallies of the man of parts and pleasure, was (however modified) but too well calculated to inflame the passions of a legislature whose authority was called in question, and who are naturally not prone to weigh the effusions of men entitled to as much freedom as themselves, while in an apparent situation of dependence. *Authority never measures liberty downwards.* Rarely is liberty supposed to mean the independence of those below us ; it is our own freedom from the yoke of superiors. The Peer dreads the King, the Commoner the Peer ; the Americans the Parliament. Each American trader thought himself a Brutus, a

---

[1] This speech will long be memorable, as it again opened the wounds scarce skinned over by the repeal of the Stamp Act. The loss of the land-tax occasioned this speech and the ensuing taxes ; those taxes produced opposition ; that opposition gave a handle to the friends of prerogative to attempt despotism in America ; and that attempt has caused a civil war in America, whence is just arrived notice of the first bloodshed, as I transcribe these Memoirs—in June, 1775.

At this later period (when thirteen provinces are actually lost) the leading steps may be summed up thus : Grenville (who had adopted from Lord Bute a plan of taxation formed by Jenkinson) had provoked America to resist. The Rockingham Administration had endeavoured to remedy that mischief by repealing the Stamp Act ; and perhaps might have prevented a further breach, though ambitious leaders, and perhaps some true republican patriots, might have entertained hopes of separating the Colonies from Great Britain ; and France had certainly fomented those designs. The pernicious mischief of lowering the land-tax gave a handle to Charles Townshend to propose his new taxes (instigated, as was supposed, by the secret cabal at Court, or officiously to make his court there). Thus the ambition of the Court began the quarrel ; Grenville was a second time, though then without foreseeing it, an instrument of renewing it ; and the Crown, that delighted in the mischief, ended with being the great sufferer, and America happily became perfectly free.

[It is not unlikely, as Sir George Colebrooke observes, 'that as the Court

Hampden, while he wrestled with the House of Commons; yet his poor negroes felt that their master, Brutus, was a worse tyrant than Nero or Muley Ishmael.[1] Had the Parliament of England presumed by one godlike act to declare all the slaves in our Colonies freemen, not a patriot in America but would have clamoured against the violation of property, and protested that to abolish the power of imposing chains was to impose them. O man! man! dare not to vaunt your virtue, while self-interest lurks in every pore!

The above speech could but expand the narrow heart of Grenville with triumph. It is a prophet's holiday when woes accomplish his prediction. As mortifying was it to Conway and Lord Rockingham's party, who had served their American brethren to so little purpose: yet they contended still for moderate measures. Dowdeswell represented that the House was not acquainted with the state of the laws in the Colonies, and which of them it would be necessary to repeal: he said, he should rather incline to enforce and amend the late Act. Beckford pleaded for the Colonies, and affirmed that they had the better of

had never intended to abandon the principle of taxation Mr. Townshend was not sorry to have an opportunity of ingratiating himself at St. James's, by proposing taxes which, though levied in America, were not laid on American growth, or American industry, and so far he hoped they would find admittance into the Colonies.'—(Sir George Colebrooke's MS. Memoirs.) Many of the Americans attached to the British connexion were also of that opinion, and told Mr. Townshend ' let it but bear the appearance of port duties, and it will not be objected to.'—(Cavendish's *Debates*, vol. i. p. 213.) At home the measure was opposed by a very slender minority in Parliament representing no powerful interests exclusive of the merchants engaged in the American trade, whose fears for the debts owing to them in the Colonies made them so tremblingly apprehensive, that their remonstrances carried less weight with the Government than would otherwise have been due to their intelligence and wealth. The country also had taken umbrage at the intemperate language of the Colonists, and regarded with some distrust the moderate policy of the Government; so that Mr. Townshend had to contend with the taunts of the Opposition, the popular voice, and the wishes of the Court—a combination far too strong for a statesman of his temperament to resist.—L. M.]

[1] Muley Ishmael, Sultan of Morocco 1672-1727, famous for his ability and ferocity. For a description of him see Walpole's *Letters*, vol. ix. p. 392.—E.

Bernard in every argument. Whether he spoke as by birth an American,[1] or whether by concert with Lord Chatham, that while the Ministers humbled the Colonies, his lordship might still be supposed favourable to them, is uncertain,—such a duplicity from his silence ran through the whole of that his second administration. He seemed to be playing the despot, and laying in at the same time for future patriotism. Burke roundly imputed the plan to him, and called it weak, as resolutions ought to be followed by deeds; and therefore, he said, he should oppose both. He arraigned the idea of dissolving their Assemblies, at the same time that the House seemed to allow them as a co-ordinate power, since the execution of the Act was to depend on their acquiescence. Yet the suspension of all their laws would fall heavier on the innocent, than the punishment could on the guilty; and what effect would the penalty have? Would not the turbulent be re-chosen? He advised a new model of their police.

Grenville opposed by outgoing the proposals of the ministry, and said, no moderation was to be suffered, when the authority of Parliament was resisted. He knew that when they saw the Stamp Act repealed, they would laugh at declarations. Lord Chatham had declared, should they still resist, he would fill their harbours with ships and their towns with soldiers. The declaration of the Lords had not been sent over. Bernard had stated the requisition in the words of both Houses—Mr. Conway had not; whether it was that he saw the fire kindled, and chose to retire. Lord Shelburne had power to control the impertinent representation of the Board of Trade. Lord Shelburne's letter should be considered hereafter. Bernard had begged for instructions in case of rebellion; no answer had been sent to him. He supposed the Secretaries of State would continue to represent the resolutions of Parliament as they had done. The encouragement the provinces had met with, had excited them to proceed in disobedience; yet, could no better be obtained, himself

[1] Beckford was a native of Jamaica.—E.

would concur even in these means of enforcing submission. If the House would support its magistrates there with no force, it were better to pass no act. On the late seizures of corn, force had been employed at home. He would advise the imposing on the Assembly-men an oath of acknowledging the sovereignty of Great Britain, and on all men in the Colonies. The taxes proposed, he thought, would be subversive of the Act of Navigation. He would lay a tax on paper currency.

Conway replied, that he had not followed Mr. Grenville from office to office to hunt out his faults or errors, nor had been employed in such mean revenge ; while men, by his orders, were dragged out of their beds by general warrants. No order had been sent to himself from the House of Lords to be transmitted to the Colonies ; yet, as appeared, that order had been transmitted. The Colonies were not mere corporations ; their charters gave them legislative power. On taxes they would always be tender. The measure proposed to be taken with the Assemblies, he thought, at once too violent and inefficient. Some provinces had actually done more than they had been required to do.

Charles Townshend declared he could not approve a general oath or test that should comprehend all the Colonies. Of a tax on paper currency he had had some thoughts. Yorke said, he thought, though the Chief Justice Wilmot was of a different opinion, that the Privy Council could and ought to annul the Act of the Massachusets.

Rigby dropped the question to satirize the Court. He wished he knew who it was that framed our ministries. He and his friends had been turned out from that ignorance. Europe must take us for a nation of ministries, while by our actions it must think we had no administration. Formerly we had annual parliaments ; now annual ministries : yet, though so many ministries were dismissed, no crime was alleged against any. Let it be known who it was possessed that latent power. He told the House

that, in the Congress at New York, it had been agreed to
erect a statue to Lord Chatham. It had been afterwards
proposed to erect one to the King ; no man had seconded
the motion.[1]

Wedderburn said it was faction that had the ruling
influence, and that Lord Bute must consequently have a
large system. Conway declared himself for a local tax on
the disobedient.

To Townshend's third resolution, Grenville proposed
an amendment for bringing in a bill to amend the late
Act.[2] On this the House divided at one in the morning,
when the Court Party rejected the amendment by 180 to
98 ; Conway voting with Grenville, and the Rockinghams
in opposition to Townshend's question, though with
different views,—the former wishing to add rigour to
the Act, the others to new-model it. It will be seen in
the votes what taxes were laid.[3] The harsher intentions
were dropped, but the taxes produced sufficient evil.
The violence of Rigby's invective against Lord Bute was
imputed to the latter's rejection of new overtures from the
Bedford faction. Wedderburn's outrage was still more
remarkable ; when he, who had been a creature of the
Favourite, pointed out his influence, who could doubt its
existence ?[4] Yet the accusation was more odious from
a tool than the crime of the accused. Conway was not

---

[1] The Assembly of New York, in June 1756, 'voted to raise on the
Bowling Green an equestrian statue of George III., and a statue of William
Pitt, "twice the preserver of his country." '—Bancroft's *History of the United
States* (1876), vol. iv. p. 10.—E.

[2] The third resolution restrained the Governor of New York from passing
any Act in that colony, till the Assembly should have made the required provision for the troops. It was strongly opposed by Thomas Pownall, M.P.
for Tregony, and late Governor successively of New Jersey, Massachusetts,
and South Carolina (*Parliamentary History*, vol. xvi. 331), who took
occasion at the same time to defend the Massachusetts' assembly from the
charge of unconstitutional action.—E.

[3] The articles taxed were glass, red lead, white lead, painters' colours,
tea, and paper (7 George III. c. 46).—E.

[4] Wedderburn had been returned for the Ayr burghs in December 1761
through Bute's influence.—E.

at all supported by his old friends, when attacked by Grenville. They were offended at his agreeing with Wedderburn in imputing all the late changes to faction; yet had he added that if there was a secret influence, nobody lamented it more than he did. Charles Townshend, at the same time, not only threatened to resign, but falsely affirmed he had offered his resignation to the King, who would not accept it. Conway dreaded its being said that he remained in place with all denominations of men. I satisfied him (and so it proved) that Townshend spoke not a word of truth; and I showed him how incumbent it was on him to carry through the East Indian business, which nothing but his temper could bring to an accommodation. In this I rendered an essential service to my country. Conway did perfect the agreement; and the Parliament at last accepted £400,000 a year for two years.[1]

On the report of the American resolutions agreed to by

---

[1] The previous discussions of the East India question are noticed in the Second Volume. They convey no exalted notion of the sagacity or virtue of the parties concerned in them. The sole object of the Ministers appears to have been to extort the largest possible sum of money from the Company, without regard to the prosperity of our commercial relations with India, the proper administration of the territories of the Company, or the welfare of the Indian population. The Company in like manner, directors and proprietors, displayed an utter unfitness for the discharge of the vast jurisdiction to which they laid claim. The venality and rapacity of their officers in India almost found a parallel in the disgraceful trafficking for votes and patronage in the Court of Proprietors, and the speculations and maladministration of the directors. Their affairs had fallen into great disorder,—the natural result of these practices on such a vicious system as the annual election of the directors and the low amount of the franchise of the proprietors. It was no wonder that all sought to escape any interference or control on the part of the Government. Strange to say, these crying evils were regarded with indifference by the public, and every effort made by Government to repress them met with determined resistance from the great mercantile interests of the City of London. Indeed the cause of the Company became so popular that many of the leading Whigs very inconsistently yielded to the general feeling, and were found among its warmest advocates. Conway wanted firmness to oppose this delusion. Of all the Ministers, Lord Chatham alone did not entirely forget that he was a statesman. He protested throughout against the rights claimed by the Company over the conquered provinces, and he did not disguise his contempt for that body. Indistinctly as his views are expressed, and extravagant as may have been his belief of the extent of the revenues of

the committee, Grenville, Conway, and the opponents, proposed to recommit them, but were overruled ; Charles Townshend making an admirably witty and pathetic speech to prevent a division.   Fitzherbert took notice that Mr. Conway's dissent would be likely to do more harm than the resolutions could do good.   Grenville then moved his test to oblige the Americans to acknowledge the sovereignty of Great Britain, but it was rejected by 141 to 40.   Three days after this, arrived an account that Georgia had refused to comply with the Act in stronger terms than any other colony, and that South Carolina would probably be equally disobedient.

At this period came to my knowledge a transaction, at which I have already hinted, and which in truth at that time persuaded me of the reality of Lord Chatham's madness.   When he inherited Sir William Pynsent's estate, he removed to it and sold his house and grounds at Hayes, a place on which he had wasted prodigious sums, and which yet retained small traces of expense, great part having been consumed in purchasing contiguous tenements to free himself from all neighbourhood.   Much had gone in doing and undoing, and not a little portion in planting by torch-light, as his peremptory and impatient temper could brook no delay.   Nor were these the sole circumstances that marked his caprice.   His children he could not bear under the same roof, nor communications from room to room, nor whatever he thought promoted noise.   A winding passage between his house and children was built with the same view.   When at the beginning of this his second administration, he fixed at North End by Hampstead,[1] he took four or five houses successively, as

the Company, he appears to have carried his views for their appropriation beyond those of mere revenue considerations to this country, and if his health had admitted of his entering further into the controversy, and he had been assisted in matters of detail, it is not unlikely that he would have struck out a scheme worthy of his genius for the government of this vast empire. —L. M.

[1] North End House, now known as Wildwood House.   For a curious account of Chatham's sojourn here, see Howitt's *Northern Heights of London* (1869), pp. 82-90.—E.

fast as Mr. Dingley, his landlord,[1] went into them, still, as
he said, to ward off the noises of neighbourhood. His
inconsiderate promptitude was not less remarkable at
Pynsent. A bleak hill bounded his view ; he ordered his
gardener to have it planted with evergreens ; the man
asked, 'With what sorts?' He replied, 'With cedars and
cypresses.' 'Bless me, my lord!' replied the gardener,
'all the nurseries in this county (Somersetshire) would
not furnish a hundredth part.' 'No matter; send for
them from London;' and they were fetched by land-
carriage. Yet were these follies committed when no
suspicion was had of his disorder. But by these and
other caprices he had already consumed more than half
of the legacy of Pynsent. His very domestic and abs-
temious privacy bore a considerable article in his house-
keeping. His sickly and uncertain appetite was never
regular, and his temper could put up with no defect.
Thence a succession of chickens were boiling and roasting
at every hour to be ready whenever he should call. He
now, as if his attention to business demanded his vicinity
to town, bent his fancy to the repossession of Hayes,
which he had sold to my cousin, Mr. Thomas Walpole.[2]
The latter, under great inquietude, showed me letters he
had received from Lady Chatham, begging in the most
pathetic terms that he would sell them Hayes again.
She urged that it would save her children from destruction ; and that her children's children would be bound to
pray for him; requesting that he would take some days
to consider before he refused. He did ; and then wrote

---

[1] This was Charles Dingley, the opponent of Wilkes at the Middlesex
election of March 1769, and the 'miserable Dingley' of Junius. He had
been a private in the Foot Guards, and by his fortunate speculations rose to
be a proprietor of sawmills at Limehouse. He died at Hampstead on 13th
November 1769.—E.

[2] The Honourable Thomas Walpole, second son of Horatio, first Lord
Walpole of Wolterton, was a merchant and banker in London, and M.P.
successively for Sudbury, Ashburton, and King's Lynn. He purchased
Hayes Place from Pitt in November 1765. For the letter in which he agreed
to resell it, see *Chatham Correspondence*, vol. iii. p. 289. He died at Chis-
wick on 21st March 1803, aged seventy-five.—E.

to her that he was very averse from parting with the place, on which he had laid out much money; but if the air of Hayes was the object, Lord Chatham was welcome to go thither directly for a month, or for the whole summer; that he would immediately remove his family, who were there, and Lord Chatham would find it well aired. This she declined accepting. Mr. Walpole then sent Nuthall[1] to her. She, who had never appeared to have a will or thought of her own, but to act with submission at her lord's nod, now received Nuthall alone, and besought him not to own to her lord that she had yet received any letter from Mr. Walpole, but to deliver it as just arrived, if Lord Chatham should ask for the answer, and then carried him to her lord. He seemed in health and reasonable; but asking if Nuthall knew anything about Hayes, and being told the contents of the letter, he said, with a sigh, 'That might have saved me.' Lady Chatham, seeming to be alarmed, said, 'My lord, I was talking to Mr. Nuthall on that subject; we will go and finish our discourse;' and carried him out of the room. She then told him they had agreed to sell the Wiltshire estate (part of Pynsent's), and with part of the produce re-purchase Hayes, which, however, they must mortgage, for they owed as much as the sale would amount to. Mr. Walpole, distressed between unwillingness to part with Hayes, and apprehension that Lord Chatham's ill-health would be imputed to him, as that air might have been a remedy, consulted the Chancellor. The latter, on hearing the story, said, 'Then he is mad,' and sent for James Grenville. Asking when he had seen Lord Chatham, Grenville replied, 'The day before, and had found him much better.' Lord Camden said, 'Did he mention Hayes?' 'Yes,' said Grenville, 'and then his discourse grew very ferocious.' No doubt there was

---

[1] Thomas Nuthall, appointed Solicitor of the Treasury, through Lord Chatham's interest, and his lordship's intimate friend and law adviser. Many letters to and from him are contained in the *Chatham Correspondence.* He was shot by a highwayman on Hounslow Heath, and expired a few hours afterwards, in March 1775.—L. M.

something in these words of Grenville that had the air of a part acted : one can scarce believe a brother-in-law would have been so frank, had there been no concerted plan in the frenzy ; yet what wonder if anything seemed more credible than the fictitious madness of a first minister in no difficult situation? From this period the few reports of the few who had access to him, concurred in representing him as sedate, conversable, even cheerful, till any mention was made of politics : then he started, fell into tremblings, and the conversation was broken off. When the session was closed, these reports wore away ; and as he remained above a year in close confinement at Hayes, unconsulting, and by degrees unconsulted, he and his lunacy were totally forgotten, till new interests threatened his re-appearance, which after many delays at length happened, though with no solution given by any friend of so long a suspension of sense or common sense. Mr. Walpole had yielded Hayes.

On the 18th the General Court of India Proprietors imitating and actuated by Members of Parliament, took a violent step, and at eleven at night when all were retired but one hundred and fifty, balloted for a petition against the Bill to regulate dividends ; and so impetuous were they, that they ordered the ballot should be closed at midnight. Two persons protested against that measure. Such indecent behaviour being stated to the House of Commons the next day, the petition was rejected ; but new proposals made by the directors were well accepted, and the accommodation was voted on the 22d.

On the 21st the Duke of Richmond moved the Lords for papers relating to a plan for a Civil Government at Quebec. It had been drawn by the last Ministers, and delivered to Lord Northington for his opinion, who had never thought more on the subject. The motion was levelled at him ; and to please the Rockinghams, the Bedfords consulted with them at Richmond House[1]

[1] Richmond House, Whitehall, the site of which is now occupied by Richmond Terrace, was burnt down, 21st December 1791.—E.

previous to the motion; but it was baffled by giving them the papers, after Lord Sandwich had been personally offensive in his speech to the Duke of Grafton. Lord Gower the next day renewed the question on the Act of the Assembly of Massachusets. It had been set aside by the Privy Council, but not declared void *ab initio*, as Lord Mansfield urged it ought to be, and as Lord Chief Justice Wilmot now maintained too, though he had twice given his opinion to the contrary; yet, though preferred by the Chancellor, he had now been gained by Mansfield. It was a day of much expectation. The Opposition had even hopes of success, having moved for papers which would resolve the House into a committee, in which proxies are never counted; and in proxies lay the material strength of the Court, who, if beaten, could only have recovered the question on the report. Lord Mansfield, to interpose solemnity, proposed, as his way was, that the judges should be consulted, and spoke with singular art and subtlety, disclaiming a spirit of opposition. The Chancellor and Lord Northington treated him most severely, the former taxing him directly with faction, and telling him the motion was complicated, involved, irregular, and yet betraying the marks of a lawyer. He quoted, too, a case in point in which the late Lord Hardwicke had been of a contrary opinion. The House sat till near ten, a late hour for that assembly, when the motion was rejected by only 62 to 56. The day was made memorable by the Duke of York, who spoke, and very poorly, against the Court, but did not stay to vote. The two other Princes voted with their brother's Administration. Seven bishops were in the minority,—the consequence of the Crown permitting great lords to nominate to bishopricks: the reverend fathers sometimes having at least gratitude, or further expectations, if they have no patriotism. The Judges said afterwards that they would have excused themselves from delivering their opinions, as the matter might come before them in the Courts below.

The same day the Earl of Radnor[1] proposed that the bishops should give in the numbers of Papists in their several dioceses, which was ordered, and much evaded by the Catholics. In fact, there was no singular increase of that sect. Many Jesuits had fled hither on the demolition of their order ; but it was not a moment to make Popery formidable. It was wearing out in England by the loss of their chief patrons, the Catholic Peers, whose number was considerably diminished. The Duchess of Norfolk,[2] a zealous, though not a religious, woman, of a very confused understanding, and who believed herself more artful than she was, contributed, almost singly, to conversions, by bribes and liberality to the poor. But Rome was reduced to be defensive ; and unless, as I apprehend, the Methodists are secret Papists, and no doubt they copy, build on, and extend their rites towards that model, Popery will not revive here, when it is falling to decay in its favourite regions.

Another motion being made on the Massachuset's Act on the 26th, Lord Denbigh[3] treated Lord Mansfield in still harsher terms than he had experienced the last day. Lord Egmont spoke well against the same person. The Duke of Bedford complained much of secret influence (Lord Bute's), and so assiduous had the Opposition been, that the Court had a majority but of three voices—65 to

---

[1] William Bouverie, 2nd Viscount Folkestone, had been created Earl of the County of Radnor, 29th October 1765. He died on 28th January 1776, aged fifty.—E.

[2] Mary, wife of Edward, Duke of Norfolk, one of the daughters and co-heiresses of Edward Blount of Blagden, in Devonshire. The biographer of the Blount family states that ' she graced that high station by the beauty and dignity of her person, and the splendour of her wit and talents.' She had lived with her husband in the south of France, until he succeeded to the dukedom on the death of his elder brother, without issue, in 1732. She died without issue in 1733. The Duke survived her, and died at the advanced age of 92, in 1777.—*Genealogical History of the Croke Family* (1823), vol. ii. p. 150.—E.

[3] Basil Fielding, 6th Earl of Denbigh, a Lord of the Bedchamber for 37 years ; died on 14th July 1800, aged eighty-one. Walpole elsewhere speaks of his ' brutality in the House of Lords.'—(*Letters*, vol. iii. p. 373.) He was known as a successful gambler.—E.

62.[1] The Duke of York was absent, as was said, by the interposition of the Princess, his mother, who had accompanied her reprimand with very bitter reproaches.

In the Commons much heat passed on the Dividend Bill, on which Dyson, as manager,—and now become a very forward manager,—grew most obnoxious to the Opposition, and the subject of many libels; but his abilities and the strength of the Court carried the Bill through, though even the Chancellor of the Exchequer, and Conway, Secretary of State, were inclined to show more favour to the proprietors. Another proof of what Lord Chatham might have done, when so subordinate a placeman as Dyson could lead the House of Commons against the chief Ministers there, when they disagreed with the measures of the Court.

These circumstances, however, the small majority in the Lords, the variations of Townshend and Conway, and the want of dignity in wanting a leader of the House of Commons, seemed to call for some speedy change. I even feared that Conway would go into Opposition. He would not, he said, resemble Lord Granby, and serve by turns under everybody. Yet was he ill content with his old friends, who persisted in a junction with Grenville for fear of Bute. The Duke of Grafton himself, who could not penetrate to Lord Chatham, thought some change necessary. Lord Northington, alarmed for himself by the attack on the Canada papers, and apt to scent decay in a ministry, told Lord Hertford the present system could

---

[1] The debate was hot and personal. Lord Denbigh threw out indirect reflections on Chief Justice Wilmot, and on being stopped as disorderly, he turned upon Lord Mansfield, and went so far as to give his lordship the lie. Eventually he was obliged to ask pardon, which Lord Mansfield seems to have given with rather unbecoming alacrity.—(Duke of Bedford's Journal, in Cavendish's *Parliamentary Debates*, vol. i. Appendix, p. 602.) On the following day, the Duke of Grafton communicated the result of the division by letter to Lord Chatham, and earnestly entreated an interview to consider what was to be done. Lord Chatham, as before, begged ' to be allowed to decline the honour of the visit,' being ' quite unable for a conversation which he should be otherwise proud and happy to embrace.'—(*Chatham Correspondence*, vol. iii. pp. 255, 256.)—L. M.

not hold. I engaged Lord Hertford to warn the King not
to open his closet precipitately on Lord Northington's
alarm. But I was not without apprehension myself on
meeting the Duke of Grafton returning very privately
from Richmond,—nothing being so unusual as his Majesty's
seeing any ministers there. The King had sent for him
and insisted on his seeing Lord Chatham the next day.
The Duke was very iniquisitive to know how Lord Chatham was : I told the Duke he would find him much disordered. The Duke said to me, 'If we can beat them
well in the House of Lords next Tuesday, perhaps we
may get the Bedfords.' I was struck, and concluded that
Lord Bute was terrified at the Duke of Bedford's and
Rigby's late attacks ; or that Lord Northington had
alarmed both him and the King ; but Lord Hertford
assured me that the Duke's own propensity lay towards
the Bedfords.

On the 1st of June, Mr. Conway moved the House to
grant £11,000 to Prince Ferdinand.[1] The Prince had
expended so much of his own money for the immediate
necessities of the army, intending to pay himself out of
the chest of contributions, with which the late King had
solely intrusted him : a German, who had the care of it,
had run away and left no money. The debt to the Prince
had been delivered in with the general accounts : and
when the debts were liquidated with the Hanoverian
Chancery, both sides pretended to a balance in their own
favour. Grenville had given notice to have all debts
brought in within a year. So many disputes had arisen
after the account was closed, that the Treasury informed
Prince Ferdinand they could not pay him, he must apply
to Parliament. Dowdeswell had prevented Mr. Conway
from applying for the debt the last year, and now, with
Grenville and Rigby, opposed the reimbursement of the

[1] Ferdinand, fourth son of Ferdinand Albert, Duke of Brunswick, and
brother-in-law of Frederick the Great, was the famous General of the Allies
during the Seven Years' War. In later years he was known for his charities
and his patronage of literature and art. He died on 3rd July 1792, aged
seventy-one.—E.

Prince, insisting the money had been paid to the Hanoverian Chancery, and that he must get it thence. Lord
Granby was violent against this refusal, but the House
was as much averse to paying the money. Samuel Martin,
who, by order of Grenville's Treasury, as their Secretary,
had written to Prince Ferdinand an approbation of his
accounts, being called upon, said very impertinently, he
had emptied his head of all that trash and trumpery—
and went out of the House. Conway, and even Grenville,
took severe notice of that expression, which Dyson defended ; he and Martin either resenting Conway's opposition to the Dividend Bill, or obeying the secret ill-will of
the Court to the House of Brunswick. Dowdeswell calling
for some necessary papers, the business was put off for
some days.

The Duke of Grafton found Lord Chatham, as he,
thought, incurably nervous, and so unfit to continue
minister, that the Duke himself talked of quitting too.[1]
He told Mr. Conway and me that he had never seen the
King so much agitated ; that his Majesty was not disinclined to take Lord Rockingham, but protested he had
almost rather resign his crown than consent to receive

---

[1] The Duke says in his MS. Memoirs :—

'Though I expected to find Lord Chatham very ill indeed, his situation
was different from what I had imagined : his nerves and spirits were affected
to a dreadful degree, and the sight of his great mind, bowed down and thus
weakened by disorder, would have filled me with grief and concern even if
I had not long borne a sincere attachment to his person and character. The
confidence he reposed in me, demanded every return on my part, and it
appeared like cruelty in me to have been urged by any necessity to put a man
I valued to so great suffering. The interview was long and painful : I had to
run over the many difficulties of the session, for his lordship, I believe, had
not once attended the House since his last return from Bath. I had to relate
the struggles we had experienced in carrying some points, especially in the
House of Lords ; the opposition, also, we had encountered in the East India
business, from Mr. Conway as well as Mr. Townshend, together with the un-
accountable conduct of the latter gentleman, who had suffered himself to be
led to pledge himself at last, contrary to the known decision of every member
of the Cabinet, to draw a certain revenue from the Colonies, without offence to
the Americans themselves ; and I was sorry to inform Lord Chatham, that
Mr. Townshend's flippant boasting was received with strong marks of a blind
and greedy approbation from the body of the House ; and I endeavoured

George Grenville again. I was much more surprised when the Duke proposed to call in Lord Rockingham and his friends as a support to the then Administration; and to make Mr. Yorke President of the Council, in the room of Lord Northington. I told his Grace that Lord Rockingham and his party would listen to no junction with Lord Chatham. The Duke was of the same opinion, and seemed to have thrown it out only to mark his fidelity to the latter, whom, he said, he could not propose to dismiss, Lord Chatham having told him that morning he would not retire but by his Majesty's command. I asked the Duke whether, if Lord Chatham continued, his Grace would not remain in place, rather than throw all again to the hazard? He seemed to allow he would: yet said, Lord Rockingham and his friends would not be sufficient addition. I replied, 'My Lord, that is what they say themselves, and therefore would bring Grenville and the Bedfords: but the fact is not so. They would now be so much stronger than last year, as the King would not now have an option to make between them and Lord Chatham; and therefore Lord Bute would be obliged to support them now, as what he hates most is the connection of Grenville and the Bedfords.' I earnestly begged the Duke to make no overtures to Lord Rockingham till the session

to lay everything before his lordship as plainly as I was able, and assured him that Lords Northington and Camden had both empowered me to declare how earnestly they desired to receive his advice as to assisting and strengthening the system he had established by some adequate accession, without which they were satisfied it could not nor ought to proceed.

'It was with difficulty that I brought Lord Chatham to be sensible of the weakness of his Administration, or the power of the united faction against us, though we received every mark we could desire of his Majesty's support. At last, after much discourse and some arguing, he proceeded to entreat me to remain in my present station, taking that method to strengthen the Ministry which should appear to me to be the most eligible; and he assured me that if Lords Northington and Camden, as well as myself, did not retain our high places, there would be an end to all his hopes of being ever serviceable again as a public man.'

Eventually Lord Chatham acquiesced in the Duke entering into a negotiation with the Bedford or Rockingham party—though he preferred the former, —a preference which explains the Duke's remark in the text of p. 37.—L. M.

was closed, as the distance of six or seven months to another session would make him and his followers more tractable. The Duke was desirous of getting rid of Lord Shelburne; and it was plain would have accorded all they could wish to the Rockinghams, if on one hand Lord Chatham and Lord Camden, and on the other Lord Bute's friends, might be suffered to remain in their places.

In the meantime the Opposition had mustered all their forces for another battle in the House of Lords. In such manœuvres Sandwich and Rigby were excellent; and Lord Rockingham himself, who had been so indolent a minister, was become as industrious a partisan as either of them. Accordingly, on the 2nd of June the Duke of Richmond made three motions; one, a resolution that there ought to be a civil government established in Canada; the others implied censure on the neglect, and were aimed at Lord Northington. The latter denied his having thrice refused to attend the Council on that business; but the Duke of Richmond proved upon him that he had even written that refusal to Lord Winchelsea, the then President of the Council. Lord Mansfield did not appear in the debate, so deeply had he felt his late treatment. The Ministers rejected the motions by 73 to 61. This was reckoned a great victory after the Court had been so hard run in the last division. Both sides agreed to adjourn for ten days, considering the heat and lateness of the season.

The King, who, to please the Duke of Grafton, had seemed to give in to the measure of sending for Lord Rockingham, now wrote to Lord Chatham to press him to continue in place. To Mr. Conway his Majesty was profuse of his favour,—told him he knew his intention of resignation was from a point of honour and adherence to a rash promise,—begged Conway not to distress him by quitting before the end of the session,—offered him any military boons,—and owned he wished Lord Edgcumbe had not been turned out. Conway replied, he hoped another time his Majesty would follow his own excellent judgment. To Lord Hertford the King declared he would submit to neither faction ; would take some of Lord Rockingham's friends, if they would be reasonable ; but Grenville he would never forgive ; and at last said, emphatically, 'My lord, you will see a strange scene!' Conway was touched with the King's behaviour, and said that, as soon as he had resigned, he would tell Lord Rockingham that he had acquitted his promises to them, and should have no further connection with them. I told him there were many independent men who would not sit still and see the closet taken by storm. No, he replied, it was what he himself and the Rockinghams had come in two years before to prevent.

Finding how unacceptable the motion in Prince Ferdinand's favour had been to the House, Conway dropped it, and the King gave the Prince a pension of two thousand pounds a year. It had been suspected that his Highness had made great advantage by the war ; but he had pressed so earnestly for this money, that Conway believed him not rich, and was afraid of his being disgusted and gained by France, from which Court he had rejected the most shining offers.[1]

After the recess at Whitsuntide the lords of the Opposition engaged warmly against the Dividend Bill, and had frequent and late sittings, which still protracted the session. The Duke of Richmond was the chief manager, and even moved for a conference with the Commons, to know why the latter had passed the bill, but was beaten by 98 to 51, the Duke of York voting in the minority : but the Bedfords were much cooled. The Duchess and Lord Gower perceiving the Court much at a loss to recruit or prop up the Administration, thought the opportunity fair for making their peace, and Lord Gower even went during the holidays to the Duke of Grafton, at Wakefield Lodge.[2]

[1] Conway was right—Prince Ferdinand realized very little property during the war, and died poor. The vast sums drawn from England fell into the hands of subordinate agents.—L. M.

[2] In Whittlebury Forest, on the borders of Northamptonshire and Buckinghamshire.—E.

The Duke, provoked at the Duke of Richmond, and already hostile to him by the rivalship of age and relationship,[1] offered Lord Gower any terms for himself and his friends, only with the exclusion of Grenville. Rigby would not abandon Grenville, and prevailed on the Duke of Bedford to say they would not come in to be turned out again in six months, and therefore should previously insist on the dismission of Lord Bute's creatures. The Duke of Grafton desired Lord Gower to reconsider his offers—if refused, the Rockinghams would accept. Mr. Conway and I saw the bad policy of this conduct, and that the Bedfords would plead merit to the Rockinghams in their refusal, and would encourage the latter to stipulate too, which they were enough inclined to do for the same dismission of Lord Bute's people.

The Dividend Bill was carried in the committee by 60 to 41. Lord Mansfield had returned to that contest, and with Lord Lyttelton and Lord Temple combated the bill eagerly.[2] In the course of it, a favourable account arrived from India of the Company's affairs; yet the Duke of Grafton would not relinquish the bill. Some few lords signed a protest drawn by Burke, and corrected by Lord Mansfield.

---

[1] They were both descendants of Charles II.

[2] A brief report of the debate is given from Lord Hardwicke's Notes in the *Parliamentary History*, vol. xvi. 350, by which it appears that Lord Mansfield's opposition was most decided and effective. He treated it as an unprecedented exertion of absolute power to set aside a legal act of private men legally empowered to dispose of their own property—they having neither violated the general principles of justice nor the bye-laws of the Company; their circumstances being amply adequate to the payment of the dividend: and he also insisted that stock-jobbing would be promoted by the bill, and left no doubt of his own impression that such was its sole object. These arguments are reproduced with great ability in the Protest, *ibid.*, vol. xvi. 353, and have never been satisfactorily refuted. The insolvency of the Company—a ground afterwards abandoned by the Government—seems to be the only legitimate defence that could have been alleged for such an arbitrary act.—L. M.

CHAPTER III

Account of the Negotiations between the Duke of Grafton's Administration and Lord Rockingham, Mr. Grenville, and the Bedford Party ; and their final Failure.

1767

THE negotiation with the Bedfords continuing, Lord Northington thrust himself into it, and prevailed on the King to allow a place to Grenville, provided it was not the Treasury ; and Grenville had acquiesced. Lord Temple put off his journey into the country. Alarmed at this, I went to Lord Holland, where finding Mr. Mackenzie, I communicated my suspicions to both, knowing how much Lord Bute would dread such a coalition ; but it came to nothing. Lord Gower said there must be great alterations : Grenville would support without a place, but Lord Temple must have a considerable one, (though acquiescing in Grafton's retaining the Treasury,) and an equal share of power as he had demanded from Lord Chatham. The Duke of Grafton said he would have nothing to do with such conditions ; yet he was exasperated against Lord Chatham, who would neither resign nor come forth, yet was continually sending Dr. Addington privately to the King to assure his Majesty he should be able to appear in a month or two. The King offered the Duke to nominate to all places, if he would remain ; but he refused, and said he had sacrificed himself for Lord Chatham, who had given him such a dose that nothing should prevail on him to be minister longer. He was not less enraged at Charles Townshend, with whom he declared he would not sit in Council. He made the same declaration against the Duke of Richmond. This increased Conway's difficulties. The Rockinghams offended him as deeply, by meditating to place Lord Albemarle, a younger general, at the head of the army. Conway complained too of the King's acquiescing to re-admit Grenville; he had been told at Court, he said, that he must stay to exclude Grenville; now even to Grenville the door was open. However, the alarm I had given remedied much: Lord Bute came to town, and Mackenzie put off his journey to Scotland. Lord Northington pressing the Bedfords on the King, received so sharp a reprimand, that he left Court, nor would stay to read the King's speech to the Council, which Conway was obliged to do.

Amidst this confusion the Parliament rose on the 2nd of July, after one of the longest sessions that was almost ever known. The City bestowed its freedom on Charles Townshend for his behaviour on the East India business and the Dividend Bill, for which in truth he had deserved nothing but censure. Somebody, a little more sagacious, inserted in the papers the following epigram :—

> The joke of Townshend's box is little known;
> Great judgment in the thing the cits have shown.
> This compliment was an expedient clever
> To rid them of the like expense for ever.
> Of so burlesque a choice th' example sure
> For city-boxes must all longing cure.
> The honour'd ostracism at Athens fell
> Soon as Hyperbolus[1] had got the shell.

As times show men, the fluctuation and difficulties of those I am describing brought forth some symptoms, though not so fully as it appeared afterwards, of the singular cast of the Duke of Grafton's mind. Hitherto he had passed for a man of much obstinacy and firmness, of strict honour, devoid of ambition, and though reserved, more diffident than designing. He retained so much of this character, as to justify those who had mistaken the

---

[1] A worthless Athenian demagogue who was the last to suffer the penalty of ostracism about 415 B.C.—E.

rest. If he precipitated himself into the most sudden and inextricable contradictions, at least he pursued the object of the moment with inflexible ardour. If he abandoned himself to total negligence of business in pursuit of his sports and pleasures, the love of power never quitted him ; and when his will was disputed, no man was more imperiously arbitrary. If his designs were not deeply laid, at least they were conducted in profound silence. He rarely pardoned those who did not guess his inclination : it was necessary to guess, so rare was any instance of his unbosoming himself to either friends or confidants. Why his honour had been so highly rated, I can less account ; except that he had advertised it, and that obstinate young men are apt to have high notions before they have practised the world and essayed their own virtue.

Mr. Conway telling the Duke that Lord Rockingham desired to treat with his Grace, he commissioned Conway to bring them together. In the meantime Lord Gower reproaching the Duke with negotiating at once with the Bedfords and Rockinghams, as Conway had foreseen, the Duke denied even to Conway the having authorized him to settle a meeting. We were struck with this, and recollected how easily his Grace had been engaged by Lord Chatham to accept the Treasury, after the most vehement protestations against it ; and how often and how lightly of late he had refused, and then consented to remain there. Now, on having seen the King at Richmond, his Grace protested against holding the Treasury if Lord Temple was to be associated to equal power.

On the 5th of July the King sent likewise for Conway to Richmond, and showed him all Lord Chatham's letters.[1] His Majesty had sent for the latter ; Lady Chatham wrote to the King that it was impossible for her lord even to *write.* In the evening the King had offered to go to him. Lord Chatham himself then *wrote* to decline that honour, pleading his health was worse than ever. His Majesty

---

[1] Many, if not all of these, are to be found in the third volume of Lord Chatham's *Correspondence.*—E.

then asked Conway's advice. The latter proposed taking
Lord Rockingham's party. The King listened, but asking
what the Marquis himself would expect, and Conway
replying, the Treasury, the King seemed surprised, protested he had heard no mention of that, and asked, what
was then to become of the Duke of Grafton? There
seemed some mystery in this behaviour. Either Grafton
had kept his eye on the Treasury, or the King had
suffered him to allure Lord Rockingham with false hopes.
The King and the Duke had misunderstood or deceived
each other; which was the more likely, the characters of
both will tell. One point, however, was clear, that the
King had had the shrewdness to penetrate the Duke's
character earlier than anybody else had, and had found
that of all the various ministers he had tried, no man
would be more pliant in the closet or give him less trouble.
In truth the Duke was the reverse of Grenville; acquiesced
in whatever his Majesty proposed, and ever was as ready
to leave the room as the King was desirous he should.
He was just the minister whose facility and indolence
suited the views of the King, the Princess, and the
Favourite.

His Majesty next commissioned Conway to treat with
Lord Rockingham, with *no* restrictions but that the Duke
of Grafton and the Chancellor should be retained in the
Administration, though the Treasury should be ceded to
Rockingham. Whether the King forgot having allowed
this last condition to be offered, or hoped to evade it, the
following negotiations made it plain that he had never
intended to fulfil it, if he could form any system without
being reduced to that necessity. Two reasons combined
to rivet in his Majesty an aversion to having Lord
Rockingham for his First Minister; the one general and
permanent, the other temporary: the Marquis and his
party had and did persist in the exclusion of Lord Bute
and his connection. If possessed of power at the eve of a
new Parliament, he would be able to influence the elections
to the exclusion of that connection. The King was not

desirous of giving himself a minister who would thus be master both of him and the Parliament.

Mr. Conway having sent for the Duke of Richmond back to London, I was desired to meet him on the subject. I was averse, as having no opinion of the abilities of that party; yet yielded, as it was thought I had most weight of any man with that Duke; but though I loved and esteemed him, I knew how much he was swayed by the intemperate and inconsiderate folly of the Cavendishes; and I accordingly declared that, should the negotiation succeed, I would have nothing further to do with that set. When Mr. Conway had opened the proposal to the Duke, the first difficulty that started was on Lord Camden. The Duke said, they would not put a negative on him, but he would be the King's man. I asked if they expected that every man should depend on King Rockingham, and nobody on King George. 'But,' said the Duke, 'he will be Lord Bute's man, as Lord Northington had been.' I said, 'If Lord Bute desires to make another breach, will he ever want a tool?' 'Oh! but they must have a permanency.' 'I know none,' I said, 'but holding the Government for life by patent.' The Duke said, a junction with the Bedfords would secure it. 'How,' said I, 'my lord, will their coming under you make them less impatient to be above you? But have they in *their* negotiation stipulated anything for *your* friends? Ask them; if they cannot say they did, it will be proof they did not. You have insisted on Mr. Conway's resigning: here he is, on the point of doing so; and now you do not know what to do with him. Will you refuse the Government now when it is offered, and yet continue to oppose and impede it?' The Duke said, he had not opposed everything last session more than Mr. Conway. 'No!' said Conway, eagerly and with warmth; 'what does your Grace think of the land-tax?' In short, we could come to no agreement. Conway was much hurt, yet persisted in his intention of resigning, though his brother and I painted to him his obligations to the Duke of Grafton, and the unreasonableness of those who claimed his promise, though they knew not to what end ; and who adhered to their resolution of proposing to the Bedfords to join them, though Conway declared against that junction, and though they had no reason to expect the King would admit them on these terms.

As we had not been able to settle even preliminaries, the King again pressed the Duke of Grafton to undertake the whole, and remain at the head of the Treasury, promising him his fullest support. The Duke replied, with vehemence, that if his Majesty proposed his being minister, he would take his horse, ride out of England, and never return. This peremptory, and, as the King thought, invincible repugnance, suggested a new plan to his Majesty, at which Mr. Conway and I were more disturbed than at all the other difficulties. It was to make Lord Hertford minister, who, we knew, was too fond of his interest, to be proper for that post. Fortunately Lord Hertford, sensible of his own unfitness, started, and said it was impossible. The King said, ' You all give me advice, but none of you will serve me in my necessity.' Lord Hertford recommended Lord Egmont. ' He will never accept the Treasury,' said the King, ' but you may confer with him ; I give you full power to do what you please.' Lord Hertford said, he himself never spoke in Parliament, and consequently could not be proper for his Majesty's service. Yet he feared losing the King's favour by refusing; and by expressions, which his son Lord Beauchamp[1] dropped, we feared he would consent to take the Treasury for a time, on the grant of a ducal title. I told him there were but three options : to take

---

[1] Francis Seymour Conway. Viscount Beauchamp, afterwards second Marquis of Hertford, was M.P. for Lostwithiel, 1766-8, and Oxford, 1768-94. He was a Lord of the Treasury, 1774-80, Cofferer of the Household, 1780-2, Master of the Horse, 1804-6, and Lord Chamberlain, 1812-21. He married, as his second wife, Isabella Anne Ingram-Shepherd, eldest daughter of Charles, tenth and last Viscount Irvine, whose relations with George IV., when Prince Regent, are the subject of so many allusions in Moore's political verse. Lord Hertford died on 17th June 1822, aged eighty.—E.

the Rockinghams, and get rid of them again as soon as possible ; to engage Mr. Conway to accept the Treasury, which I could scarce think practicable ; or to place the Duke of Northumberland there, since, if Lord Bute *would* govern, he and his friends ought to stand in the front of the battle, instead of exposing others to danger for him. It would, besides, encourage others to list, as marking certainly that the King's favour would accompany the Administration. Lord Hertford said the King would not take that step before the new elections, lest the unpopularity should affect them ; though no doubt he would willingly make the Duke of Northumberland minister afterwards.

I went at night to Lord Holland. He ranted for an hour ; said the King might make a page [1] first minister, and could maintain him so ; that Mr. Conway, when turned out, ought never to have been replaced ; that it had been wrong to restore General A'Court and others ; and that a king of England could always make what ministry he pleased ;—he had forgotten that himself had tried for six weeks in the last reign with all the influence of the Crown, and could not succeed. All I could get from him was, that Lord Bute had not seen the King in private for two years—an assertion I believed as much as the rest.

[1] Lord Holland had long vented this maxim, though he himself and Lord Chatham had proved the futility of it in the last reign, when they had successfully attacked the Duke of Newcastle's Administration, on his setting Sir Thomas Robinson to lead the House of Commons. Lord Bute at the same instigation had erected himself into Minister, with Sir Francis Dashwood for his substitute, and though it is true the nation bore it for one session, it was so ridiculous an Administration, that the Earl took fright, resigned himself, and deposed his deputy. The King not having courage to repeat the system, though he liked it, had recourse to an artful expedient, which answered his purpose—which was to set up an ostensible Minister, but govern by his secret junto. Lord Rockingham had really been Minister for one year, but found he could not gain the King's confidence without submitting to the junto, and he was removed for Lord Chatham, another real Minister, whose madness or mad conduct left the King at liberty to revert to his own system, and then the Duke of Grafton and Lord North submitted to be ostensible Ministers.

In the meantime Lord Rockingham, on the strength of
the overtures made to him, had sent a formal message to
Woburn to invite the Bedfords to enter into the Administration with him.   The Duke of Bedford returned for
answer, that he was not averse to Lord Rockingham
having the Treasury ; for the rest, he would consult his
friends.

If Lord Rockingham thus exceeded the offers made to
him, the King laboured no less to prevent their taking
place.   The Queen asked Colonel Fitzroy if he had any
weight with his brother, and whether the Duke of Grafton
would leave the King in that distress ?   The King told
Fitzroy he had rather see the devil in his closet than Mr.
Grenville.

Lord Rockingham himself then went to Woburn,
whence Rigby had been despatched to settle measures
with Mr. Grenville.   The answer given to the Marquis
was, that Lord Temple and Mr. Grenville desired nothing
for themselves ; would support the future Administration,
and hoped their friends would be taken care of ; but could
give no further answer, till they knew if the bottom was to
be wide enough.[1]   This oracular and evasive reply did not
yet open the eyes of the Marquis, who had so fixed it in
his idea that Bute would betray him, and, indeed, had
made it so natural he should, that the most flimsy veil
could hide from him what no art ought to have been
able to conceal.   What imaginable reason ought to have
persuaded Rockingham that Grenville was willing to be
his substitute ?

This negotiation, and these general terms, Lord Rockingham communicated to the Duke of Grafton ; who,
whether offended at the indecency to the King, or
affronted at the slight put on himself by their treating
through him for his own place, grew much reconciled to

----

[1] The reply of the Grenvilles on this occasion seems to have been more
cordial than would be gathered from Walpole's account. See Duke of
Bedford's Journal in Cavendish's *Parliamentary Debates*, vol. i. pp. 604-5;
and the *Grenville Papers*, vol. iv. pp. 43-4, 50-1.—E.

keeping it himself. The Duke said to Lord Rockingham :
—'Your Lordship would not leave his Majesty one nomination. He had excepted nobody but the Chancellor,
and I told your Lordship he ordered me to except myself
too ; but I told you from myself I would give up the
Treasury to you. By the terms you now ask, you certainly
do not mean to come in.' Lord Rockingham had sense or
irresolution enough almost to own he did not. On the
report of this conference, the King said he would be at
liberty to alter, accept, or reject any part of their plan as
he should see cause.

The negotiation having gone so far, it was necessary to
proceed till it should produce either agreement or rupture.
The Duke of Grafton and Mr. Conway accordingly were
empowered by his Majesty to treat in form with the
Marquis. On the 15th of July they asked his terms. He
spoke vaguely, but highly. At night, Lord Hertford
showed me the following notes of a letter, which he, his
brother, and the Duke had drawn to send in the Duke's
name to the Marquis :—

'My dear Lord,—After having delivered to his Majesty
the answer which your Lordship communicated to General
Conway and myself this morning, I was commanded to
acquaint your Lordship that the King will expect to
receive from your Lordship the plan on which you and
your friends would propose to come in, in order to extend
and strengthen his Administration, that his Majesty may
be enabled to judge how far the same shall appear consistent with his Majesty's honour and the public service.'

I by no means liked this letter. Grenville and Rigby
I knew wished to prevent Rockingham's acceptance, as
they must come in under him, or remain out of place. If
he declined, they would become more united, and Grenville would attain the ascendant. A list I could not
imagine they would deliver, which would disgust all that
were to be proscribed ; nor could they easily agree to
form a list. All they could wish was, an opportunity to
break off the treaty, and impute the rupture to the King's

defence of Lord Bute's tools.   This letter furnished every
one of these opportunities.   *To extend and strengthen*,
implied a resolution of retaining the present system, of
which both the Rockinghams and the Bedfords complained.   *Consistent with his honour*, bespoke fidelity to
Lord Bute's friends ; and *expect*, sounded harsh and
peremptory.   Mr. Conway had already objected to
that word.   I wished to have the letter so expressed
that the King's friends might be able to show it, and
exasperate mankind against the unreasonableness of
the Opposition.   I accordingly altered it thus :—

'My dear Lord,—After having delivered to his Majesty
the answer which your Lordship communicated to General
Conway and myself this morning, I was commanded to
acquaint your Lordship that the King *wishes your Lordship
would specify to him* the plan on which you and your
friends would propose to come in, in order *to form an
extensive and solid Administration* ; that his Majesty may
be enabled to judge how far the same *may be advantageous
to his Majesty's and the public service.*'

These corrections were approved by the Duke, Lord
Hertford, and Mr. Conway ; yet the Duke came and told
me the next day that he had restored the words *extend and
strengthen the Administration*.   This had been done no
doubt by his Majesty's order ; but though I wished, as
much as his Majesty, to break off the negotiation, I saw
how improper the method was : it was treating for a
change and refusing to make it at the same time.   Accordingly Lord Rockingham returned an answer as understanding it in that manner ; but, withal, nothing could surpass
the insolence of that answer.   It was long, and, in our
hurry, I forgot to keep a copy of it ; but it concluded
with hoping his Grace had explained to the King that
he (Rockingham) had laid down for a principle that this
Administration was at an end ; and, therefore, if his
Majesty liked *he* should form a new one, he desired
previously to have an interview with his Majesty.

Impertinent as the body of the letter and the assumption

to himself of forming an Administration were, it seemed but reasonable that the King should see the man whom he had sent for to be his minister : and to have refused him an audience on the arrogance of his style, would, probably, bc falling into the snare they had laid for breaking off the treaty. Under this dilemma, the Duke of Grafton desired me to draw up an answer. I did, and was so lucky as not only to please all the persons concerned—the King, the Duke, and Mr. Conway, but to embarrass Lord Rockingham and his Council so entirely, that they could neither answer it nor get out of the perplexity with tolerable honour or conduct. Here is the letter :—

'My dear Lord,—I have laid your Lordship's letter before his Majesty, and have the satisfaction of acquainting your Lordship that his Majesty's gracious sentiments concur with your Lordship's in regard to the forming a comprehensive plan of administration ; and that his Majesty, desirous of uniting the hearts of all his subjects, is ready and willing to appoint such a comprehensive Administration as may exclude no denomination of men attached to his person and government. When your Lordship is prepared to offer a plan of administration formed on these views, his Majesty is willing your Lordship should yourself lay the same before him for his consideration.'

Lord Rockingham having received this letter, owned to the Duke of Grafton and Mr. Conway that it was the most artful letter he ever saw, and would puzzle him and his friends to answer. The Chancellor told Lord Hertford he never saw anything so ably drawn ; not a word could be mended. As it passed for the Duke of Grafton's composition, I allowed for what quantity of applause might be attributed to that belief. The letter, however, remained unanswered : Lord Rockingham only pressing the Duke for an audience of a quarter of an hour with the King ; but the Duke told him it could not be obtained.

At night, Mr. Conway and I going home with Lord

Hertford to supper, the latter found a most pathetic letter from the King, which said the Duke of Grafton had just been with him, and had peremptorily declared he would not go on without Mr. Conway ; and therefore his Majesty called upon Mr. Conway, in the most earnest manner, not to leave him exposed to Lord Rockingham, who had insulted him so much.   The Duke of Grafton, the latter said too, had promised the King to desire Mr. Walpole would use all his interest with Mr. Conway ; to whom his Majesty engaged to give the Blues on Lord Ligonier's death, and any civil place, if he did not like that of Secretary of State.   Mr. Conway cried out at once, it was impossible.   I immediately saw that if I persuaded him *then* to stay, he would dispute, and thence would confirm himself in his resolution.   I determined, therefore, to let the first burst of his feeling pass over without contradiction, that I might work on him another way.   I walked about the room with as melancholy an air as I could put on, only dropping now and then, that it was the most serious crisis I ever knew.   At supper I spoke not a word.   When the servants were retired, his brother, Lady Hertford,[1] and his own wife, Lady Ailesbury, attacked him in the most eager manner, pressing him to comply with the King.   He resisted as firmly ;   I jogged Lord Hertford privately, who understood me, and said no more : but the two ladies were out of patience, thinking me on Mr. Conway's side.   Still I would not speak, but seemed to be lost in thought, though I attended to every word he said, to learn where his principal objection lay, and soon found it was to Lord Chatham.   When we rose up to go away, the ladies pressed me to give my opinion, which I had expected, and intended to bring them to do.   I then spoke with tears in my eyes ; said I was sensible of the honour the King had done me ; but, for the King nor anybody, would I give Mr. Conway any advice in so important a moment, till I had considered the question most coolly

---

[1] Lady Isabella Fitzroy, the youngest daughter of Charles, 2nd Duke of Grafton.—E.

and thoroughly. He was much pleased, and said that was very fair. I then knew I should do what I would; Lord Hertford proposed that he and his brother should go early the next morning to the Duke of Grafton, but I shifted that off, and winked to Lord Hertford, who then said, he would go first, and Mr. Conway should come to me in the morning to talk the matter over. The moment I got home, I wrote back to Lord Hertford to explain my meaning, and desired he would not come to me till an hour after the time appointed for meeting his brother at my house.

The next day (the 18th), Mr. Conway came to me. I told him he had convinced me that while the treaty was going on, he could not with honour engage to the King to undertake a share of the Administration, which would encourage the King to break off the treaty; but if Lord Rockingham and his friends continued unreasonable, I thought him bound in honour to extricate the King from the difficulties in which he had, by his promise of resignation, involved him. That if he (Conway) refused, his Majesty, rather than give up all Lord Bute's friends, would certainly set up some one of them: such a step would drive the Opposition into the last violences, and might end in a civil war. That the nation was now quiet and satisfied; and that all sober men, not ranked in any faction, would not bear to see the King taken prisoner. That all men saw through the pretences of the several factions; that all danger of arbitrary power was over, when the most Lord Bute pretended was, to save a few of his friends from being displaced: but that another danger was growing upon us, a danger I had always feared as much as the power of the Crown,—danger from aristocracy, and from those confederacies of great lords. I showed him that the present dissatisfactions were nothing but combinations of interested and ambitious men; that Lord Rockingham and his party had deserted their principles by adopting Grenville and the Bedfords, who had been the instruments of Lord Bute's bad measures, besides

having been criminal in other excesses without his partici-
pation.   I dwelt on the outrageous behaviour of the Duke
of Richmond the day before, who had told me that if
Conway should refuse to act with Grenville when united
with them (the Rockinghams), they would bid him go
about his business; and that he himself would tell Conway
so to his face (the greatest excess, in truth, of which I
ever knew the Duke of Richmond guilty ; whose friendly
heart was uncommonly unaccustomed to resent a difference
of opinion in those he loved, and who in a few days after
this heat gave a clear proof of his firm attachment to Conway).   I continued to say to the latter, that I saw he must
do something, though I did not well know what : if anything, I thought that, to show he did not act from interest,
and to strike a great stroke in character, he must resume
the seals of Secretary of State, but refuse the salary.   The
Rockinghams might then say what they pleased ; that I
myself had always defied all parties on the strength of my
disinterestedness : and I then offered him half my fortune,
which he generously refused, but he was exceedingly struck
—as I knew he would be—by a proposal that would place
his virtue in so fair a light.   How well soever I knew the
method of drawing him to my opinion, it is but justice to
say that, had I been so inclined, I never could have
swayed him to any wrong act; nor had I so often occasion
to lead him towards my sentiments as to fix his irresolution, which wandered constantly from one doubt to
another, and paid too much deference to what men would
say of him.   This was the case in the transaction I am
relating.   Lord Rockingham and his friends did not weigh
a moment what Mr. Conway owed to the King, to the
Duke of Grafton, to his country, or to himself.   They
availed themselves of what had been more a threat than
a promise, in order to blow up the Administration and
create confusion.   To Conway they had not paid the least
deference, acquiesced in nothing he proposed to them or
for them, and most arrogantly pretended to involve him,
against his repeated declaration, in a system composed for

their own convenience, and by their own wilful blindness
with his and their country's most grievous enemies. Could
I employ too much art to set him above such treatment?
He told me he had had some such thought as I mentioned,
and would certainly follow my advice; but he would
resign first on the next Wednesday (this was Friday), and
then he should be able to talk with more authority to the
Rockinghams. We agreed to keep this a secret from all
the world; and I was only to give the Duke of Grafton
and Lord Hertford hopes. I said he might be sure I
would keep the secret for my own sake; circumstances
might change, and I would not pledge myself to the King,
and be reproached afterwards if he was disappointed. I
said, too, that I would not go to Court (as I ought to have
done after the King's letter), that I might give no jealousy;
but would let the King know the reason of my absenting
myself. 'I like policy,' said I, 'but I will always speak
truth, which I think the best policy.' Conway grew impatient at his brother's not coming, and went to the Duke
of Richmond. Lord Hertford arrived the next moment.
I bade him be satisfied, but would not tell him on what
grounds. He did not approve his brother's resigning, but
I convinced him it was necessary to yield that point in
order to carry the greater. We agreed, indeed, that to
his brother he should not give it up, that his brother might
not suspect our being too much in concert. We then
went to him. The Duke of Richmond told him that they
had sent for the Bedfords to town. Lord Hertford and I
disputed about the resignation before Mr. Conway; and
as I wanted to prepare the Duke of Grafton, I said I was
sure I could convince the last. Lord Hertford said I
could not. 'Well,' said I, two or three times, 'you shall
see I can. I will go to him—shall I?' Conway said,
'Well, go.' Lord Hertford kept his brother in dispute. I
went, gave the Duke hopes; told him he himself must
retain his place, but must let Mr. Conway resign. He
said, if it would satisfy Mr. Conway's delicacy, he would.
I thus carried all my points, and knew I was doing right.

At the same time I must confess there was a moment in which, reflecting on my success, and on the important service I had rendered to the King in so distressful and critical an hour, I was tempted to think of myself. I saw I might have written to the King, or asked an audience, or made any terms I pleased for myself. My brother had just been at the point of death, and presented me with the near prospect of losing half my income.[1] What would remain, would depend on the will of every succeeding First Lord of the Treasury; and it was determined in my own breast that I would pay court to none. I resisted, however; and in this favourable shining hour, resolved to make no one advantage for myself. I scorned to tell either my friend or myself, and sat down contented with having done the best for him, and with shutting the door against a crew I hated or despised: yet I had one more struggle to come before the victory was complete.

At night the two brothers and I saw the Duke of Grafton again. Our intelligence agreed that Grenville had said to his friends that he had reserved himself at liberty to oppose. This showed what headlong voluntary dupes Lord Rockingham and his friends had made themselves.

On the 20th, a meeting was held at the Duke of New-castle's, of Lord Rockingham, the Duke of Richmond and Dowdeswell, with Newcastle himself, on one part; and of the Duke of Bedford, Lord Weymouth, and Rigby on the other. The Duke of Bedford had powers from Grenville to act for him, but did not seem to like Lord Rockingham's taking on himself to name to places. On the latter asking what friends they wished to prefer, Rigby said, with his cavalier bluntness, 'Take the Court Calendar and give them one, two, three thousand pounds a year.' Bedford observed that they had said nothing on measures: Mr.

---

[1] This refers to the collectorship of customs from which Walpole drew an income of about £1400 a year. It had been granted to the 1st Earl of Orford for his own life and the lives of his two elder sons Robert and Edward. Robert the 2nd Earl died on 1st April 1751, but Sir Edward Walpole, in spite of Horace Walpole's alarms, survived until 12th January 1784. The payment of his salary as Usher of the Exchequer appears to have been irregular. (See *Letters*, 1857, vol. i. pp. lxxxii-iv.)—E.

Grenville would insist on the sovereignty of this country over America being asserted. Lord Rockingham replied, he would never allow it to be a question whether he had given up this country: he never had. The Duke insisted on a declaration. The Duke of Richmond said, 'We may as well demand one from you, that you never will disturb that country again.' Neither would yield. However, though they could not agree on measures, as the distribution of places was more the object of their thoughts and of their meeting, they reverted to that topic.[1] Lord Rockingham named Mr. Conway; Bedford started; said, he had no notion of Conway; had thought he was to return to the military line. The Duke of Richmond said, it was true Mr. Conway did not desire a civil place; did not know whether he would be persuaded to accept one; but they were so bound to him for his resignation, and thought him so able, they must insist. The Duke of Bedford said, Conway was an officer *sans tache*, but not a minister *sans tache*. Rigby said, not one of the present Cabinet should be saved. Dowdeswell asked, 'What! not one?'—'No'—'What! not Charles Townshend?' 'Oh!' said Rigby, 'that is different; besides, he has been in opposition.' 'So has Conway,' said Dowdeswell; 'he has voted twice against the Court, Townshend but once.' 'But,' said Rigby, 'Conway is Bute's man.' 'Pray,' said Dowdeswell, 'is not Charles Townshend Bute's?' 'Ay, but Conway is governed by his brother Hertford, who is Bute's.' 'So is Charles Townshend by his brother,[2] who is Bute's.' 'But Lady Ailesbury[3] is a Scotchwoman.' 'So is Lady Dalkeith.'[4] From this dialogue the assembly fell to

[1] The public opinion of the day on this subject may be gathered from a letter of Gilly Williams (2nd December 1766), who while referring to the late resignation of Admiral Saunders on conscientious motives, speaks of 'these childish indiscretions of quarrelling with two or three thousand a year.' (Jesse's *George Selwyn and his Contemporaries*,' 1843, vol. ii. p. 91.)—E.

[2] George, Lord Townshend.

[3] Lady Caroline Campbell, wife of General Conway.

[4] Lady Caroline Campbell, wife of Charles Townshend. These two ladies were daughters of two Johns, Dukes of Argyle, and were widows of the Earls of Ailesbury and Dalkeith.

wrangle, and broke up quarrelling. So high did the heats go, that the Cavendishes ran about the town, publishing the issue of the conference, and taxing the Bedfords with treachery.

Notwithstanding this, the same evening the Duke of Bedford sent to desire another interview, to which Lord Rockingham yielded ; but the Duke of Richmond refused to be present. So much, however, were the minds on both sides ulcerated by former and recent disputes, and so incompatible were their views, that the second meeting broke up in a final quarrel ; and Lord Rockingham released the other party from all their engagements. The Duke of Bedford desired they might still continue friends—that was, at least, agree to oppose together. Lord Rockingham said, No ; they were broken for ever.[1]

It was at this meeting that the Duke of Newcastle appeared for the last time [2] in a political light. Age and feebleness at length wore out that busy passion for intrigue, which power had not been able to satiate, nor disgrace correct. He languished above a year longer, but was heard of no more on the scene of affairs.

Chance and folly having thus dispersed those clouds that were only formidable by their assemblage, the task grew easier to re-establish some serenity ; yet the principal actor could not help distinguishing his superior absurdity before the act was closed.

The Duke of Richmond acquainted me, on the 22nd,

---

[1] According to the Duke of Bedford's Journal, this meeting originated with the Duke of Newcastle ; it took place at Newcastle House on the 21st, at 9 o'clock in the evening. The two Dukes, the Marquis, and Messrs. Rigby and Dowdeswell were the only persons present. The point on which they finally disagreed was Mr. Conway's continuing Secretary of State with the lead in the Commons. ' This,' says the Duke, ' necessarily put an end to any further possibility of going on, and we broke up with our declaring ourselves free from all engagements to one another, and to be as before this negotiation began.'—Cavendish's *Debates*, vol. i. Appendix, p. 606.—L. M.

[2] At the beginning of the ensuing year, being in great danger, and recovering to some degree, he resolved to give over politics ; he was then seventy-four. This determination he notified by letter to Princess Amelie, Lord Rockingham, and others ; for he could not quit folly but in a foolish manner. He languished near ten months, and died November 17, 1768.

that Lord Rockingham was going to the King to thank
his Majesty for his gracious offers, to ask pardon for
having dealt with Grenville and the Bedfords, and to
acquaint him that he could not undertake the Administration. One should rather have expected that when he
confessed his error in applying to them, he would propose
to accept without them. I said, not with much ardour,
that I hoped they would now accept alone ; and I asked
what was to become of Conway? The Duke replied,
They had told him he must go on. 'Well, my lord,' said I,
'but then you cannot continue to oppose.' 'No,' replied
the Duke, 'if the King should offer us full power, he
might be sure now that we could not make use of it
against his friends ; yet I do not know whether we should
undertake. I think we must at least allow our friends to
take on with the Court.' I commended this noble behaviour, and approved the admission of their friends ; but
their first thoughts had been too right to last.

Lord Rockingham went to Court, and asked an audience ;
but instead of the decent part he had meditated, he sillily
entered into former complaints against Lord Bute. The
King, as unnecessarily frank, owned that he had never
intended to give him the Treasury, but to keep the Duke
of Grafton. Thus they parted, each more soured than
they had met. The King complained that Lord Rockingham had taxed him with breach of his word, and that
he had not offered to accept without Grenville, etc.
Lord Rockingham, that the King had not asked him to
undertake—as if the language he had held had been
conciliatory. His party resented highly what they called
the King's insincerity ; and the Duke of Richmond, dining
with Conway and me, expressed the utmost warmth,
declaring they would accept nothing under as full powers
as had been granted to Lord Chatham. Conway endeavoured to moderate ; but as I could go further than it
was proper for Conway to do, I ridiculed the ascribing as
much importance to Lord Rockingham as to Lord
Chatham ; and said the former could only compose an

Administration in dumb show, so few of the party being speakers, and none of any rank among them, but his Grace, having any parts. I asked how they could treat Mr. Conway so ill? They had called on him to resign; had that very morning acknowledged he must stay, and had advised him to stay; and now the Duke said, they had only meant he should stay just for the present moment. But there was no allaying the Duke's heat; and indeed, unless they would have acquiesced in the only rational plan, a junction with the Administration, without insisting on the pre-eminence of Rockingham, it was indifferent to me whether they were pacified or not. The difficulty, however, was increased to Conway by the regard they had paid to him, and which had widened their breach with the Bedfords. But besides their having allowed the necessity of his staying in place, their struggle for him was not only what he had deserved at their hands, but had much the appearance of having been but a decent tribute, since they had owned to the Bedfords that they doubted his accession; and what was yet stranger, they had stickled for him, when they were morally certain he was not only averse to, but would not accede to, their coalition with Grenville. Every part of the miscarriage had flowed from their own fault. They had conjoined men to their plan without the King's leave, even without asking it, had refused on the terms he had offered; and had concluded by affronting him to his face; had owned they had no excuse for opposing any longer; and now were desirous Mr. Conway should oppose with them, only because they had been to blame. Such inconsistencies could not be wiped out by their having made use of his name against his consent. Yet, as Conway's delicacy was great, I told the Duke of Grafton, when he sent for me the next morning, that it was of absolute necessity that his Majesty should once more offer the Administration in form to Lord Rockingham, as nothing but the positive refusal of the latter would induce Mr. Conway to go on. I knew, I said, it was not very civil to his Grace to advise him to propose again a successor to himself; but my confidence that Rockingham would again refuse, and the benefits resulting thence, encouraged me to press that advice. The Duke, though disinclined to the measure, was persuaded. I sent Lord Hertford to the King with the same counsel : said, I was sure they would refuse ; if they did, I besought his Majesty to express no resentment, but to soothe them, and say, that though they would not undertake the Administration, he yet hoped they would support it, and suffer their friends to enlist, which at least would produce a defection from their party.

The Duke acquainted the King with my advice, who expressed extreme repugnance to it, yet consented to follow it, though it was very grievous, he said, to humble himself again to Lord Rockingham, who, but the preceding day, had taxed him with an ancient breach of promise. To Lord Hertford his Majesty observed, that it was very extraordinary advice to come from me. Lord Hertford explained that my reasons were founded upon the hopes of carrying Mr. Conway clearly from Lord Rockingham, on a new refusal of the latter ; and for fear his Majesty should be reduced, if Conway wavered, again to deliver himself up to Mr. Grenville. The King replied, he would sooner meet Grenville at the end of his sword than let him into his closet ; and that there must be men in England who would form an Administration for him, and not let him be reduced to that mortification. His Majesty would not yield to send for Lord Rockingham, but allowed the offer to be once more renewed,—a consent from which I drew a remarkable observation : as his Majesty yielded on the first proposal (for he saw the Duke before the conversation with Lord Hertford), it was plain he did not always consult the Princess or Lord Bute, having now allowed the Duke to make the offer, before the latter quitted the closet.

The Duke, Mr. Conway, and I, consulted on the best method of delivering the message. Conway thought it was best to do it, as I had advised, in a free, friendly way, exhorting the Marquis to let them all re-unite in their old system; and Conway added, 'If they refuse, your Grace and I must then do the best we can.'

At night, the Duke, Conway, and Lord Rockingham met. The Duke, in the King's name, offered him the Treasury, in the amicable way agreed on. Lord Rockingham was all reserve, and would only say, this was no message. The Duke offended, and naturally cold and shy, would not repeat positively that it was; and thus the meeting broke off.

Having engaged the King and Duke in so bold and hazardous a step, I trembled lest it should take another turn than I expected: and though my advice had not been completely followed, yet as it sufficed to disgust Conway, I rejoiced that it had ended so fortunately, especially as I doubted from recollecting circumstances and from Lord Rockingham's demand of a precise message, whether he would not have accepted; in which case the King would probably have flown off, and Conway have been offended the other way, if the terms, when offered and accepted, had not been granted. That Rockingham fluctuated between ambition and distrust was evident, for late that very night the Duke of Richmond came to Lord Hertford's door and sent for me down to his chariot, when, though ashamed of the silly message imposed upon him, he made me this frantic and impertinent proposal from Lord Rockingham, which I was desired to deliver to Mr. Conway,—that the latter would engage the King to allow the Marquis to try again to get the Bedfords—the Bedfords whom, two days before, Rockingham and all his party had absolutely broken with, and published as the most treacherous of men, and who had proscribed Conway himself. Should the Bedfords again refuse, the Marquis notified that he would then deign to accept the Administration. I neither wished his acceptance, nor chose to run any further risks of it. Conway, to whom I communicated it, treated this senseless proposal as it deserved; and the Duke of Richmond did not attempt to defend it.[1]

[1] For further particulars as to these negotiations and the motives of the parties concerned, see Dowdeswell's *Memoir* and the Duke of Bedford's *Journal* in Cavendish's *Parliamentary Debates*, vol. i. Appendix, pp. 582-5, 604-7; *Bedford Correspondence*, vol. iii. pp. xlviii.-l., 365-89; Burke's *Correspondence* (1844), vol. i. pp. 132-49; Almon's *Political Register*, vol. i. pp. 201-8 (said to be written by Lord Temple); Rockingham's *Memoirs*, vol. ii. pp. 46-58; *Grenville Papers*, vol. iv. pp. 35, *et seq.*; Walpole's *Letters*, vol. v. pp. 54-62.

Walpole regarded any one likely to become Prime Minister as a rival to Conway; hence his bitterness towards Rockingham, who adhered firmly throughout to his 'fundamental principles,' viz., opposition to the Bute system, and to the policy formerly pursued by Grenville. The latter and Lord Temple were probably really responsible for the failure of the scheme; but the three sections of the Opposition had but little in common except distrust of Bute and the King.

The two points on which the negotiations were broken off—the questions of American policy and of Conway's leadership in the Commons show, says Lord John Russell, 'that this powerful confederacy was not agreed either upon measures or upon men.' He adds: 'Fifty small intriguers, Mr. Horace Walpole among the busiest, carried tales from one party to the other, inflamed animosities, betrayed confidences, assailed or thwarted the King, as their fancy or interest suggested.'—(*Bedford Correspondence*, vol. iii. xlix.-l.) —E.

CHAPTER IV

General Observations.—Attempt to procure an Earldom for Lord Holland.—
Reconstruction of the Administration.—Death of Charles Townshend—
Of the Comte de Guerchy.—Of the Duke of York.—Characters of the
Royal Dukes.—French Travellers in England and Ireland.—Generosity
of Conway.—Conduct of Lord Townshend in Ireland.—Meeting of
Parliament.—Debates on the Address.—Fresh Negotiations with the
Bedford Party.

1767

NOTHING now remained but to resettle the Administration as we could on its old bottom, no new forces being to
be had.   But I must make a few observations.

In all my experience of the King or knowledge of his
measures, he never interfered with his Ministers, scarce
took any part in his own business (I speak of the past
years of his reign), unless when he was to undo an
Administration.   Whether hating or liking the persons he
employed, the moment he took them, he seemed to resign
himself entirely to their conduct for the time.   If what
they proposed was very disagreeable to him, at most he
avoided it by delay.   How far he had entered into his
mother's and Lord Bute's plans while they were all-
powerful at the beginning of his reign, cannot be known.
Afterwards he had, undoubtedly, confidence in none of
his Ministers ; which according with his extreme indolence
and indifference to all men, his Ministers found little
obstruction to their views from the closet, till the greater
indolence of the Duke of Grafton and Lord North taught
his Majesty to act on his own judgment, assisted by the
secret junto of the creatures of Lord Bute.   The sensible
disgrace that fell on the Crown from so frequent a change

of Ministries, had, at last, alarmed the King, and made a lasting impression. And yet the ruling principle of the reign, which had been, by breaking and dividing all parties, to draw attention and dependence only to the King himself, had succeeded so happily, that even these storms tended to strengthen the unbounded influence at which the King aspired, and which he pursued invariably on every returning calm. The ductility and congenial indolence of the Duke of Grafton, accompanied with much respect and good breeding, fixed his Majesty in preferring him to all the men whom he *could* employ : and though the Duke not long afterwards fell into a connection of very ill-odour at Court,[1] *yet* the tedious tyranny of Grenville, and the inveteracy of Rockingham to Bute, were so much more dreaded, that Grafton did not cease to be almost a favourite ; with the additional comfort to the King, that if forced to sacrifice him, it would be the loss of an useful tool, rather than of a Minister for whom he had any fondness.

Another observation is, that during the whole preceding negotiation the names of Lord Chatham and Charles Townshend were scarce mentioned, so insignificant had both rendered themselves to the nation and to every faction in it.

I cannot help reflecting, too, that had the Duke of Cumberland or the Duke of Devonshire lived, men in the prime of their age, many of the follies I have been recounting had probably been avoided. The excellent sense of the former would have kept Lord Rockingham and the Cavendishes within bounds ; and the deference of his Royal Highness for the Crown would have restrained them from the excesses into which they fell against the King, the Princess, and the Favourite ; for though nobody had less partiality to the two latter, he would not have encouraged a useless inveteracy, when himself would have enjoyed so much credit in the Government. The Duke

---

[1] His connection with Nancy Parsons, which has been rendered famous by Junius.—E.

of Devonshire, though inferior in parts even to Lord Rockingham, must have had the precedence of him in Administration ; and being diffident, timid, decent, and fond of court, no man would have been more alarmed at the violent and obnoxious counsels of his brother John. The latter would undoubtedly have enjoyed much credit with the Duke ; but as men govern others by humouring their tempers, not by driving them into contrary extremes, I question whether Devonshire would not oftener have checked than have been impelled by Lord John's visions. As either the Prince or the Duke would probably have prevented many scenes that I have related, so both, I am persuaded, would have obstructed and discountenanced the frenzy into which their friends were hurried in the subsequent Parliament.

The share I had had in these transactions could not be totally a secret, especially to those who looked narrowly into or had connections with the Court ; yet it did surprise me, I own, when the first person I beheld at my feet was Lord Holland.   He sent for me, and weakly pretending that it was to gratify his wife, of all women the most indifferent to grandeur, he supplicated me in the most flattering terms to obtain him an earldom from the Duke of Grafton.   In a long intimacy, and during every period of his power, he had barely once, and that when he foresaw I should not accept it,[1] offered me a faint attempt to serve me conditionally.   I had the strongest presumption for believing that he had afterwards essentially injured me for declining to assist his bad measures.   I was not at all sorry to have this opportunity of repaying both debts by forgiving both, and by endeavouring to obtain what he desired.   The King had declined his request, pleading the state of his affairs.   I told Lord Holland I would use all

---

[1] It was after Mr. Pelham's death, when he had joined the Duke of Newcastle, and was made Secretary of State.   He came to me and told me he believed that he could procure for my own life the place I held during my brother's, if I would be well with the Duke of Newcastle.   I replied warmly and peremptorily, 'Mr. Fox, do you think that, after laughing at the Duke of Newcastle all my life, I will stoop to accept a favour from him?'

my interest with the Duke of Grafton to oblige him, but
that I was not so vain as to think I could obtain the
earldom for him, if his own importance could not. I did
earnestly labour it, and really believe the Duke of Grafton
did too, as he promised me he would : but the King could
not be persuaded to grant it : I know not why. Lord
Holland had well earned it. He read to me at the same
time a long letter from Lord Bute, dated September 1st,
1766, in which in the strongest terms the Favourite disclaimed having been made acquainted with the last
promotion of Lord Chatham, and the restoration of his
own brother Mackenzie ; adding that a *great lady*, to
whom he (the Earl) often paid his court, had been as
ignorant and incredulous of those steps as himself ; and
protesting that himself had not seen the King since the
preceding July. I knew not how to give entire credit to
this epistle : however, as it owned the continuation of his
visits to the Princess, it imported little what embargo it
was thought prudent to lay on his actual commerce with
the King, nor by what channels the intercourse was kept
up. The credit which Mackenzie soon gained with the
Duke of Grafton spoke the duration of favour : and as no
symptoms appeared of the Queen having acquired any
political ascendant over her husband, the old connections
probably subsisted still, though the clamours of the times
inspired great caution in conducting them.[1]

On the 28th Lord Hertford, Mr. Conway, and I supped
with the Duke of Grafton, when he and Conway were to
take their final resolutions, and to fix their future Administration. Conway appeared by far the more determined ; yet

---

[1] A distinct confirmation of Lord Bute's statement may be found in the
Memoirs of Lewis Dutens, the Secretary to Mr. Mackenzie. His Lordship
assured that gentleman 'that since the year 1776 he never interfered, directly
or indirectly, with public affairs, nor had privately seen the King during that
period. He continued to visit regularly the Princess of Wales ; but when
the King came to see his mother, Lord Bute always retired by a back staircase.'—(*Memoirs of a Traveller now in Retirement*, vol. iv. pp. 182-3.)—
L. M. [See also Lord J. Russell's *Memorials and Correspondence of Fox*,
vol. i. p. 36, and the *Bedford Correspondence*, vol. iii. p. 329.—E.]

both agreed to go on, though the Duke laid in a specious salvo, that it should only be till Lord Chatham should recover.   From that moment there was no further question of him.   Conway, who desired his own liberty, willingly subscribed to that condition.   The list was next to be adjusted.   I proposed the Duke of Northumberland should be President of the Council, as an indication that the King intended this Administration should last.   Both the Duke and Conway objected as savouring too much of Bute : for, however Rigby had charged Conway with being sub-servient to the Favourite, no man living was less propense to him, nor had less connection with him.   I myself, who wished the Administration should have his support, had never been within his doors after he had been First Lord of the Treasury ; and when I wished he should traverse any counsels of any faction, I was reduced to drop notices accidentally to such of his friends as I happened to have a common acquaintance with.   Even Lord Hertford, though connected with him by his son's marriage,[1] had not the slightest intercourse with him—not from disin-clination, but from the shy, uncommunicative, and now timid disposition of that unpopular man.   A greater diffi-culty presented itself,—the Chancellor[2] of Ireland was dying.   Lord Chatham, wishing to gain the support of Norton, had wanted to purchase and appoint the latter to succeed to those Seals.   Conway had already strongly objected to Norton on the flagrancy of his character, and renewed his opposition now, fearing abuse from the Rock-inghams.   I said, When *they* had adopted even Sandwich, could they reproach him with taking Norton ?   If Norton was not for the Ministers, he would be against them, and was too able to let it be indifferent on which side he acted. I proposed the Duke should take the deed on himself. Conway finding the Duke would not go on, unless this

---

[1] Lord Beauchamp and Lord Mountstewart, sons of the Earls of Hertford and Bute, had married the two daughters of the late Lord Windsor.

[2] John Bowes, who died 22nd July 1767. On 9th January 1768 James Hewitt was appointed to the post with the title of Baron Lifford. See vol. i. p. 285, note.—E.

was done, gave it up. We then sketched out other arrangements; and it was settled that Conway should be either
Cabinet-Counsellor and Lieutenant-General of the Ordnance, or third Secretary of State for America.

The Lieutenancy of the Ordnance was pitched upon, as
Lord Townshend, to please his brother Charles, was destined to be Viceroy of Ireland in the room of Lord Bristol.
The last, whose stately manners and delicate form were
ill-adaped to please so rude and turbulent a people as the
Irish, and who was now deprived of the support of his
patron, Lord Chatham, had been alarmed at the rough
reception that he heard was preparing for him; and fearing
he should be turned out if Lord Rockingham or Grenville
became Minister, had declared he would resign his government. He now wrote to the Duke of Grafton, that if his
Majesty still laid his commands on him, he would go and
take possession, but should not be sorry to be excused.
He was taken at his word, and Lord Townshend appointed
his successor. The latter yielded the Ordnance handsomely to Conway, who was obliged to retain his old
Seals, it having been observed that a third Secretary of
State being a new office could not sit in the House of
Commons. The Duke of Grafton persisted in not dismissing Lord Northington, being desirous of keeping some
post in his power that could facilitate his introducing the
Bedfords. Thus no room was left for Lord Egmont or
Lord Edgecumbe, with whom we were all willing to
strengthen the Administration. Its recovering its permanency at all was a signal disappointment to Grenville
and Rockingham, who had flattered themselves that
Grafton and Conway could not be induced to go on, and
who had certainly quarrelled upon the presumption that
either the one or the other must succeed. Conway was
indeed most averse to accept the Ordnance and retain the
Seals, and wished heartily to give up the latter; and when
compelled to keep both, would not accept the very lucrative emoluments of Secretary, as I had suggested: but of
that hereafter.

Having thus contributed once more to a settlement
agreeable to my wishes, fatigued with so long anxiety and
suspense, torn from all the amusements I loved, and de-
testing details after my point was accomplished, nor more
inclined than formerly to profit of the consideration I had
acquired, I once more broke from politics, and set out for
Paris, where I stayed six weeks. In that little interval an
unexpected event happened, which both shook and prevented a shock to the Administration.

• On the 4th of September died Charles Townshend, of
a neglected fever, in, I think, the forty-second year of his
age. He met his approaching fate with a good humour
that never forsook him, and with an equanimity that he
had never shown on the most trifling occasions. Though
cut off so immaturely, it is a question whether he had not
lived long enough for his character. His genius could
have received no accession of brightness; his faults only
promised multiplication. He had almost every great
talent, and every little quality. His vanity exceeded
even his abilities, and his suspicions seemed to make him
doubt whether he had any. With such a capacity he
must have been the greatest man of this age, and perhaps
inferior to no man in any age, had his faults been only in
a moderate proportion—in short, if he had had but common truth, common sincerity, common honesty, common
modesty, common steadiness, common courage, and common sense.[1]

---

[1] This portrait has the broad lines of truth, and is more to be depended
upon than Mr. Burke's splendid and affectionate panegyric (Speech on
American Taxation, Burke's *Works*, 1815, vol. ii. pp. 422-8), and yet who
can blame the warmth with which this great man claims admiration for a
genius which in some points resembled his own? It is to be regretted that
of the many eminent literary men who enjoyed Mr. Townshend's intimacy,
none should have left behind any memorial by which his wonderful qualities
might be justly appreciated. In the absence of all biographical information,
the following loose memoranda from Sir George Colebrooke's Memoirs are
not without value :—

'The ambition of Mr. Townshend would not have been gratified but by
being Minister; and doubtless, had he lived to see the Duke of Grafton
resign, he must have had the offer which was made to Lord North, who suc-

A month before he died, he told Rigby he would resign, and would never rest till he brought him and his friends into place ; and asked how he should do it.   On the very day his wife kissed hands for a barony,[1] Townshend had threatened Conway to resign unless the peerage was granted.   The very next day he told Conway that the

ceeded him as Chancellor of the Exchequer.   But he never would have remained Premier as long as Lord North did.   Though much his superior in eloquence and abilities, he wanted the nerve necessary to conduct business with steadiness ; and instead of engaging in hostilities with America, he would have been the first to flinch from them, had he lived and been allowed to guide.   So far, therefore, his death may be considered as a public loss.   As a private man, his friends had used to say that they should not see his like again.   Though they were often the butts of his wit, they always returned to his company with fresh delight, which they would not have done had there been either malice or rancour in what he said.   He loved society, and in his choice of friends preferred those over whom he had a decided superiority in talent.   He was satisfied when he put the table in a roar, and he did not like to see it done by another.   When Garrick and Foote were present, he took the lead, and hardly allowed them an opportunity of showing their talents of mimicry, because he could excel them in their own art.   He shone particularly in taking off the principal members of the House of Commons.   Vanity was his ruling passion, and he sacrificed, even before his wife and daughter, all sense of decorum to a joke : I have seen instances of this which would have shocked Lord Rochester.   Among the few he feared was Mr. Selwyn ; and at a dinner at Lord Gower's they had a trial of skill, in which Mr. Selwyn prevailed.   When the company broke up, Mr. Townshend, to show he had no animosity, carried him in his carriage to White's ; and as they parted, Mr. Selwyn could not help saying, " Remember, this is the first set-down you have given me to-day."   As Mr. Townshend lived at considerable expense, and had little paternal fortune, he speculated occasionally both in the French and English funds.   With regard to the first, he had a concern with me in *contrats sur le cuir,* in which we lost, and he gave me his bond for his share of the difference, which was paid after his death.   When he was Chancellor of the Exchequer the Duke of Grafton gave a dinner to several of the principal men in the City to settle the loan.   Mr. Townshend came in his nightgown, and after dinner, when the terms were settled, and everybody present wished to introduce some friend on the list of subscribers, he pretended to cast up the sums already admitted, said the loan was full, huddled up his papers, got into a chair and returned home, reserving to himself by this manœuvre a large share in the loan.   Where he was really a great man was in Parliament.   Nobody, excepting Mr. Pitt, possessed a style of oratory so perfectly suited to the House.   He read sermons, particularly Sherlock, as models of eloquence and argumentation.'—L. M.

[1] Of Greenwich ; a title that had been borne by her father, John, Duke of Argyle.

peerage had been offered by the King. As soon as he was dead, Lord Mansfield owned that Townshend had assured him he would blow up the newly resettled Administration. His brother, the Viscount, who shared nothing with him but his duplicity, repaired to Rigby and desired to be directed by him in his Irish Administration, Rigby having much weight there through his friend the Provost.[1]

On the 17th of the same month died at Paris the Comte de Guerchy, their Ambassador to England. His death was occasioned by a former ill-cured complaint, but hastened by the various mortifications he had received from D'Eon, and the recent neglect and ill-usage of his own Court. He had been a lover of the Duchesse de Grammont, the Prime Minister's sister, who, aspiring at rank, had fixed on the Duc de Grammont as a man suited to her purposes. It was said that having consulted Monsieur de Guerchy, he, without considering that her resolution was probably taken, inveighed with too much sincerity against the choice of so contemptible a man, and was never forgiven. Certain it is that, his embassy being finished, he found nothing but coldness at home, and no hopes of reward or recompense for his services or mortifications. This cruelty being censured, pensions were granted to his widow and son.

On the very same day departed, at Monaco, Edward, Duke of York, next brother of the King. His immoderate pursuit of pleasure and unremitted fatigues in travelling beyond his strength, succeeded without interruption by balls and entertainments, had thrown his blood, naturally distempered and full of humours, into a state that brought on a putrid and irresistible fever. He suffered considerably, but with a heroism becoming a great Prince.

---

[1] Francis Andrews, Provost of the University of Dublin, M.P. for the City of Londonderry, a man of talent and accomplishments, which he disgraced by his subserviency to the Castle and the Ministerial leaders. His agreeable conversation and conviviality made him very influential in Irish society. He died suddenly at Shrewsbury in 1774.—(Hardy's *Memoirs of Lord Charlemont*, 1812, vol. i. pp. 147-150.)—L. M.

Before he died, he wrote a penitential letter to the King (though, in truth, he had no faults but what his youth made very pardonable), and tenderly recommended his servants to him. The Prince of Monaco, though his favourite child was then under inoculation at Paris, remained with and waited on him to his last breath, omitting nothing that tenderness could supply or his royal birth demand. The Duke of York had lately passed some time in the French Court, and by the quickness of his replies, by his easy frankness, and (in him) unusual propriety of conduct, had won much on the affection of the King of France, and on the rest of the Court, though his loose and perpetually rolling eyes, his short sight, and the singular whiteness of his hair, which, the French said, resembled feathers, by no means bespoke prejudice in his favour. His temper was good, his generosity royal, and his parts not defective : but his inarticulate loquacity and the levity of his conduct, unsupported by any countenance from the King, his brother, had conspired to place him but low in the estimation of his countrymen. As he could obtain no credit from the King's unfeeling nature, he was in a situation to do little good ; as he had been gained by the Opposition, he might have done hurt—at least so much to the King that his death was little lamented. Nor can we judge whether more years and experience would have corrected his understanding or corrupted his heart, nor whether, which is most probable, they would not have done both.[1]

The Duke of Gloucester, of as fair complexion, as short-sighted, of worse health, but of a more manly form, was a Prince of a very different disposition. Reserved, serious, pious, of the most decent and sober deportment, and possessing a plain understanding, though of no brilliancy, he was of all his family the King's favourite, though

---

[1] A more detailed account of the Duke of York is given in *George Selwyn and his Contemporaries*, 1843, vol. ii. pp. 194-200. He seems to have been a frivolous, dissipated youth, in all respects unlike the King, whose disapprobation of his conduct deserves praise rather than censure.—L. M.

admitted to no confidence, intimacy, or credit. An honourable amour which totally engrossed him, and of which I shall have occasion to speak hereafter, preserved him from the irregularities into which his brothers Edward and Henry fell, and which the severity of confinement in which they were held by their mother until they attained the age of twenty-one, did much excuse.

Henry, Duke of Cumberland, though not tall, did not want beauty, but with the babbling disposition of his brother York, he had neither the parts nor the condescension of the latter; familiarizing himself with bad company, and yet presuming on a rank which he degraded, and, notwithstanding, made an annoyance. His youth had all its faults, and gave no better promises.

In the room of Charles Townshend, Lord North, son of the Earl of Guilford, was appointed Chancellor of the Exchequer. He had sound parts, wit, and, it was thought, industry; an ungracious manner, a voice untuneable, and a total want of polish in his behaviour. He had been an active and ready agent in the whole cause against Wilkes, and was not a man that the friends of the Constitution could regard with partiality: but there were so few upright, that it was become almost eligible to select the exceptionable, in order to lessen confederacies amongst those whose union would be formidable should they return to power in a body. Lord North's (supposed) application and facility of access repaired in some degree the negligence and disgusting coldness of the Duke of Grafton.[1]

At my return from France, where I had perceived how

---

[1] Lord North at first refused the Exchequer from a distrust of his ability to encounter Mr. George Grenville on financial questions. Lord Barrington was then applied to, and had consented, when Lord North agreed to accept. —(Lord Barrington's *Political Life*, 1814, pp. 105-112.) The latter proved perfectly equal to his office, and had he risen no higher would have left a considerable name as a statesman of extensive 'knowledge, of a versatile understanding fitted for all sorts of business, and a most accomplished debater.' Unhappily for himself and his country, he wanted firmness to resist the solicitations of his Sovereign, and submitted to be the instrument of carrying into effect measures which have stamped his Administration with indelible disgrace.—An interesting account of Lord North is given in Lord

much it behoved us to be on our guard against the designed hostilities of that Court, as soon as their finances should enable them to renew the war, I laboured to infuse attention to our situation. We not only had little intelligence, but scarce suspicion. Our safety rested alone upon our fleet. No care was observed in watching the intercourse between the two kingdoms. The French, under pretence of curiosity, grown fashionable amongst them for the first time, resorted hither in considerable numbers. They visited the counties; and, under colour of studying commerce and manufactures, familiarized themselves with our weakness. Except Portsmouth and Plymouth, we had not a fortification in South Britain that could afford us time to recover from the panic of the first successful invasion. A few of the new travellers even visited Ireland—no subject of curiosity, if political reasons were out of the question. It was there, I did not doubt, but the first storm would burst. In vain I painted over and over this our defenceless situation; I could raise no attention, or at most was told we were not in a condition to do anything great. Methought it was just the position in which a great man would have attempted to exert genius—it was more true that we had no great man.

We had small bickerings with both France and Spain; but as we made no hurry to amend our circumstances, they took the leisure we afforded to recruit theirs. In the meantime the busy ambition of the Duc de Choiseul was preparing from a distance a general conflagration. France having refused the title of Imperial Majesty to the Czarina, her Ambassador, Prince Gallitzin,[1] received

Brougham's *Statesmen of the Time of George the Third*, 1839, vol. i. pp. 48-69, and above all in Lady Charlotte Lindsay's Letter in the Appendix, pp. 391-7.—L. M. [Lord North at the time of his appointment to the Exchequer was M.P. for Banbury and Joint Paymaster-General. He succeeded his father as 2nd Earl of Guilford in August 1790, and died on 5th August 1792, aged sixty.—E.]

[1] Dimitri Alexeievitch, Prince de Gallitzin, subsequently Russian Ambassador at the Hague, was a friend of Voltaire, and was well known for his literary and scientific pursuits. He died at Brunswick in March 1803, aged sixty-four.—E.

orders to quit Paris in a fortnight.   As she intermeddled in the affairs of Poland (which come not within my plan), the Duc de Choiseul intrigued at Constantinople till he poured an army of Turks into Russia; but that scene was not yet opened.   Portugal and Spain quarrelling about some American possessions, the former seized Rio Grande. This was thought a desperate act of D'Oyeras to involve us in their protection ; or, if we abandoned them, as an excuse for leaning towards the family compact.   His subsequent conduct was so little favourable to our trade, that the conjecture seemed not unfounded.[1]

Mr. Conway grew impatient to give up the profits of the Seals.   The Duke of Grafton and Lord Hertford disapproved it ; but I drew them into consent by asking them, before him, whether, if he got a regiment, he would keep the salary of Secretary of State, of the Ordnance, and of Colonel, at once?   He said, Certainly not; nor could they encourage him to keep all three.   On this it was agreed he should immediately sacrifice the income of his place : he did ; generously begging the King to bestow five hundred pounds of it on the clerks of the office, which was granted.   Such noble disinterestedness shut the mouths of Opposition, but did not open any in commendation,—an indication, that, however corruption was censured in this age, it was envy, not disapprobation of the practice, that raised clamour.

Lord Townshend, the new Lord-Lieutenant, was favourably received in Ireland.   He carried with him the consent of the King that the Judges there should hold their places, as in England, *quamdiu se bene gesserint*.   Impatient to acquire popularity, he notified this grace in his speech to

---

[1] The differences between Portugal and Spain were subsequently adjusted by an agreement that each nation should maintain the undisputed enjoyment of the country in its possession on the 28th of May 1767.   The plans of Pombal for the encouragement of the domestic trade of Portugal, such as his establishing the Oporto and other great companies, were necessarily most injurious to the interests of foreigners, and especially of the English, many of whose merchants were utterly ruined.   Mr. William Henry Lyttelton was employed to obtain redress of these grievances, without success.—L. M.

that Parliament, though he had been positively instructed not to mention it in that place, only to promise it in private. Lord Mansfield and the lawyers here censured this conduct warmly, as a direct breach of Poyning's law. The Chancellor being dead, and no successor appointed (for Sewell the Master of the Rolls refused it, nor would any great lawyer here accept the post without an additional pension, which Conway and others opposed), the Irish Speaker,[1] Lord Shannon,[2] and Tisdall[3] the Attorney-General, who aspired to that great seal, all acquainted Lord Townshend that there would be a motion of complaint that no Chancellor was appointed. Lord Townshend represented the indecency of such a step, and exciting the King's servants to oppose it, the others promised to stop what they had secretly instigated. The alarm, however, caused the Government at home to send over for Chancellor Judge Hewet, an able lawyer, but much despised for his deficiency of parliamentary talents. Trifling as this first success was, it was the greatest service which the Lord-Lieutenant rendered to the Government. Obstinate against advice, thirsting for low popularity, and void even of decorum, he soon lost all consideration. Drunkenness and buffoonery, unsupported by parts or policy, rendered him the scorn even of the populace. That he might exempt himself from the reproach of whatever in his instructions was disagreeable to the Irish, he spoke of

[1] The Right Hon. John Ponsonby, brother of William, second Earl of Bessborough.—E.

[2] Richard Boyle, second Earl of Shannon, succeeded to the vast political influence of his father in Ireland. He married Catherine, daughter of the Speaker Ponsonby, held various offices under the Crown, and died on 20th May 1807, aged eighty.—E.

[3] Philip Tisdall never obtained the object of his ambition ; probably because the Government would not venture to promote an Irishman to such a post. He represented the University of Dublin for over thirty years, was a successful lawyer, and could hardly be termed an unsuccessful politician, for he steered a steady course through the tumults of his day, maintaining amidst occasional fluctuations of popularity great personal influence to the last. It is said of him that his countenance was never gay, his mind never gloomy. He died in 1777.—(Hardy's *Memoirs of Lord Charlemont*, 1812, vol. i. pp. 152-7.)—L. M.

himself as intrusted with no power ; and giving a loose to
his own turn for caricature, he drew ridiculous pictures
of himself in ignominious attitudes with his hands tied
behind him ; thus shunning opposition by meriting contempt.[1]

At home there appeared no symptoms of dissatisfaction
among the people. The patrons of general warrants were
still the only obnoxious persons. The Court, profiting of
that disposition, exerted a little authority, the King
dismissing the Earls of Buckingham[2] and Eglinton, who
were devoted to the Grenvilles, from his bedchamber.

[1] Far from interfering, as Walpole states, to defeat the intrigues of Tisdall
and the Irish Council, Lord Townshend wholly lent himself to them, and
nearly prevailed on the Cabinet to raise that ambitious lawyer to the Chan-
cellorship. (Duke of Grafton's MSS.) He afterwards yielded other points
with equal facility, and indeed seldom showed any vigour throughout his
Administration, except in his disputes with his colleagues in England. He
enjoyed advantages which had been denied to his predecessors ; for the
English Government were at length beginning to feel ' that the time must
come when a different plan of government ought to take place in Ireland.
Lord Chatham had intended to begin it ; and, to enable himself to contend
with the powerful connexions there, proposed to establish himself upon the
basis of a just popularity, by shortening the duration of Parliament, and granting other measures which the Irish appeared to have most at heart. These
views went far beyond the reach of Lord Townshend.'—(MS. Letter from
Lord Camden to the Duke of Grafton.) Instructions were accordingly given
to Lord Townshend in a spirit of great liberality for that day ; but he
frittered away their effect by the indiscretion with which he executed them.
The firmness, consistency, and judgment—the constant exercise of perseverance and self-denial, requisite for contending with the factions that stood
between the Crown and the people, did not belong to him. If he could only
enjoy his ease and his pleasures, and receive the homage usually paid to his
station, he was content ; the patronage of the Castle continued to be applied
to the same unworthy purposes as before, and the interests of the people to be
equally neglected. If neither harsh nor oppressive, he held the reins of
Government with too careless a hand for its course to be attended with real
benefit to the country.—L. M.

[2] John Hobart, second Earl of Buckinghamshire ; he had already been
Ambassador in Russia, and in 1777 succeeded Lord Harcourt as Lord-
Lieutenant of Ireland. His Administration partook of the weakness of Lord
North's Government, as was too plainly shown by the embodying of the Irish
volunteers, and the concessions made to Irish trade ; the latter, however just,
being too evidently extorted from the Government to obtain any lasting gratitude. Lord Buckinghamshire was an amiable nobleman of fair intentions and
pleasing manners. He died in 1793, without male issue.—L. M.

They were succeeded by the Duke of Roxburgh[1] and
Lord Bottetort.[2]

On the 24th of November the Parliament met. The
Duke of Bedford and Lord Lyttelton talked much against
the Ministers and the outrages of the Americans. In the
other House Dowdeswell observed that the King in his
speech the last session had mentioned the encouragement
of commerce, but took no notice now of having given any.
He proposed to add to the address words that should give
that encouragement. He asked, too, if the Ministers had
any plan for lowering provisions, the dearness of which
were become a capital grievance. Conway answered, No:
he could not find that any man could point out such a
method of reduction. The Manilla ransom having been
mentioned, he wished, as the affair was pending, the House
would not meddle with it. He had already, he said, received favourable answers on that subject. Himself was
now accused of neglecting that business; formerly he had
heard a minister (Grenville) pleading *for* Spain against
the captors. Burke spoke with great and deserved
applause, chiefly on the dearness of provisions; to remedy
which, he said, if Ministers could form no plan, it would

[1] John, third Duke of Roxburgh, born in 1740, succeeded his father in 1755.
He was one of the handsomest men of his day, and not less remarkable for
the grace and nobleness of his manners. In early life, during his travels he
visited the small court of Mecklenburg, where he is said to have gained the
affections of the Princess Christiana, the Duke's eldest daughter. Indeed,
their marriage was believed to have been prevented only by the application
of George the Third for the hand of her younger sister. This belief was
strengthened by the Princess and the Duke remaining unmarried through life.
Notwithstanding this incident, the Duke became a favourite companion of
George the Third. His name is now best known as an eminent collector of
books. He died in 1804, and was succeeded by his cousin, Lord Bellenden,
on whose death the title was claimed by Sir James Innes, and, after a
long process, the House of Lords pronounced him the fifth Duke of Roxburgh in 1812.—(Douglas's *Peerage of Scotland*, edited by J. P. Wood,
vol. ii. p. 455.)—L. M.

[2] Norborne Berkeley, M.P. for Gloucestershire 1741-63, in April 1764
established his claim to the Barony of Botetourt, which had been in abeyance
since 1406. He was sent to Virginia as Governor in 1768, where he died on
15th October 1770, and the title again fell into abeyance. It is now merged
in the Dukedom of Beaufort. See *infra.*—E.

teach the people to undervalue Parliament.[1] He dwelt, too, on the discontents of the *nobility*—a new topic in a popular assembly! Wedderburn spoke well, too, and with greater acrimony. Conway, he said, when in Opposition, had been one of the loudest to censure the neglect of recovering the Manilla ransom, now had done nothing in it. Had been violent on being turned out; now Lord Buckingham and Lord Eglinton, very respectable men, had been dismissed. This philippic was coldly received, and the amendment rejected without a division. Grenville then, to mark that he had not and would not support Dowdeswell's motion, rose with affected coolness, but betraying how much he was hurt. He had declared, he said, in the summer, that he desired no place; his friends knew he desired none. The King, he thought, had better keep the present Ministry than change so often. That the whole state of our affairs was not laid before Parliament: himself had in his pocket a *Boston Gazette* inciting the people to rebel. The governor there had no power to punish the printer. Himself had been much misrepresented in libels. Conway, too, had misrepresented him; he supposed, if by forgetfulness, would recant. It was but six months after the peace when Conway had attacked

---

1 Mr. Burke's speech may be found in the *Parliamentary History*, vol. xvi. 386, where it is stated to be the first of his speeches of which a report has been preserved. The opinions he entertained on the dearness of provisions are stated with more force and perspicuity in his celebrated *Thoughts and Details on Scarcity.*—(*Works*, vol. vii. p. 375.) A petition from the City was presented on the first day of the session, in which, after soliciting the continuance of the temporary acts passed in the preceding session, prohibiting the exportation of corn, and allowing its free importation, the petitioners ascribe the high price of meat in a great degree to the recent increase in the breeding of horses, owing partly to the growing practice of employing them instead of oxen in tillage, and partly to the exportations to the Continent; whereby the number of cattle for slaughter was necessarily diminished; secondly, to the unlimited consumption of ewe lambs and cow calves in all seasons of the year, merely to gratify the unreasonable appetites of the rich and luxurious. The consolidation of small farms was also deprecated in the strongest terms.—(*Journals of the House of Commons*, xxxi. pp. 423-4.) The Duke of Grafton was opposed to unlimited importation of corn, on the ground that it would encourage smuggling. (Bedford MSS.)—L. M.

him on the affair of Manilla ; now three or four years had
elapsed. He offered to read the Spanish answer, but if he
did, desired not to be called an advocate for Spain. He
would appeal to the Spanish Ambassador if he had ever
given up that ransom.

Nothing could be less justly founded than Grenville's
complaint of libels. Himself wrote one on American
affairs, in which Lord Rockingham and Conway were
treated with contempt and bitterness. His friend, the
Dean of Norwich,[1] Thomas Pitt, and Rigby, not to
mention his brother Lord Temple, dabbled continually
in that way. Rigby had even revised Almon's last
Political Register, in which was an account of the conference between the Duke of Bedford and Lord Chatham
at Bath.

Conway answered that he had been struck at the time
with the idea that Grenville was pleading in behalf of
Spain : himself might have been too warm then ; was not
ashamed to recant and ask his pardon, if he had misrepresented him. He had heard, he said, that Mr. Grenville desired no place ; but wondered he was so much
wounded by libels. He himself was abused by one
Almon once a month for being avaricious ; he believed
it was pretty well known how unjustly. He always
bought the pamphlet,—the only hurt he did to the
printer. Almon had lately been so modest, as to solicit
him for a patent for printing a book ; he had spoken to
the King and obtained it. Everybody must live by
their trade ; abuse was Almon's trade. He himself sometimes differed with the other Ministers ; he was pinned on
no great man's sleeve. He now warned his colleagues
that he should differ with them whenever he was of a
different opinion.

The conduct of Grenville in this debate was extremely
remarkable. He not only seemed transported into very
impolitic separation from the Rockinghams by his
violence against the Americans, but even by personal

[1] Dr. Lloyd, Dean of Norwich, who had been tutor to Mr. Grenville's sons.

resentment against the former: while at the same time his affected moderation had the appearance of having taken a new part, that of standing detached and waiting to see whether he could not penetrate with more facility into the closet when standing alone, than by the joint effort of two discordant factions. Whatever were his motives, he soon fell a sacrifice to this very conduct.

On the report of the address, Grenville engaged in a hot altercation with Dowdeswell and Burke on their different ideas of what ought to be done with respect to America. Rigby, provoked at Grenville's unseasonable disputation, and perhaps not sorry to offend him, could not help saying he saw no use in that contest unless it were to tranquillize the Administration, who might have apprehended the union of the two Oppositions. The younger Onslow diverted the House with proposing, in imitation of the Romans, who used to send senators to inquire into the state of their provinces, to despatch Grenville to America on that errand. Two days after Grenville complaining in form of the *Boston Gazette*, the elder Onslow moved to put off the consideration for six months, which the House, with a laugh, approved.

On the 27th, Lord Weymouth, observing invidiously that the Ministers were only in the House of Lords, moved to inquire into the state of the nation on the Tuesday sennight.

Thomas Townshend, the younger, succeeded Lord North as half-paymaster; and Jenkinson in Townshend's room was appointed a Lord of the Treasury.

On the 29th opened another new scene. Mr. Conway told me, as the greatest secret, that the Bedford faction had offered themselves to the Duke of Grafton on these limited, though few, conditions,—that Lord Gower should be President of the Council; that Rigby should have a place, and that Lord Weymouth should divide the Secretary's place with Lord Shelburne, taking either the European or American department. Conway added that he could not object to so considerable an accession of strength to the Government, but had pressed the Duke of Grafton to suffer him to resign. He was unwilling to expose himself to more abuse from the Rockinghams, though they would not speak to him, and all except Richmond and the Cavendishes censured him in all places. I warned him to put the Duke of Grafton on his guard: and advised that his Grace should demand from the Bedfords a specific renunciation of Grenville, lest their view should be to introduce him afterwards, as they might hope Conway would quit and leave the Seals open. But, in truth, I did too much honour both their honesty and policy. I saw this reinforcement would establish the Government, would diminish Conway's trouble if he stayed in employment, or would facilitate his retirement, which he wished; and to which his irresolution and the impossibility I had found of making him take the first part, had perfectly reconciled me. I was weary of sacrificing myself for others, and wished as much as he did to withdraw from politics. At the same time I was desirous that the Bedfords might disgrace themselves as much as might be in this transaction. The motives to their new conduct were these :—

Rigby had passed over to Ireland in hopes of obtaining to have his place of Master of the Rolls there confirmed in the Act for establishing the Judges for life, but had not succeeded. This disappointment, the rupture with the Rockinghams, and the precarious state of the Duke of Bedford's health, who was breaking, and on the point of being totally blind,[1] had suggested to Rigby the thought of abandoning Grenville, whose tedious gravity mixed ill with so bacchanalian a junto; and, which was more important, was so obnoxious to the King. It was not difficult to infuse these ideas into his associates, Rigby being the only one who had prevented their deserting

---

[1] He was couched during this negotiation, in which he took little or no part, though his name was often made use of. He recovered a small degree of sight, and went into public and played at cards, yet, as he said himself, saw very imperfectly.

Grenville long before. Grenville's American frenzy, and his absurd breach with Dowdeswell and that party on the opening of the session, and his avoidance of hostilities towards the Court, which alarmed the Bedfords lest he should anticipate them and make his peace first, drove Rigby into immediate negotiation, which the unpromising state of their Opposition could but make desirable. Lord Temple was not come to town ; and as Grenville told Rigby, would not come before Christmas, unless the Duke of Bedford sent for him : but that Court were not desirous of laying their chief under such an obligation. The Duke of Newcastle had in vain tried to renew the negotiation between the two opposing factions. Grenville's wrong-headedness, and many civil professions towards the Duke of Bedford dropped by the Duke of Grafton the first day of the session, encouraged Rigby to make the overtures above mentioned. They were conveyed by Vernon and Meynell,[1] jockeys and gamesters of Grafton's society ; the latter his intimate in private, the other, brother-in-law of the Duchess of Bedford.[2]

Among the various and precipitate changes of the Duke of Grafton at which I have hinted, and which afterwards constituted so capital a part of his character, it was not the least astonishing the partiality he had taken up for Lord Gower, who had been in love with the Duchess of Grafton ; and a principal reason assigned by the Duke for their separation was his wife's attachment to Lord Gower and the Duchess of Bedford—at the same time acquitting her of any criminal partiality. To policy and to the fear of attacks from Lord Gower and that set in the House of Lords, the world imputed Grafton's facility in meeting the

---

[1] Hugo Meynell was M.P. for Lichfield, and the Duke's intimate friend, as appears in his Grace's Memoirs. He was a man of high fashion, in which service he spent a large portion of a noble estate on the turf and other expensive amusements and vices so popular with the aristocracy of that day. —L. M.

[2] The last letters which passed between the Duke of Bedford and George Grenville previously to their political separation, will be found in the *Bedford Correspondence*, vol. iii. pp. 394-9.—E.

overtures. But it was not then known how little policy and how much sudden caprice influenced his Grace's most important steps.

The Duke of Bedford (for the message was sent in his name) demanded a solemn promise that it should never be known if no treaty was concluded. They desired, too, that the proposal should not be carried directly to the King, but that the Duke of Grafton would sound his Majesty's inclinations. The Duke answered that he would take no step without consulting Mr. Conway, and even declared that he would acquaint him with the offer. They replied civilly that they were confident of Mr. Conway's honour and secrecy, and would trust him, confessing also that there was nobody else fit to conduct the House of Commons,—that is, they would stick at nothing to get into place, nor at nothing afterwards to show ingratitude and insolence to the man to whom they had stooped to be obliged, as soon appeared. The negotiation being so prosperously advanced, Rigby went out of town for three days, as was his way on such occasions, that if it miscarried he might to Grenville plead ignorance.

Having thus far sacrificed to seeming decency, they began to say that the Duke of Bedford had not quite surmounted his objection to acting under Conway, but did not doubt but he would. It seemed extraordinary that they should have commenced the negotiation before that difficulty was removed. It alarmed me the more as I had conceived peculiar pleasure in thinking what a triumph it would be to Conway to see the Bedfords suing to act under him so soon after having proscribed him. It was no less satisfaction to have Grenville experience what I had often and often announced to him, that the Bedfords would betray him the first instant they should find their advantage in it. Yet I again apprehended that he was behind the curtain, when I heard that, on opening their views further, they had not only asked some place for Lord Sandwich, but for Lord Lyttelton; yet they were so sincere in their treachery, as to relinquish the

latter early.   Nor had I occasion to warn Mr. Conway
against acting with Grenville, which he had refused to do
when requested by Lord Rockingham.   But as Lord
Sandwich was now mentioned, I thought it necessary to
alarm the Duke of Grafton for the Cabinet, into which I
saw they meant to force too large a number.   He said he
was on his guard.   I thought, too, that Lord Shelburne
ought not to be discontented.   The Duke agreed, and
talked of fidelity to Lord Chatham.   All this was conveyed to him at my desire by Mr. Conway, for as yet the
Duke had not imparted the negotiation to me.   Hearing,
however, that he was inclined to bestow a vacant seat at
the Admiralty on one of the Duke of Bedford's friends,
though promised to Lord Lisburne,[1] I recommended the
Duke's adhering to all the engagements he had entered
into for the ensuing elections.   Lord Sandwich and Rigby
were great traffickers in that trade, and the Duke, on the
contrary, was ill-suited to it.   He had lost Suffolk and
Kent by not exerting himself, and Liverpool because he
would neither see Sir George Maccartney, nor trouble
himself to give an answer.   If admonished, he would say
he did not like his post and would resign.   Many irre-
concilable enemies he made on this single article of
elections by imperiousness, and refusing himself to all
access.   In this negotiation alone he outwent even the
promptitude of the Bedfords ; and they saw themselves so
sure of success that their demands were not only swelled,
but Lord Weymouth, as a prelude to their laying down
all pretensions to patriotism, moved to put off the consideration of the state of the nation.   The nation was
safe and flourishing as soon as that faction had even an
antepast of emoluments.   But in or out of place, their
conduct was void of decency.   The first day of this

---

[1] Wilmot Vaughan succeeded his father as fourth Viscount Lisburne in
January 1766, and was created Earl of Lisburne on 18th July 1776.   He was
M.P. for Cardiganshire, 1755-61 and 1768-96, and for Berwick-upon-Tweed,
1765-8.   He held a seat at the Board of Trade from 1768 to 1770, and was
a Lord of the Admiralty from 1770 to 1782.   He died at Mamhead, Devonshire, on 6th January 1800, aged seventy-two.—E.

session, but five days before their message, the Duke of
Bedford had threatened that the King's debts should not
be paid.   This his Majesty resented with warmth, and
said, the Duke of Bedford, when last in place, had been
the first to propose it to him.   This menace from Bedford,
and Weymouth's motion for the state of the nation, were
proofs that it was Grenville's preposterous conduct that
had fixed Rigby's determination to treat.

December 4th.—Happening to go to Mr. Conway, I
met the Duke of Grafton at the door.   I waited, but was
called in immediately.   The Duke said he was sure he
could trust me with their great secret; wished to know
my opinion on it, and then related the negotiation.   I
seemed much surprised, approved of taking the Bedfords,
but expressed great suspicion on their having named
Lord Lyttelton.[1]   The Duke said that point was given
up; that George Grenville had been with the Duke of
Bedford, who had declared he was weary of opposition,
and that his friends were so too; and that himself and
Mr. Grenville were free to take any part they pleased.   I
heard this with few replies; but the Duke adding that
they proposed Mr. Conway should resign the Seals, as
they heard he was desirous to do, I broke out, and treated
the proposal as an unheard-of impertinence in a fragment
of a minority.   I told the Duke roundly that he and
Mr. Conway were *the* ministry, and that his Grace could
not in honour give up Mr. Conway; and that it was
ridiculous in the aspirants not to have surmounted the
Duke of Bedford's pretended point of honour before they
offered themselves; and as they allowed their not doubt-
ing but it would be surmounted, it ought not now to be
insisted on.   The Duke answered, it was not they but
Meynell who had said he thought they would give it up:
that himself had said he could not treat on it, but would
refer it to Mr. Conway.   To my utter astonishment Mr.
Conway acknowledged himself ready to give up the Seals.
It should not be told, he said, that his place prevented so

---

[1] He was entirely in the Grenville interest.—L. M.

great an event for the King's service. I grew warmer, and
said, it was being turned out by them. He said, No;
they had only proposed it, as he had expressed dislike of
his place. It would be pride and obstinacy to keep it
only out of contradiction. I replied, such pride would be
well-founded when they took upon themselves to remove
him. The Duke seemed, though with indifference enough,
to be on my side; and I saw Conway was hurt that the
Duke, as he ought to have done, did not take it upon
himself to reject the motion; and I believe, adhered the
more to his opinion from that just scorn. The Duke said
the City's confidence was only in him and Conway, and
was increased by the accession of Lord North instead of
Charles Townshend, of whom he related a thousand tricks.
Seeing I could make no impression on Conway, I asked
the Duke what Lord Chatham would say. He replied, if
Lord Chatham would do nothing, and left them to do the
best they could, they *must* do the best they could. He
seemed very willing to part with Lord Shelburne, who,
he said, did not communicate with him, and whose part
Conway honourably took. I was so much provoked at
the insolence of the Bedfords, and at the facility with
which the Duke, after so often having declared he would
not go on without Conway, and after so many obligations
both to him and to me for Conway's assistance, gave him
up, that after repeating to the Duke in strong terms how
much his honour was concerned not to sacrifice Conway,
he said at last he would send word to the Bedfords that
Mr. Conway was ready to give up his place, but that he
himself would not consent, as it would be changing the
Administration. I asked how the King would approve
the plan? 'Oh!' said the Duke, 'we shall ask him when
it is settled.' He pleaded in his own defence that these
recruits were necessary, as from the weakness of the
Administration, all men were exorbitant in their demands,
and threatened to resign if not gratified: and he read
some letters to us, the arrogance of which I found
had much offended his haughty temper. I stayed with

Mr. Conway till the Duke was gone, but soon left him, telling him he thought nothing a virtue but his own moderation.

If I lost my temper on the notification, reflection did not reconcile me to the measure. Not to mention the impertinence of the supposed point of honour in the Duke of Bedford, who, because he had excepted to Conway in the meeting with the Rockinghams, pretended to think it necessary to adhere to it in the very instant of deserting Grenville, I was shocked at the indifference and levity of the Duke of Grafton and the indecency of his making the proposal in such bare-faced terms to Mr. Conway. I had expressed that indignation with so little management, that the Duke, I am persuaded, did not forgive it. That was the least part of my concern. His mutability was so glaring, that I determined never to have anything to do with him more; and, in fact, did not see him again in private afterwards. It was yet more lasting reflection that I made on the futility of politics. All my success and triumph in the preceding summer had lasted but five months. Conway was desirous to quit, and the Bedfords were to come into place. It determined me to busy myself no more in such delusive scenes. I had in the preceding winter notified to my constituents at Lynn, that I would serve no more in Parliament. The door was thus already favourably open to me. Mr. Conway's resignation would leave me at liberty to have done with politics. I took my resolution to abandon them with the present Parliament—a happy determination, and which I never found one moment's cause to repent. For, if the alarming designs of the Court have since forced me at any time to encourage opposition to their measures, I still had seen too much of parties, factions, and their leaders to embark with any. Still, the weakness of the human mind, and the difficulty of bursting from all one's passions at once, did not suffer these reflections to strike root directly, but occasioned my making a few more struggles to thwart the overbearing arrogance of the Bedfords.

After parting from Mr. Conway, I saw Lord Hertford, who talked of going out of town. I said, he absolutely must not. He asked, Why? I replied, I could not tell him; but go he must not. I was resolved to keep the secret, but yet to disappoint the full effect of the plan, so far as to reduce the Bedfords to come in under Mr. Conway.

He himself came to me the next morning, saying, I had quitted him in such a passion, that he wished to talk the affair more coolly over with me. I said, I had never in my life been so much hurt as at seeing him submit to such an affront. He denied that it was one. At last I almost engaged him to say he would keep the Seals till the end of the session, and then resign them. All I desired was to finish with that triumph.

Lord Hertford, impatient to learn the meaning of my mysterious behaviour, came to desire an explanation of it. I told him I had received private intelligence that the Bedfords would soon make an offer of themselves; and that, therefore, he must go to the King, and tell him he came to put his Majesty upon his guard, for Lord Gower had got such an ascendant over the Duke of Grafton, that he could do what he would with him: but his Majesty must ask time to consider; and, above all things, insist that nobody that had stood by him should be given up, lest it should look more like changing than strengthening the Administration. 'Oh!' said he, '*that* I am sure the King will not hear.' 'Ay,' replied I, 'but he must insist too that there shall be no alteration in the plan of elections.' This, I knew, would strike Lord Hertford, who was dealing largely for boroughs—and so it did. He fired, and said he would press it strongly; but he was sure no offers had yet come, for the King would have told him. I suspected by this that the King did not trust him so much as he thought, or wished to have thought, for I did not doubt but the Duke had already broken the matter in the closet. I said, 'My Lord, be not too sure.' 'Why?' said he; 'have any offers been made?' I replied, My intelligence could not go so far as that; but I suspected there had : and I added, 'When you tell the King, watch his countenance. If any offers have been made, he will tell you on this opening; or, at least, you will discover it in his face.'

CHAPTER V

Affair of Colonel Brereton with the Duke of Grafton.—Tax on Absentees.—
Character of Lord Weymouth.—Attempted Treaty with Grenville.—
Successful one with the Bedfords.—Case of the Duke of Portland.—
Dunning made Solicitor-General.—Resignation of Conway.—Affair of
Lord Bottetort.—Corruption of the Corporation of Oxford.—Bill for
Septennial Parliaments in Ireland.—Attempts to repress Bribery at
Elections.—Bill to restrain the Recovery of Crown Lands.—Dissolution
of Parliament.

1767

IN the midst of this treaty the Duke of Grafton embarked
himself in a very ugly affair. One Brereton, a gamester,
and not of the best character even in that profession,
which he had assumed on quitting the army, declared
publicly that, as he was betting on a game at whist at
Newmarket, he had seen Vernon and Meynell, the two
negotiators, then playing the game, cheat in concert. He
offered to prove his assertion with his sword, or in a
court of justice. The accused bore the insult. Brereton
then wrote to Vernon, that having borne the King's
commission he ought to have acted with more spirit, and
demanded satisfaction. Vernon declined giving it. It
was not believed that they had cheated ; but their want
of spirit was notorious. Other circumstances were unfavourable to them. Meynell's father had created a large
fortune by play, and nobody doubted but by unfair play.
Vernon supported a great expense by his skill in horse-
racing. The Duke of Grafton took up their cause with
zeal ; and summoning the Jockey Club[1] at a tavern in

---

[1] The Jockey Club was composed of noblemen and gentlemen, frequenters
of Newmarket. [It appears to have originated during the reign of George II.
The first mention of it is to be found in Heber's *Racing Calendar* for
1758.—E.]

Pall Mall, where it was usually held, he, at the head of a great many men of the first quality, set their names to the expulsion of Brereton, and caused their act to be printed in the public newspapers,—a proceeding so unbecoming the dignity of the Duke's situation and so likely to expose him to Brereton's resentment, that I had still so much regard for him left, as to engage Mr. Conway to persuade him from taking so indecent a step; but the Duke was inflexible.

About the same time arrived from Ireland a bill for imposing a tax of four shillings in the pound on the pensions and places of all who resided in England. It was undoubtedly a great grievance on Ireland, that so much of their treasure was spent out of the country. The Opposition there wished even to extend the tax to estates. The English Government was become so indulgent as to intend allowing Septennial Parliaments to that kingdom— but this bill was exceedingly unwelcome here. The Commons of Ireland had passed it, hoping the Lords would throw it out. The Lords, trusting in the same manner to the extreme probability of its not receiving the assent of the Lord-Lieutenant, had, in hopes of popularity, suffered the bill to pass through their House too. Lord Frederick Campbell, Lord Townshend's secretary, had made no objection; and Lord Townshend himself, not to risk the odium which all the rest had shifted from themselves, gave his assent likewise. Councils were held here to seek means of defeating the bill, but to no purpose. The Privy Council of England must either reject or correct the bill. Should the Irish Parliament reject the amendments, the bill must drop entirely; and as they had tacked the new imposition to the bill for settling the revenue, the Crown would lose its whole revenue for two years if the bill did not pass. The King was obliged to give his consent.

As this bill not only fell heavy on Rigby's post of Master of the Rolls in Ireland, but would likewise affect that of Vice-Treasurer, which was destined to him in the new arrangement, he grew difficult and began to throw obstructions in the way of the treaty he had set on foot. He should be ridiculed, he said, for acting under Mr. Conway, and, therefore, if he did, would be well paid for it; that the Ministry might yet have him, if they would make him Paymaster. To back his game with threats, he notified his intention of proposing a call of the House against the day on which the land-tax was to be voted, as if he meant to reduce it lower, and called on Lord North to specify the day. The latter said, he had already given notice that it was to be voted on the following Wednesday.

Lord Hertford now told me he had acquainted the King with my intimation of an intended treaty, who was much surprised, and protested he had heard nothing of it. The Duke of Grafton had signified to Mr. Conway that he had in general apprised his Majesty,—but his Grace was not always strictly correct in what he said. He had certainly encouraged the Bedfords to expect Mr. Conway's resignation, and had imparted to them his own desire of dismissing Lord Shelburne. On this they had flattered themselves with obtaining the Seals of both Secretaries, intending that Sandwich should be one. In truth, the preference they gave to Lord Weymouth was both unjust and injudicious. Lord Sandwich, by age, rank, experience, by having already been Secretary of State, by having suffered with them in a common cause, and by very superior abilities and activity, had every pretension to take place of Lord Weymouth: and, though the unpopularity of Lord Sandwich was, I believe, the sole reason of their having set him aside (unless might be added that Rigby knew he could more easily govern Weymouth), there was nothing in Weymouth's character that recommended his morality. He was a prompt and graceful speaker of a few apt sentences, which, coming from a young and handsome figure, attracted more applause than they merited. Yet, considering the life he led, his parts must naturally have been very good; for sitting up nightly, gaming and drinking till six in the morning, and rising thus heated after noon, it was extraordinary that he was master of himself, or of what little he knew. His great fortune he had damaged by such profuse play, that his house was often full of bailiffs ; and he had exposed himself to receive such pressing letters and in such reproachful terms, that his spirit was as much doubted, as what is called his point of honour among gentlemen-gamesters. He was in private a close and sound reasoner, and good-humoured, under a considerable appearance of pride ; but having risen on such slender merit, he seemed to think he possessed a sufficient stock, and continued his course of life to the total neglect of the affairs of his office, the business of which was managed, as much as it could be, by Mr. Wood, his under-secretary.[1]

Whether Grenville had got wind of the negotiation, or whether he acted in consequence of the separate plan he had formed, he and Lord Temple attempted a private negotiation with Lord Hertford by the means of Calcraft and Governor Walsh.[2] The latter beating about for an opening, though he had desired a private meeting, told Lord Hertford that the Duke of Bedford had declared to Mr. Grenville that his friends were impatient for places ; and then asked Lord Hertford whether his Lordship did not think it best for Mr. Grenville to remain detached, and whether there were no hopes of the Court pardoning him ? Lord Hertford, who was all caution, had kept on the reserve ; but I persuaded him to encourage these overtures. If the Bedfords were not to be had on moderate terms, it would be wise to get the Grenvilles, and break the Opposition that way : that Lord Temple might be President, and Grenville Paymaster. He answered, that Lord Temple's ambition now was a Dukedom. I said, that would be a cheap purchase. Lord

---

[1] See more of Lord Weymouth, vol. ii. p. 126, note 3.—L. M.

[2] John Walsh, M.P. for Worcester city from 1761 to 1780, was an intimate friend of Lord Clive, through whom he probably was thus employed by Mr. Grenville, that nobleman's political patron.—-L. M.

Hertford readily consented to court the Grenvilles. This negotiation seemed to explain Grenville's late conduct, and intimated that his intentions had not been much more faithful to his connection than Rigby's actions; unless Grenville had suddenly resorted to this new plan on the Duke of Bedford's declaration—which, indeed, would acquit him, the declaration, I think, having been made the very day, or the day before the meeting of Parliament. But Rigby got the start by plunging at once into the treaty, while Grenville was preparing to soften the Court by affected moderation.

The negotiation now growing public, I urged Mr. Conway to tell it to his brother. He said he would in general; on which I thought myself at liberty, but I own with not very justifiable casuistry, and communicated the whole to Lord Hertford, who agreed to prevent the King from making too large concessions.

On the 9th, Mr. Conway proposed an increase of the troops in Ireland, which was indeed in a most defenceless state. The motion was much liked, though Wedderburn made a pompous speech against standing armies. The latter, too, attempted to put off the land-tax, on pretence that Mr. Grenville was ill; but he had sent Lord North word that he did not disapprove it, and it passed unanimously for three shillings in the pound. About the same time came an account from Boston, that they had agreed to take no more of our manufactures.

On the 11th, the Bedfords, fearing too great obstinacy would mar their traffic, consented to submit to Conway, but insisted on removing Shelburne, at least from half his department, with some lesser demands. Conway stickled for the latter; but Grafton, wishing to get rid of him, told Lord Shelburne himself that he must not keep both America and the southern province. Shelburne asked him, with a sneer, how Lord Chatham would approve that arrangement? The Duke replied, He was reduced to do the best he could. Shelburne desired till next day to consider, and then made his option of the southern department: but though the Duke had left him his choice, he now told him he must stick to America; on which Shelburne desired another day, and in the meantime sent an express to Lord Chatham, and by his advice, probably, persisted in retaining the southern province; on which the Duke of Grafton again grew desirous that Conway should resign soon after Christmas, and leave the northern province open for Lord Weymouth.

The King expressed no repugnance to admitting the Bedfords, but declared against their having more than two places in the Cabinet, lest they should obtain influence there. He told Conway he would not have yielded so far, if he (Conway) would have stayed in; but that knowing his determination of quitting, he had consented to admit Gower and Weymouth; 'though,' added his Majesty, 'I have tried that party once before, and never can trust them again.' In fact, though the capital objection at Court was to Grenville, and though Lord Bute and his friends advised the acquisition of the Bedfords, to separate them from Grenville, yet the Butists lamented the loss of Conway (whose temper, void of ambition, self-interest, and animosity, interfered so little with their views), and declared on every occasion that no other man was so proper to be at the head of the House of Commons. The King, too, finding a Garter was demanded for the Duke of Marlborough amongst other new conditions, suddenly called a Chapter of the Order before the treaty was concluded, and gave the only vacant riband to his brother, the Duke of Cumberland: an evidence of his dislike of the Bedfords, the more marked, as I do not remember an instance of a single Garter given but to Lord Waldegrave.

The Chancellor was much offended at not being either consulted or informed of the treaty in agitation; yet he prevented Lord Chatham from resigning on the meditated disgrace of his creature, Lord Shelburne. Lord Chatham had set out from Bath in great wrath: yet being persuaded to acquiesce, his wife gave out that he had not returned on Lord Shelburne's message, but was coming before. He was, however, displeased enough to remain in his old state of seclusion and inactivity.

Neither Sandwich nor Rigby were contented with Post-master and Vice-Treasurer, the posts designed for them; and the latter openly paid Court to Grenville, and in private disavowed to him having either conducted or approved the treaty; yet, on a question relative to East Indian affairs, Rigby left the House, and Grenville, Burke, and Wedderburn, were beaten by 128 to 41.

The negotiation was at length completed on the 18th of December on these terms:—Mr. Conway was to remain Secretary of State till February, and then resign the Seals to Lord Weymouth. Lord Gower to be President; Lord Sandwich, Postmaster; Rigby, Vice-Treasurer of Ireland, with the promise of Paymaster on the first opportunity; a Garter to the Duke of Marlborough, and a Baron's Coronet to Mr. Brand,[1] when any Peers should be created; with some less considerable places for others of their dependants. Yet did even this arrangement cost nine thousand, others said, fifteen thousand pounds, a year to Government. Lord Northington, who enriched himself by every distress and change, got three thousand pounds a year for ceding the post of President. Lord Hilsborough obtained as much for that of Post-master, and Oswald was indemnified for the temporary admission of Rigby to the Vice-Treasurership; yet was Lord Bute displeased with Oswald's dismission, though the latter was fallen into a state of dotage, and appeared no more.[2]

On the 21st the House of Commons adjourned to the 14th of January for the holidays; the Lords to the 21st, to

---

[1] Thomas Brand, Esq., of the Hoo in Hertfordshire, had married Lady Caroline Pierrepont, half-aunt of the Duchess of Bedford. He died before any creation of Peers, which did not happen till ten years after this date. [Mr. Brand was M.P. for Gatton, and died in 1770; his son married Gertrude Roper, sister and heir of Lord Dacre, on whose death she succeeded in that ancient barony, which descended to her son, Thomas Brand, in 1819. —L. M. This barony is now merged in the Viscounty of Hampden.—E.]

[2] See *supra*, vol. i. p. 284, note 4.—L. M.

avoid entering on Lord Weymouth's motion for considering the state of the nation, which was fixed for the 14th.

Grenville and his few remaining friends, whether lulled
by Rigby, or too weak to show resentment, declared they
had no cause to complain. I asked Lord Temple's friend,
Mr. W. Gerard Hamilton, if the Grenvilles and Lord
Chatham would not now be reconciled? He replied, Lord
Temple and Lord Chatham might, but George Grenville
never would; that his love of business and love of money
would both yield to his obstinacy.

Many persons ascribed the suggestion of the treaty to
Lord Mansfield, and to his weariness of opposition, which
was not his turn, and in which his aversion to Lord
Chatham had solely embarked him. He wished to obtain
a seat among the sixteen Scotch Peers in the new Parliament for his nephew, Lord Stormont.[1] But it had been
sufficient cause to Lord Mansfield to promote this new
settlement that it would, as it did entirely, give the
finishing blow to Lord Chatham's Administration. The
Bedfords saved Lord Eglinton in the succeeding Parliament from being omitted of the sixteen; but his place in
the Bedchamber they did not recover for him, promising
their friend, Lord Bolingbroke,[2] that office on the first
opportunity. Lord Eglinton was shot two years afterwards on his own estate by a poacher.

On the 23rd, Lord Gower kissed hands. The King,
to show how well he could dissemble, told him he had
never been happy since they parted. This was over-
acting insincerity.

[1] Ambassador at Vienna, and afterwards at Versailles. He was a Secretary
of State from November 1779 to March 1782, and President of the Council
in 1783. He succeeded his uncle as second Earl of Mansfield in March
1793 and died on 1st September 1796.—E.

[2] Frederic St. John, Lord Viscount Bolingbroke. [He was nephew and
successor of the famous Henry St. John, Viscount Bolingbroke, to whom he
bore some resemblance, in personal graces and vivacity, as well as in laxity
of morals. Several of his letters are given in *George Selwyn and his
Contemporaries*, and show a smattering of literature. His marriage with
the accomplished Lady Diana Spencer, afterwards Beauclerc, was dissolved
more from his fault than hers in 1768, and he died in 1787.—L. M.]

The year concluded with his Majesty making his second son, the Bishop of Osnabrugh, Knight of the Bath.

The new year was opened by the publicity of an affair which, though in agitation for some months past, had been known to very few persons. It was common, particularly in Wales, for private jobbers to apply to the Treasury, and offer to make out the title of the Crown to certain lands which had been usurped from the domain, under pretence of having been grants, though often the grantees had occupied much more than had been granted. On these occasions a new grant was the condition and reward of the informer. As these suits had regarded inconsiderable property, or rather inconsiderable persons, such transactions had never occasioned clamour. The precedent was now employed by so obnoxious a man, and to the prejudice of so puissant a lord, that no marvel it occasioned loud murmurs. Among the grants bestowed by King William on his Dutch favourite, the Earl of Portland,— grants that in their day had been sounded high by Opposition, and many of which had been cancelled by Parliament,—the Duke of Portland still enjoyed the honour of Penryn, adjoining to which he likewise possessed the forest of Inglewood, which, having been part of Queen Caroline's jointure, she had held after Penryn had been granted to Lord Portland,—a strong presumption that it made no part of what he had obtained—though on her death he or his son had entered upon it, and had enjoyed the forest to the present time. It was estimated at about eight hundred pounds a year; but whether of that value or not, included within its precincts a large number of freemen, a material article to the Duke, who was then contesting the interest of Cumberland and Westmoreland at an unbounded expense with Sir James Lowther, one of the most opulent subjects in Britain, and who, till now, had exercised almost sovereignty over the voters of those counties. Sir James discovered the flaw in the Duke of Portland's title, and made the usual application to the Treasury for leave to prove the defect, on condition of being gratified with what he should recover to the Crown. The application being made some months before, while Charles Townshend was alive and Chancellor of the Exchequer, he, rash and thoughtless as he was, had yet been struck with the inconveniences likely to follow from such indulgence, and had stopped it. Sir James Lowther was not only a man of a hateful character, but lay under the unpopularity of being Lord Bute's son-in-law. The affair, too, though simple in its own nature, ultimately regarded elections, and must revive against the Scotch favourite the odium which had attended the Dutch one, when the grant was originally made. That the Duke of Portland was in Opposition was, in prudence, an additional reason for not exerting the power of the Crown in so ungracious an act; nor was it wise in the Favourite to countenance his son in so hostile a step; a possession of land and of interest in elections ravished from a potent family was a violence that no time could obliterate. I speak of the Favourite's connivance hypothetically, for Lowther was of so mulish a nature, that I question whether he, who treated the Favourite's own daughter, a very amiable woman, but hardly, would have paid much deference to his father-in-law's remonstrances. However, as Norton was supposed to have hit the blot, and certainly was the conductor of the business, it may be presumed that Lord Bute, though he denied having given his approbation, was not sorry to see the Duke of Portland's inveteracy punished. That the King countenanced the suit may be presumed from the unparalleled wantonness and inconsideration with which the Duke of Grafton had now given it the Treasury's sanction. The Duke of Portland, who could not ascertain his right, had desired to see the collection of grants in the office of the Surveyor-General. The Duke of Grafton had allowed it, but Mr. Herbert,[1] the surveyor, refused to communicate them,

---

[1] Robert Sawyer Herbert, uncle of the Earl of Pembroke. [He was Surveyor-General of the Land Revenue from 1751 and M.P. for Wilton from 1722 until his death in April 1769.—E.]

pleading that others would claim the same indulgence. Grafton would not overrule the surveyor's objection, on which Portland reproached him, by letter, with breach of promise, in terms which the Duke of Grafton said he could scarce take as a gentleman. The Duke of Portland, though asserting his right, could never prove it, and probably had none. More of this affair will appear hereafter. Mr. Conway, who maintained his friendship with the House of Cavendish, of which the Duke of Portland had married a daughter, was much hurt at this exertion of the Crown's power, and at the Duke of Grafton's total silence to him on that transaction.[1]

On the 14th of January the House of Commons met. Dunning was declared Solicitor-General in the room of Willes,[2] who was made a Judge to make room for him. This was an extraordinary promotion, as Dunning was connected with Lord Shelburne, and was to be brought by him into the ensuing Parliament. The affair indeed had been agitated before the accession of the Bedfords, who wished to raise Wedderburn to the Solicitor's place ; but the great reputation of Dunning decided it in his favour. He was the most shining pleader then at the bar, and being a zealous Whig, had distinguished himself greatly as counsel for Wilkes. The fame of his eloquence sunk entirely and at once in the House of Commons, so different is the oratory of the bar and of Parliament. Lord Mansfield, Hume Campbell, and Lord Camden, maintained a superior reputation in both kinds. Wedderburn shone brightest in the House. Norton had at first disappointed the expectation entertained of him when he came into Parliament ; yet his strong parts, that glowed through all the coarseness of his language and brutality of his manner, recovered his weight, and he was much dis-

---

[1] A clear and impartial statement of this great case is given by Mr. Adolphus, in his *History*, vol. i. p. 308.—L. M.

[2] Edward Willes, second son of Sir John Willes, Lord Chief Justice of the Common Pleas in the reign of George the Second. [He died in January 1787 after twenty years of judicial life, and was buried at Burnham in Berkshire. He was never knighted.—E.]

tinguished. But Sir Dudley Rider,[1] the soundest lawyer, and Charles Yorke,[2] one of the most reputed pleaders, talked themselves out of all consideration in Parliament —the former by laying too great stress on every part of his diffusive knowledge, the latter by the sterility of his materials.

Dunning soon neglected the House; whether embarrassed by his attachment to Lord Shelburne, or by the affairs of Wilkes, which again became so capital an article of parliamentary debates, and in which he could take no part without offending the Crown or deserting his ancient client, or whether sensible of his own ill-success, I do not pretend to determine.[3]

---

[1] Attorney-General to King George the Second.

[2] Second son of Lord Chancellor Hardwicke.

[3] Dunning's relations with Wilkes and with Lord Shelburne furnish abundant reasons for the undistinguished figure he made in the House during the short period that he remained Solicitor-General. He was of course distrusted and slighted by Lord North, who would have obtained his dismissal within a few months after his appointment, but for the intervention of Lord Camden.—(Duke of Grafton's MS. Memoirs.) Few men could have succeeded under such circumstances. As soon as he was released from this constraint, his great powers obtained the full recognition of the House. Wraxall describes him (after the date of these Memoirs) as one of the leaders of the Opposition, the constant associate, and not unworthy fellow-labourer of Burke, and says, that 'so powerful was reason, flowing from his lips, that every murmur became hushed and every ear attentive. . . . Dunning rather subdued his hearers by his powers of argumentative ratiocination, which have rarely been exceeded, than he could be said to delight his audience.'—(*Historical and Posthumous Memoirs*, 1884, vol. ii. pp. 39-40.) His success was more remarkable from the extreme meanness of his person, and the badness of his voice. At the bar he excited universal admiration. Hannah More, in a letter on the Duchess of Kingston's trial, wrote of him,—'Dunning's manner is insufferably bad, coughing and spitting at every three words, but his sense and his expression pointed to the last degree; he made her Grace shed bitter tears.'—(*Memoirs of the Life and Correspondence of Hannah More*, 1835, vol. i. p. 82.) A great authority (Lord Brougham) has recorded that the fame of his legal arguments still lives in Westminster Hall—(*Historical Sketches*, etc., vol. iii. p. 158), and one of the most accomplished of his contemporaries has left a tribute to his memory, so beautifully worded that one cannot read it without pleasure. 'His language was always pure, always elegant, and the best words dropped easily from his lips into the best places with a fluency at all times astonishing, and when he had perfect health really melodious. . . . That faculty, however, in which no mortal ever surpassed him, and which all

Mr. Conway, who, as I have said, was disgusted at the Duke of Grafton's not communicating to him the step taken against the Duke of Portland, received a new affront from the Bedfords, Rigby declaring he would not kiss hands till after Conway's resignation : he would not have been so squeamish, had the post allotted to him been adequate to his desires. Of this impertinence Conway took, properly, only this contemptuous notice. He bade Grafton tell the Duke of Bedford that he ought to send for Rigby and whip him ; but the impertinence was so childish, he himself should take no other notice of it. Grafton sent Weymouth to Rigby, who denied the fact, said it was too absurd, and that he would kiss hands on the 18th : but even 'that was an evasion, for the 18th being the Queen's birthday, he could not kiss hands on that day ; and on the 20th, Conway, impatient to be released, resigned the Seals. The King would have exceeded his usual graciousness if he had not lately showered it so insincerely on Lord Gower. He told Conway he had never liked any man so well : insisted on his continuing Minister of the House of Commons, and in the secret of affairs, and that he should depend on him for the report of what passed in Parliament : that he wished to give him the best regiment, and would give him the first that fell : did not take his resignation ill ; and ordered him to attend him in his closet once a week : asked him how the Duke of Grafton remained with regard to the Bedfords : hoped the Duke would confine them to their agreements : did not, he said, know whether Rigby spoke truth, but that he had recanted on his (Conway's) subject.

found irresistible, was his wit. This relieved the weary, calmed the resentful, and animated the drowsy ; this drew smiles even from such as were the objects of it, scattered flowers over a desert, and, like sun-beams sparkling on a lake, gave spirit and vivacity to the dullest and least interesting cause. Not that his accomplishments as an advocate consisted principally of volubility of speech, or liveliness of raillery. He was endued with an intellect sedate yet penetrating, clear yet profound, subtle yet strong. His knowledge, too, was equal to his imagination, and his memory to his knowledge.'—(Sir William Jones's *Works*, 1799, vol. iv. pp. 577-8.)—L. M.

It appeared that these professions were not empty words. The King continued to distinguish Conway by favour, confidence, and benefits. He was constantly called to the most secret counsels of State, and remained, as much as he would, a leader in the House of Commons. The Queen, too, told him she had seen many kiss hands, but wished to see him soon kiss hands again. But this favour was no recommendation to Grafton and his new allies, though Conway, who bore no rancour to them, behaved with cordiality ; and to introduce Lord Weymouth to the succession he left him, made a dinner for him to meet the foreign Ministers. But Grafton's countenance grew so changed to him, that even the Chancellor, who was but half a politician, perceived it at Council, where the Duke paid no deference to Conway's opinion. But though this estrangement was probably owing to Rigby's machination, joined to the Duke's fickleness, the secret lay deeper, and will appear hereafter, should I continue these Memoirs, of which I am weary, and fear the reader must be more so ; though, as I was not engaged in the ensuing transactions, and having quitted Parliament, am not able to detail the debates there, my narrative will be less prolix, and the events lie in a narrower compass. At present I mean to close this part with the dissolution of the first Parliament of this reign.

The same day that Conway resigned the Seals, Lord Weymouth was declared Secretary of State. At the same time Lord Hillsborough kissed hands for the American department ; but nominally retaining the Post Office, the salary of which he paid to Lord Sandwich till the elections should be over,—there being so strict a disqualifying clause in the bill for prohibiting the Postmasters from interfering in elections, which Sandwich was determined to do to the utmost, that he did not dare to accept the office in his own name till he had incurred the guilt.

Another affair of a private nature became politics, though of little consequence. Lord Bottetort, of the Bedchamber, and a kind of second-rate favourite, had engaged

in an adventure with a company of copper-workers at
Warmley.[1] They broke. Lord Bottetort, in order to
cover his estate from the creditors, begged a privy seal, to
incorporate the Company, as private estates would not
then be answerable. The King granted his request, but
Lord Chatham, aware of the deception, honestly refused
to affix the Seal to the Patent, pleading that he was not
able. Lord Bottetort, outrageous at the disappointment,
threatened to petition the House of Lords to address for
the removal of Lord Chatham, as incapable of executing
his office. The Earl would not yield, but in the middle
of the next month, did acquiesce in resigning the Seal for
a short time, that, being put into commission, it might be
set to the grant;[2] after which he resumed it again,—to as
little purpose as he had held it before. Lord Bottetort,
not able to retrieve his losses, obtained the Government
of Virginia in the following summer, and repaired thither,
where he died.

The bill for restraining the Dividends of the East-India
Company was renewed, and after great debates carried by
130 to 41. Wedderburn opposed it strongly, and took
occasion to ask, Who was the Minister of the House of
Commons, now General Conway had resigned? He complained, too, of the erection of a third Secretary of State.

The nearness of a general election had now turned the
attention of all men that way; and such a scene of profligacy and corruption began to display itself, that even
the expiring House of Commons thought it became the
modesty of their last moments to show indignation, if they
showed no repentance: and while they were separately
pursuing the same traffic, much of their public time was

---

[1] In the parish of Sutton Coldfield, Warwickshire.—E.

[2] Lord Bottetort's proposal was absolutely monstrous, being nothing less
than a gross fraud on his creditors. In the present day it would not have
been entertained for a moment. Neither the Attorney-General nor the Home
Office, however, raised any objections, and it would seem from the Duke of
Grafton's Memoirs that the case was heard before the Commissioners of the
Privy Seal, and the claim allowed; but on referring to the Records in the
Privy Seal Office, I find that the patent *did not* pass.—L. M.

consumed in stigmatizing the practice. Beckford, on the 26th of January, moved for leave to bring in a bill to oblige the members to swear that they had not bribed their electors—a horrid bill, likely to produce nothing but a multiplication of perjury! It came out now, that the city of Oxford had acquainted Sir Thomas Stapylton[1] and Mr. Lee,[2] that they should be chosen for that town if they would contribute £7500 towards paying the debts of the Corporation. The two gentlemen refused, and Oxford sold itself to the Duke of Marlborough and Lord Abingdon. Lord Strange took up the matter with zeal, and Sir Thomas was ordered to produce to the House the letter by which the offer had been made. It is not worth returning to this subject, and therefore I will conclude it briefly here. The Mayor of Oxford, and ten more of the Corporation, appearing at the Bar, confessing their crime, and asking pardon, Lord Strange moved to commit them to Newgate for a short time. This, after a debate, was agreed to. Beckford proposed an address to the Crown, that the Attorney-General might be ordered to prosecute them ; but the House did not come into it, and they were discharged after confinement for five days. Dowdeswell proposed that Sir Thomas Stapylton should be thanked for rejecting the offer, and for telling the Corporation, that, as he did not intend to sell them, he could not afford to buy them ; but Conway objecting that a mere rejection of corruption did not deserve the thanks of the House, which ought not to be rendered too common, the motion was dropped. The Duke and Earl not having been so scrupulous, and their agreement with the town having been entered into the book of the Corporation, the town-

---

[1] Sir Thomas Stapylton, Bart., of Rotherfield Greys, Oxon, married Mary, daughter of Mr. Fane of Wormsley, and niece of the Earl of Westmorland. His eldest son became in 1788 Lord le Despencer, the abeyance of that ancient barony having been determined in his favour.—L. M.

[2] The Honourable Robert Lee, uncle to the Earl of Lichfield, whom he succeeded in that title in 1772. He died without issue in 1776, and was the last of his family. The title became extinct and Ditchley has descended to Lord Dillon.—L. M

clerk was sent off with it to Calais; and Lord Strange was prevailed upon to absent himself from the House till the matter was hushed up.[1]

The Irish Parliament, which it was not so easy for the Crown to gratify, was consequently less tractable; and since the tax on places and pensions had sent over a bill for making their Parliaments, which lasted during the life of each reigning King, septennial,—this, in truth, had been a grievous concession made by the members to popularity, and in which both Houses had again trusted to the negative of the Crown. The members of the House of Commons, who might look on themselves, under so young a Prince, as seated for life, could not taste a measure that rendered those seats precarious, or, if renewed, expensive. To their surprise and grief, the Council here advised the King to pass the bill—but with these alterations: instead of septennial, they made those Parliaments octennial, that both kingdoms might not be in tumult and confusion at the same time every seven years: and whereas the bill, as sent over, was not to take place under seven years; to punish those who had sent it, it was to operate immediately. If accepted on its return to Ireland, the Members would suffer for their promptitude in passing it; if rejected, they would lose their popularity—or should they start any method of rejection hostile to the Court, it would still be in the power of the Court to dissolve them. Lord Camden was the principal adviser of the King's assent being given, from his affection to liberty and a free constitution— laudable motives, but productive afterwards of much inconvenience; for the Irish, who were pushing to throw off all dependence on England, looked on the concession as a symptom of weakness, and consequently hurried further from that union which was necessary to both kingdoms.

[1] The proceedings are reported in *Parliamentary History*, vol. xvi. 397. Mr. Adolphus says in a note to his *History*, vol. i. p. 337: ' The whole matter was treated with great ridicule by writers of all parties,' a statement which may easily be believed if Mr. Grattan's story be true, that the peccant alderman completed their bargain with the Duke of Marlborough during their imprisonment in Newgate.—L. M.

Scotland had been averse to union, but reaped the fullest benefits from it; and it was likely to confer many on Ireland, and to remove that narrow spirit by which we had been influenced to treat them with injustice. Mr. Grenville's imprudence and rash economy had drawn such another line of separation between Great Britain and America; and he and Lord George Sackville Germaine [1] will long be remembered as the authors or causes of those divisions which have embroiled the mother-country and its members. The King's assent to the Octennial Bill was received with such transports of joy all over Ireland, that the Parliament did not dare but pass it with its corrections, and were obliged to thank his Majesty for having passed it.

Marshal Sir Robert Rich [2] dying on the 1st of February, the King, who learnt the news on coming from Richmond, would not dine till he had written to Mr. Conway that he gave him the vacant regiment, and intended him a better —meaning the Blues, after Lord Ligonier.

On the 4th of January, the bill to regulate dividends was carried in the House of Lords by 70 to 30. Lord Weymouth apologized for himself, the Duke of Bedford, and their friends, saying, ' that to be consistent, they must vote against the Court, as they had warmly opposed the same bill the last year.' Lord Temple told them they were pitifully silent now.

On the second reading of Beckford's Bribery Bill, Dowdeswell and Burke opposed it for multiplying oaths, and while it restrained the Commons, left a power of corruption in the Crown and nobility. By the clause to

---

[1] When this was written, it alluded only to the opposition occasioned by Lord George in Ireland. He has since engrafted himself on Mr. Grenville's persecution of America.

[2] Sir Robert Rich, Bart., had been made Field Marshal in 1757. His Brigadier's commission is dated as far back as 1727, so that he must have been very aged when he died. His name does not appear as having ever been employed on active service. He was succeeded in his baronetcy and estates by his eldest son, General Rich, who had lost an arm at Culloden; one of his daughters became the second wife of Lord Lyttelton.—L. M.

disqualify those who bribed, it would subject the rights of elections, they said, to the courts below. The bill, however, was committed. But before the day came, the House went on new matter of the same species. Boroughs had been publicly advertised for sale in the newspapers; and there was a set of attorneys who rode the country and negotiated seats in the most indecent manner. Reynolds and Hickey, two of them, were taken up by order of the House, and some of those borough-brokers were sent to Newgate.

When the Bribery Bill was read in the committee, the oath appeared horrid to everybody, and was so rigorously worded, that it would have excluded every neighbourly act of kindness or charity. This was universally disapproved. The disqualifying clause met with not much better success. It would have encouraged informers without being a check on the Crown and Treasury. Dowdeswell proposed a clause to take away their votes at elections from all officers of the revenue. Upon this, one Fonnereau, a peevish man, who had all his life been a Court tool, complained that Chauncy Townshend,[1] a brother-dependant, but more favoured, had so much interest with the Ministers, that one Bennet, parson of Aldborough, and attached to Townshend, had vaunted that he could obtain the dismission of any officer of the revenue who should vote for Fonnereau.[2] Grenville

---

[1] Chauncy Townshend was M.P. for the Wigtown district of burghs. He died in 1770. The *Annual Register* states that he was the first Englishman that represented a Scotch burgh (vol. xiii. p. 114). His son became an Alderman for the City of London, and a politician of sufficient notoriety to be often noticed in this work.—L. M.

[2] Thomas Fonnereau, of Christ Church Park, near Ipswich. He was out of humour with the Minister for having refused him the place of Receiver-General of Suffolk. It is said that he had the offer of being Joint Postmaster-General, which did not suit or satisfy him. He had the reputation of being very acute and persevering in business; the Lizard Lighthouses were projected and erected by him, and he had a lease of the tolls, which must have been very productive; but his expenses at Aldborough and Sudbury, for which he also returned a member, kept him poor. He had made himself remarkable for his loyalty in the rebellion of 1745, when he made a speech to the grand jury of Suffolk, which was publicly distributed at their request.

caught artfully at this complaint, and with Blackstone and Dowdeswell insisted on inquiring into the affair. The Ministry made but a bad figure, though Lord North shone greatly, and was ably supported by Dyson. But the House was empty, few of the new courtiers were there, and of them Rigby took no part, till Grenville had left the House. Conway added to their distress by threatening to pursue up the affair of Fonnereau's complaint.

Arthur Onslow, the late Speaker, who died on the very day of this Committee, had ordered the House to be acquainted that he died in peace on hearing of that bill. But though the good old man's detestation of corruption did him honour, the House reasoned too soundly to attempt a vain cure by increasing a blacker crime—perjury. When the bill was again read in the Committee on the 19th, it was so ill received, that Beckford, the author, left the House in the middle of the debate. Dowdeswell and all his party resisted the bill; but Grenville, to flatter the country gentlemen, who can ill afford to combat with great lords, nabobs, commissaries, and West-Indians, declaimed in favour of the bill; but the courtiers moving for the Chairman to leave the Chair, Dowdeswell said, he could approve that proposal no more than the bill, as there had been instructions given to the committee on his clause for disqualifying officers of the revenue. On this he was reduced to vote with Grenville ; but they were beaten by 96 to 69, and the bill was thrown out.

Bradshaw, the Duke of Grafton's favourite secretary of the Treasury, having been concerned in the business at Aldborough complained of by Fonnereau, the Opposition hoped to reach the Duke himself, and ordered the parson to their bar. He demanded counsel. Grenville vociferously ranted against allowing counsel on so enormous a crime as bribery, but was put to shame for his tyranny

He was obstinate rather than peevish, and his manners were generally very agreeable. He died a bachelor in 1779, in the eightieth year of his age. —L. M.

by Sir Gilbert Elliot, who showed that even on treason and murder, counsel was allowed to prisoners. Dunning, the new Solicitor-General, but not yet in Parliament, appeared as counsel for Bennet, who was a jovial, sporting young parson, neither very moral, nor very modest. Dunning exerted himself with great lustre. Fonnereau, to save £40 (for he was a very miser) had refused counsel, and behaved so obstinately and absurdly, that though Grenville, Wedderburn, and Dowdeswell supported, and gave him hints, with all their parliamentary craft, he counteracted his own witnesses; and it came out that he had not only been more criminal himself than the clergyman, but for a series of years had established and profited of Ministerial influence in the borough in question. Conway was converted by the rancour of the charge, and with Hussey, as they were the two most candid men in the House, threw such disgrace on Fonnereau, that the parson was acquitted by 155 to 39; the most remarkable event of the debate being a warm dispute between the late friends Rigby and Grenville, in which the former attacked and treated the latter without management.

Though this was the last debate in that Parliament, another had intervened of more weight, but I chose not to intermingle the subjects.

On the 17th of February Sir George Savile moved to renew a bill drawn by Lord Chief Justice Coke, and passed in the reign of James the First for quieting the minds of those who possessed Crown lands, by preventing the Crown from suing for the recovery of them after they had been enjoyed by private persons for sixty years. Sir George made the proposal in very general terms, and with great decency, though in a style too metaphoric. The intention was evidently suggested by the recent case of the Duke of Portland, but he affected not to allude to it, nor to pass any censure on that act. The case they knew would present itself to every man, and the less animosity they discovered the more easily they hoped the bill would find its way through the House and be at once a silent

reproach to and a real check upon the Crown. Sir
Anthony Abdy seconded the motion. Lord North objected on the impropriety of the time, the very end of a
parliament; and he urged that such bills should only
arise out of grievances: he called to know if any such
existed. Lord Clare said, that the Crown having actually
in contemplation to give up or sell to the public many
forests and wastes for cultivation and increase of provisions, such a bill would impede that scheme. Charles
Yorke, in a very long deduction, argued against vexatious
revisals. Himself, when Attorney-General, he said, had
been consulted by persons who had obtained such grants
and had condemned them. So had Lord Mansfield,
whose abilities and merits were only exceeded by slander.
He then stated the case of the Duke of Portland, which,
he said, had been treated with incaution and precipitation;
and that the Duke ought to have had the preference
given to him, as being in possession, over Sir James
Lowther. Norton replied that the case had been four
months in agitation; that the preference could not be
given to the Duke, who contested the right of possession
with the Crown, and did not sue for it. That though his
Grace's grant dated sixty-three years before the dispute,
the encroachment was not of equal antiquity, the lands in
question having appertained to the Queen Dowager, who
had granted them on lease, which had not expired till the
year 1724, when the Dukes of Portland had appropriated
them to themselves. He challenged Yorke to meet him
in any court in England, and fight out that cause. Yorke
evaded the challenge; though Norton and Rigby again
called on him to be explicit. Much complaint was made
of the surveyor's refusal of the sight of necessary papers.
Sir William Meredith spoke, with more applause than he
had ever done, in behalf of the bill. Grenville trimmed
with all his art, not to offend Lord Bute and Sir James
Lowther. Lord Barrington, in order to get rid of the bill
at that time, approved of passing it in another Parliament,
and said he should be desirous of taking away the *nullum*

tempus[1] from the clergy likewise.   Lord John Cavendish, throwing out insinuations against the Duchy Court of Lancaster for issuing vexatious notices, Stanley said he had been desired by Lord Strange to defy in his name any accuser.   Lord North, to avoid putting a negative on so popular a bill, moved for the orders of the day, and at eleven at night his motion was carried by 134 to 114, many courtiers voting in the minority as favourers of the bill.

On the 11th of March the Parliament was dissolved. Thus ended that Parliament, uniform in nothing but in its obedience to the Crown.   To all I have said I will only add that it would have deserved the appellation of one of the worst Parliaments England ever saw, if its servility had not been so great, that, as the times changed, it enacted remedies for the evils it had committed with the same facility with which it had complied with the authors of those evils.   Our ancestors, who dealt in epithets, might have called it the *impudent* Parliament.

[1] Nullum tempus occurrit regi et ecclesiæ : an old absurd maxim of law.

CHAPTER VI

On the Literature of the Early Part of the Reign of George the Third.

1768

IT may not be amiss, by way of appendix, to say a few words on the state of literature during the period I have been describing. It will be the less improper as the controversies and politics of the age gave the principal, almost the whole tone to letters of that time. I do not mean to send the reader to the gross and virulent libels of Wilkes and his still coarser imitators. As a writer, Wilkes's chief merit was an easy style,—the vehicle of little knowledge, of not much more wit, and of extreme boldness.[1] He was so far an original as being the first who dared to print the most respected names at full length. In imitation of him, the daily and evening newspapers printed every outrageous libel that was sent to them. Till that time the abuse of the week was generally confined to essays in the journals on Saturdays. Bolingbroke and Pulteney were content with battering the Administration once in seven days.

The contests that arose out of Wilkes's case produced much disquisition into the laws and Constitution; and amidst much party invective, some grave and serious treatises appeared, especially one I have mentioned, the masterly tract called *An Inquiry into the Doctrine of Libels.*[2]

---

[1] *Vide* The Character of Wilkes as a Politican and a Writer, in Lord Brougham's *Statesmen of the Time of George the Third*, vol. iii. p. 181.—L. M.

[2] *An Enquiry into the Doctrine, lately propagated, concerning Libels, Warrants, and the Seizure of Papers; with a view to some late proceedings, and the defence of them by the majority; upon the principles of the Constitution. In a letter to Mr. Almon from the father of Candor.* (London, 1764, 8vo.) In the later editions it is intituled *A Letter concerning Libels*, etc.,

Several other good pamphlets were written on national affairs, particularly relative to the East India Company; and to the heats occasioned in America by the Stamp Act. Among the latter were justly distinguished *A Farmer's Letters from Pennsylvania*, written by Dr. Franklin.[1]

The state of our finances, and the properest methods of conducting and restoring them, were much discussed: never more ably than in Mr. Edmund Burke's answer to a (supposed) pamphlet of Mr. Grenville, in 1769.[2]

Politics not only occupied our prose but inspired our poets. I have taken notice of Churchill's works; and will only say here that he did not so much prove himself a great poet, as he showed how great he might have been.

The politics of the times gave birth to two other poems of uncommon merit, both in the burlesque style, but one in that of *Hudibras*, the other in the graver march of *The Dispensary*. The first called *Rodondo*,[3] of which only two cantos appeared, though a third was promised, was written by a Mr. Dalrymple, a Scot, and contained a

and both Almon and 'the father of Candor' are removed from the title-page. 'Candor' is the signature of a very clever letter to the *Public Advertiser*, published a short time before by Almon on the same subject, severely attacking the Government under the pretence of defending it.—L. M. [The *Enquiry* is said to have gone through five editions in a few months. The name of the author is unknown, but it was probably revised by Dunning and Lord Chatham.—E.]

[1] *Letters from a Farmer in Pennsylvania to the Inhabitants of the British Colonies* (Boston [U. S.], 1768, 8vo). These letters were not written by Franklin, but by John Dickinson, who was born in Maryland on 13th November 1732, and died at Wilmington on 14th February 1808. Dickinson was successively President of the State of Delaware, and of the Commonwealth of Pennsylvania. His political writings were published in 1801 (Wilmington, 8vo, 2 vols.).—E.   [2] See *infra*.—L. M.

[3] The first and second cantos of *Rodondo; or the State Jugglers* were published separately in 1763 (London, 8vo). The third canto did not appear until 1770 (London, 8vo). The author of these three cantos 'was Hugh Dalrymple, Esq. He also wrote *Woodstock: an Elegy*, reprinted in Pearch's *Collection of Poems*. At the time of his death he was Attorney-General for the Grenades, where he died, 9th March 1774. His daughter married Dr., afterwards Sir John Elliott, from whom she was divorced,' etc.—(MS. note on fly-leaf of copy of *Rodondo* in the British Museum.) *Rodondo* was reprinted in Ruddiman's *Collection of Scarce, Curious, and Valuable Pieces* (Edinburgh, 1783, 8vo).—E.

severe satire on Mr. Pitt, not much inferior in wit to Butler,
and like his work, liable by temporary allusions to lose
many beauties in the eyes of posterity.

The second, called *Patriotism ; a Mock Heroic,*[1] by
Mr. Richard Bentley, though full of negligences and
crowded with intricate and sometimes too far-fetched
metaphors,—nay, in some places pushed to nonsense by
the confusion of those metaphors, in sense and imagination excelled Churchill ; and though less sonorous, did not
breathe a spirit less poetic. The flattery was profuse and
indelicate ; the satire rarely unjust. The imitations of
Milton, Dryden, and Garth, though frequent, were always
happy ; and the whole poem, though much more incorrect
than *The Dispensary* or *The Dunciad*, has beauties that
rank it next to them in merit : in the dignity of its heroes it
precedes both. One of its greatest faults seems to be, that
though all the personages appear under allegoric names, all
were meant for living characters, till the last canto, when
Fate is introduced in its own essence, and though maintained with as sublime dignity as the nature of burlesque
would allow, still produces a confusion by not being of a
piece with the rest of the work. It has the same misfortune with Rodondo of being written on transient ridicules.

Two other poets of great merit arose, who meddled not
with politics ; Dr. Goldsmith, the correct Author of *The
Traveller* ;[2] and Mr. Anstey, who produced as original a
poem as *Hudibras* itself, *The New Bath Guide.*[3] The

---

[1] *Patriotism ; a Mock Heroic, in Five Cantos* (London, 1763, 4to). The
author, Richard Bentley, was the youngest son of Dr. Bentley, the famous
scholar. He lived on terms of great intimacy with Walpole for several years,
and died in October 1782. His contemporaries had a higher opinion of his
abilities than his writings are capable of sustaining.—E.

[2] The first edition of the *Traveller* was published in December 1764. *The
Vicar of Wakefield* appeared in March 1766, and *The Deserted Village* in
May 1770.—E.

[3] *The New Bath Guide, or Memoirs of the B—r—d [Blunderhead] Family,
in a series of Poetical Epistles* (Cambridge, 1766, 4to). Christopher Anstey
died in 1805, aged eighty-one, and was buried in Walcot Parish Church, Bath.
His Poetical Works, with an account of his life by his son John Anstey,
were published in 1808.—E.

easiest wit, the most genuine humour, the most inoffensive
satire, the happiest parodies, the most unaffected poetry,
and the most harmonious melody in every kind of metre,
distinguished that poem by their assemblage from the
works of all other men.   It was a melancholy proof of
how little an author can judge of the merit of his own
compositions, when he afterwards produced *The Patriot*,
in which nobody could discover his meaning, or whether
he had any meaning ; and in which, amidst various but
unsuccessful attempts at humour, nothing remained but his
sonorous numbers.   He afterwards sunk to no kind of
merit at all.

   I do not know whether this period may not be said to
have *given birth* to another original poem ; for notwithstanding its boasted antiquity, and the singularity of the
style, it remains a doubt with me and many others, whether
Fingal[1] was not formed in this age from scraps, perhaps
not modern, but of no very early date.   Its sterility of
ideas, the insipid sameness that reigns throughout, and
the timidity with which it anxiously avoids every image
that might affix it to any specific age, country, or religion,
are far from bespeaking a savage bard, who the more he
was original, the more he would naturally have availed
himself of the images and opinions around him.   Few
barbarous authors write with the fear of criticism before
their eyes.   The moon, a storm, the troubled ocean, a
blasted heath, a single tree, a waterfall, and a ghost ; take
these away and Cadmus's warriors, who started out of the
earth, and killed one another, before they had time to conceive an idea, were as proper heroes for an epic poem as
Fingal and his captains.

   [1] *Fingal, an ancient Epic Poem in six books, together with several other
poems. Composed by Ossian, the son of Fingal. Translated from the Gaelic
language by James Macpherson.* (London, 1762, 8vo.) The 'translator' of
the Ossianic poems was born in Ruthven, Inverness-shire, in 1738. The long
and fierce controversy respecting the authenticity of these poems is well
known. He was M.P. for Camelford from September 1780 until his death
on 17th February 1796. He was buried within a few feet of his sturdy
opponent, Samuel Johnson, in Westminster Abbey.—E.

I will mention but two other authors of this period, Dr. Robertson,[1] and Mrs. Macaulay. The first as sagacious and penetrating as Tacitus, with the perspicuity of Livy, and without the partialities of his own countryman, Hume, gave a perfect model of history in that of Scotland. In biography, his method and style were still preserved, though his Charles the Fifth fell far short of his other works. The female historian, as partial in the cause of liberty as bigots to the Church and royalists to tyranny, exerted manly strength with the gravity of a philosopher.[2] Too prejudiced to dive into causes, she imputes everything to tyrannic views, nothing to passions, weakness, error, prejudice, and still less to what operates oftenest, and her ignorance of which qualified her yet less for a historian,—

---

[1] William Robertson's *History of Scotland* was published in 1759 (London, 4to, 2 vols.). It passed through fourteen editions in his lifetime. The first editions of his *History of the Reign of the Emperor Charles V.* and of his *History of America* appeared respectively in 1769 and 1777. He died at Edinburgh on 11th June 1793.—E.

[2] It may appear strange to us that a work of so little merit as Mrs. Macaulay's *History* should be mentioned by Walpole almost in the same sentence with Robertson's *Charles the Fifth*, but other writers of that day have bestowed on it equally elaborate and still more complimentary criticism. Indeed, it met, on its original publication, with a warmth of praise that presents a striking contrast to the discouraging reception of the early volumes of Hume. Madame Roland regarded it as hardly inferior to Tacitus. The adventitious events which produced this perversion of judgment in a large portion of the public have long ceased to operate, and the discredit which deservedly attaches to Mrs. Macaulay's *History* has extended rather unjustly to her talents. She was a vain, self-opinionated, and prejudiced, but also a clever woman. Her works show occasionally considerable power of writing, especially in description; and carelessly as she consulted original authorities, and unfairly as she used them, she may in that respect bear no dishonourable comparison with Smollett, and others of her contemporaries. She is at least entitled to the praise of having been the first, in order, of our female historians. Mrs. Macaulay died in 1791, aged fifty-eight. An imprudent marriage, late in life, with a man much younger and in a much lower station than herself, alienated from her most of her friends, and hastened the downfall of a literary reputation, which had barely survived the wreck of the small section of politicians with whom she was connected.—L. M. [Catherine Macaulay was the sister of Alderman Sawbridge and the wife first of George Macaulay, M.D., and secondly of a Mr. Graham. Her *History of England from the Accession of James I. to that of the Brunswick Line* was published between 1763 and 1783 in 8 vols. (London, 4to.)—E.]

to accident and little motives. She seems to think men
have acted from no views but those of establishing a
despotism or a republic. As a mixed government clashed
with her system, she forgot the nation had been habituated
to it, and she could not forgive the victors in the civil war
for not abolishing all *established* order, and for not shutting
their ears and hearts against every connection and interest,
in pursuit of a model which mad Harrington had chalked
out, though impracticable, and which she was not then
born to preach up. In this wild pursuit of a vision which
must have rooted up every law, she is reduced to declare
for the army [1] that tore out of the House of Commons the
very Parliament to whom the nation had owed the first
assertion of its liberties. To such absurdities are they
reduced whose prejudices hurry them to extremes! If the
Parliament were not the legal authority for controlling the
King, where shall we say legality resides? She would
answer, In the natural right of mankind to be free. That
right, then, must be vindicated by force. Thence we
revert to a state of nature. What did that state of nature
produce? System-builders will tell me, it produced de-
liberation on the right method of governing nations. The
answer is not true. Time, accident, and events produced
government ;—but no matter, I will allow the position,
with this proviso, that a victorious army shall sheathe
their swords, and allow the wisest and best citizens to
form a new Constitution: who sees not the absurdity and
impracticability of this proposition? When did an army
bestow freedom? Did that army which raised Cromwell
to the throne—those republican heroes of Mrs. Macaulay?
The Parliament was the truer barrier against the King's
usurpations, and had done its duty nobly. Reformation,
not destruction of the constitution, was its aim : and therefore in her eyes, it was not less guilty than the King. I
worship liberty as much as she does, detest despotism as
much ; but I never yet saw or read of a form of govern-

---

[1] This is the case in her fourth volume ; in the fifth, she takes the contrary
extreme.

ment under which more general freedom is enjoyed, than under our own. Republics veer towards aristocracy or democracy, and often end in a single tyrant,—not that nobles are not tyrants. For the people, they are not capable of Government, and do more harm in an hour, when heated by popular incendiaries than a king can do in a year. It is a government like ours, in which all the three parts seeks augmentation of their separate powers, and in which King, Lords, and Commons, are a watch and a check upon the other two, that best ensures the general happiness. Mrs. Macaulay will allow that there is no check upon an absolute monarch. In an aristocracy, the pride, ambition, and jealousy of the nobles are some check upon each individual grandee. But what is a check upon the people in a republic? In what republic have not the best citizens fallen a sacrifice to the ambition and envy of the worst? God grant that, with all its deficiencies, we may preserve our own mixed government!

CHAPTER VII

1768

As I had rather disparage these Memoirs than disappoint the reader by promising him more satisfaction than he will find, let me remind him that I had now quitted my seat in Parliament; and consequently, what traces of debates shall appear hereafter must be mutilated and imperfect, as being received by hearsay from others, or taken from notes communicated to me. As I had detached myself, too, from all parties, I was in the secrets of none: and though I had curiosity enough to fathom some, opportunities of learning others, and made observations on what was passing, in which I was assisted by the clue of what I had formerly known; yet it will doubtless be perceived that my information was often incomplete, and that the mysterious springs of several events never came to my knowledge. In those situations I shall be far from decisive: yet that very ignorance may guide future historians to the search after authentic papers; and my doubts may lead to some certainty. It may yet be asked why I choose, under these impediments, to continue my narrative, while I allow that it must fall short of the preceding parts? The honestest answer is the best: it amuses me. I like to give my opinion on what I have seen : I wish to warn posterity (however vain such zeal) against the folly and corruption and profligacy of the times I have lived in ; and I think that, with all its defects, the story I shall tell will be more complete than if I had stopped at the end of the foregoing Parliament, which was no era of anything but of my own dereliction of politics ; and not having been the hero of my own tale, I am desirous at least of bringing it down to the termination of the political life of some of the principal actors in the foregoing pages. I propose to carry the work down to the pacification with Spain in 1771, when not only all our foreign quarrels were terminated, but when the Court had surmounted every domestic difficulty, had pacified the Colonies and Ireland ; and by the aid of fortune and by the folly of opposition, had little to disturb them but their own indiscretion, and the restless, though timid desires of ascertaining and extending a prerogative which the King enjoyed effectually by less obnoxious, though less dangerous, means than force. Whether I shall live to complete this plan, or whether, if I do, I shall not again be tempted to prosecute it further, I am equally ignorant. The reader, that is amused, may perhaps be glad if I proceed. If I am tedious, the most delicate of my readers will always have that facile remedy in his power, of ceasing to read me the moment he is tired. To such, therefore, I make no apology. To please the other sort, if I can—at least to employ some vacant hours, I continue my journal.

The Parliament having been dissolved on the 11th of March, 1768, and the writs issued for the general election of another, the memorable John Wilkes, who had resided for some time at Paris, and had fallen almost into oblivion, came suddenly over, and declared himself a candidate to represent the City of London. His first step, indeed, was to write a submissive letter to the King, imploring pardon ; but his Majesty refusing to read the letter,[1] Wilkes, bold

---

[1] The letter was delivered at the Palace by Wilkes's footman, and as unceremoniously returned. It is not disrespectfully worded. It is printed in Almon's *Memoirs of Wilkes*, vol. iii. pp. 263-4.—L. M.

from his desperate situation, and fond of extraordinary daring, opened his new campaign by this attack on the metropolis itself, though an outlaw, and subject to be sent to prison on his former sentence. Men wondered at the inactivity of a Government that had by no means shown itself indifferent to the persecution of so audacious a criminal, and expected every day to hear he was taken up. But whether the Court looked with contempt on a measure that promised so little success, or whether, which I believe was their true motive, they feared that new severity would enhance the merits of the martyr in the eyes of the people, neither the Government nor the courts of law interposed to check his career. Alderman Sir William Baker was the only citizen of note and fortune that countenanced his pretensions; yet Wilkes persisted, appeared openly on the hustings, and contested a seat with the most popular of the City's magistrates. The lower people[1] embraced his cause with ardour; and he soon appeared to have so many partisans, that his fortune became combined with that national frenzy, stock-jobbing. Bets on his success were turned into stock; and in the phrase of the times, *he was done*, like other wagers on the funds. The credit of the candidate Alderman was, however, too firmly established to be shaken so suddenly. Wilkes was every day the lowest on the poll, and the very first evening as he left the court, he was arrested for debt —probably by the underhand direction of the Ministry; but his attorney answered for his appearance; and preferring to be a prisoner to the Government, as more likely to create pity, than to lie in prison for debt, Wilkes acquainted the Solicitor of the Treasury, that he intended to surrender himself to his outlawry. He returned each day to the hustings, but lost his election; Harley, the Lord

---

[1] Going to ask the vote of a petty shopkeeper in Wapping, the man desired Wilkes to wait a moment, went up-stairs and brought him down a bank-note of £20. Wilkes said he wanted his vote, not his money. The man replied, he must accept both or neither.

Mayor, Sir Robert Ladbrooke,[1] Beckford, and Trecothick,[2] being elected ; the last, a West-India merchant, who, at the time of the Stamp-Act, had signalized himself by procuring petitions against it from Bristol, Liverpool, and other commercial towns. Sir Richard Glynn,[3] Paterson, the unpopular creature of Lord Holland, and Wilkes, being thrown out. During the struggle, Beckford and Trecothick behaved towards Wilkes with much civility ; the Lord Mayor with sullen coldness, and occasionally with spirited resistance.

Far from dismayed, Wilkes, like an able general, rallied his forces, and declared himself a candidate for the county of Middlesex—nay, threatened to stand for Surrey, too, in opposition to George Onslow,[4] one of his deserting

[1] Sir Robert Ladbroke was elected an Alderman in January 1741, and served the office of Sheriff 1743-4, of Lord Mayor 1747-8. He was M.P. for the City of London from May 1754 until his death in October 1773.—E.

[2] Barlow Trecothick was an opulent merchant in the American trade, and not, as Dr. Johnson supposed, an American. He supported Wilkes with less warmth, but more judgment than Beckford, Mawbey, and Townshend, and Sawbridge, and the other prominent City patriots. Probably he had the penetration to see deeper into his character and views. Wilkes, in consequence, appears not to have lived on any intimate footing with him. He spoke well in Parliament. He was by far the ablest man of the party that ruled the City in that day. He died at Addington in Surrey, where he had a considerable estate, in 1775. His epitaph states, with more truth than elegance of expression, 'that he was much esteemed by the merchants for his integrity and knowledge of commerce, truly beloved by his fellow-citizens, who chose him as their representative in Parliament, and sincerely lamented by his friends and relations, who looked up to and admired his virtues.'—L. M.

[3] Sir Richard Glyn, an opulent banker in the City, and alderman. He had been Lord Mayor in 1758-9, and was created a baronet in 1759. He died in 1773 : he was the founder of the great banking-house which still bears his name. He married twice, and left issue by both marriages. His eldest son by his second marriage was created a baronet in 1800.—L. M.

[4] Son of the late Speaker. Colonel George Onslow was the son of the General, brother of the Speaker. [George Onslow, son of Speaker Onslow, M.P., Rye, 1754-61, Surrey, 1761-74, Lord of the Treasury, 1765-77, was created Baron Cranley in May 1776, and in the following October succeeded his cousin as fourth Baron Onslow. He was Comptroller of the Household, 1777-9, Treasurer of the Household, 1779-80, and a Lord of the Bedchamber, 1780-1814. In June 1801 he was created Earl of Onslow, and died 17th May 1814, aged eighty-three. He was the mover of the resolution in April 1769 declaring Colonel Luttrell M.P. for Middlesex.—E.]

friends; yet hitherto he had no eminent patronage. Lord Temple, linked with Grenville, abandoned him. Humphrey Cotes,[1] an old ally, but who in his absence, it was said, had cheated him of some money, made amends by warm activity; and the Duke of Portland, incensed by his late affair with Sir James Lowther, on Wilkes's pretensions to Middlesex, espoused his cause. Lord Mansfield, equally revengeful, timorous, and subtle, pretended that it was the office of the Chancellor to bring this outlaw to justice; but the Chancellor and the Duke of Grafton did not care to increase their unpopularity by adding persecution to the complaints Wilkes had already made of their giving him up. Still less was Lord Camden solicitous to save Lord Mansfield from danger and odium. The Chancellor went to Bath, and the Duke to Newmarket.

On the 28th of March the election began at Brentford; and while the irresolution of the Court and the carelessness of the Prime Minister, Grafton, caused a neglect of all precautions, the zeal of the populace had heated itself to a pitch of fury. They possessed themselves of all the turnpikes and avenues leading to the place of election by break of day, and would suffer no man to pass who bore not in his hat a blue cockade inscribed with the name of Wilkes and Number 45,[2] or written on paper. The other candidates were, Sir William Beauchamp Proctor[3] and Mr. Cooke, the former members. Cooke was confined with the gout: a relation who appeared for him was roughly handled at Hyde Park Corner, and Sir William's carriage was demolished. At Brentford the mob was

---

[1] Cotes became a bankrupt in February 1767.—L. M.

[2] It was for the forty-fifth number of the *North Briton* that Wilkes had been prosecuted.

[3] Sir William Beauchamp Proctor, of Langley Park, Norfolk, had represented the county from 1747 to 1768. He had been made a Knight of the Bath on the King's accession. He made a fruitless application for Lord Chatham's support in this contest; his Lordship's answer being that he did not meddle with elections. Sir William Beauchamp Proctor died in 1773, aged forty-nine.—L. M.

more peaceable, but had poured in in such numbers, that on the first day's poll the votes for Wilkes were 1200, for Proctor, 700, for Cooke, 500. At night the people grew outrageous; though when Wilkes first arrived in town, I had seen him pass before my windows in a hackney chair, attended but by a dozen children and women; now all Westminster was in a riot. It was not safe to pass through Piccadilly; and every family was forced to put out lights: the windows of every unilluminated house were demolished. The coach-glasses of such as did not huzza for *Wilkes and liberty* were broken, and many chariots and coaches were spoiled by the mob scratching them with the favourite 45. Lord Weymouth, Secretary of State, sent orders to Justice Fielding to have constables kept in readiness. He begged his Lordship not to tell it, but there was not a constable in London—all had been sent for to Brentford. On this the guards were drawn out. Lord Bute's house was attacked, but the mob could not force an entrance, nor at Lord Egmont's in Pall Mall. The Duke of Northumberland the mob obliged to appear and to give them liquor, and to drink with them to Wilkes's success. Some ladies of rank were taken out of their chairs, and ordered to join the popular cry; and to Lady Holderness they cried, 'No King! No regal Government! In the City they attacked the mansion house and broke the windows. The Lord Mayor, a zealous anti-Wilkite, sent for the trained bands, but they were not sufficient to disperse the tumult. Six thousand weavers had risen in behalf of Wilkes, and were the principal actors. Some of the regimental drummers beat their drums for Wilkes, who finding his election secure, dismissed the weavers, and by the next morning all was quiet, but the poll was at an end. Wilkes was too triumphant to be resisted; and, master to act as he pleased, he threw his supernumerary votes in to Cooke, who was elected with him.

The second night was less tumultuous; but the Scots, sullenly persisting in not celebrating their enemy's triumph by illuminations, had their windows broken. The Dowager Duchess of Hamilton,[1] one of the beautiful Gunnings, though born in Ireland, had contracted such hatred to Wilkes from her two Scotch marriages, that though with child, and though her husband, Lord Lorn, was in Scotland, and all her young children by both matches were in the house with her, she resolutely forbade her house to be lighted up. The mob assaulted it, broke down the outward gates with iron crows, tore up the pavement of the street, and battered the doors and shutters for three hours, but could not surmount her courage. The Count de Seilern, the Austrian Ambassador, the most stately and ceremonious of men, they took out of his coach, and chalked 45 on the sole of his shoe. He complained in form of the insult; it

[1] Elizabeth Gunning, sister of the celebrated Countess of Coventry, had first married the Duke of Hamilton, and afterwards John Campbell, Marquis of Lorn, eldest son of John, Duke of Argyle, whom he succeeded in the title, and thus became mother of the two heirs of the great rival houses of Hamilton and Argyle. She was Lady of the Bedchamber to Queen Charlotte, and had gone to fetch her from Mecklenburg, with the Duchess of Ancaster, Mistress of the Robes. Her eldest son, [the] Duke [of] Hamilton, died before he was of age. Lord Douglas Hamilton, his brother, succeeded him. The Duchess Elizabeth, as guardian of her sons, carried on the famous law-suit against Mr. Douglas for the succession of his (supposed) uncle, the Duke of Douglas, of which more will be said hereafter. By [the] Duke [of] Hamilton she had one daughter, Lady Elizabeth, afterwards married to the Earl of Derby. By Lord Lorn she had two sons, the eldest of which died an infant, and two daughters. [There were three sons, the eldest of whom died an infant, while the other two succeeded as fifth and sixth Dukes of Argyll.—E.] In her widowhood she had refused the hand of the Duke of Bridgewater. She was entirely governed by the artful Lady Susan Stuart, daughter of the Earl of Galloway, afterwards Countess Gower, on whose account she much offended the Queen, as will be said hereafter; but recovering her favour, was created an English Baroness, for the benefit of her eldest son, [the] Duke [of] Hamilton. It is very remarkable that this great lady and her sister, Lady Coventry, had been originally so poor, that they had thoughts of being actresses; and when they were first presented to the Earl of Harrington, the Lord-Lieutenant, at the Castle of Dublin, Mrs. Woffington, the actress, lent clothes to them. They no sooner appeared in England than their beauty drew crowds after them wherever they went. [The] Duke [of] Hamilton married the second in such haste, that, having no ring ready, they made use of one from the bed-curtain. The Duchess was more delicate than her sister, with the most beautiful hands and arms in the world; but Lady Coventry was still handsomer, had infinite life and vivacity, the

was as difficult for the Ministers to help laughing as to give him redress.

Elate with success, the triumphant tribune assumed a tone that heaped new mortification on the Court. In his printed thanks to his constituents he besought them to give him their instructions from time to time, promising that he would always defend their civil and religious rights. Hearing that the Privy Council intended to issue a proclamation against riots, the new defender of the faith instructed his committee or privy council to preserve the peace, and ordered them, as they returned in procession from Brentford, not to pass by St. James's Palace, that no insult or indecency might be offered to the King. He vaunted that his Committee had patroled the streets of the capital on the night of the 30th and had kept all quiet.

The Court received another defeat of less consequence. They had set up Jenkinson, one of the favourite cabal, for

---

finest eyes in the world, nose, and mouth, excepting that both had bad teeth. Lady Coventry danced like a nymph, and was too kind a one. The Duchess always preserved her character. Lady Coventry died young, of a consumption. Till within a few days of her death she lay on a couch with a looking-glass in her hand. When she found her beauty, which she idolized, was quite gone, she took to her bed, and would be seen by nobody—not even by her nurse, suffering only the light of a lamp in her room. She then took leave of her husband, who had forgiven her errors, and died with the utmost resignation. It was in October. I had dined with her in the foregoing June with my niece, the beautiful Lady Waldegrave, then just married, since Duchess of Gloucester. They stood in the window in the full sun, and though Lady Coventry was wasted and faded, and Lady Waldegrave in all her glow of beauty, in spite of my partiality to my niece, I could not but own to myself that Lady Coventry was still superior. It was a less triumph, as Lord Pembroke was so fickle, that Lady Coventry gave great uneasiness to his lovely wife, Lady Elizabeth Spencer, who, in the Madonna style, was divinely beautiful. As the Gunnings made so much noise, it may be excused in a note if I mention another anecdote. Soon after Lady Coventry was married, I was at an assembly at Bedford House, and drew together, her, the charming Lady Emily Lenox, then Marchioness of Kildare, and since Duchess of Leinster, and Mrs. Penelope Pitt, since Lady Rivers (the two last celebrated in my poem of *The Beauties* ;) I said I wanted to decide which was the handsomest. They said I should declare. I replied that was hard, but since they insisted, I would—and 'I give it,' added I, 'to Lady Kildare, because she does what you both try to do—blush.' These trifling anecdotes may at least be as amusing as the more serious follies committed by and about Wilkes.

Oxford, where he had been bred, but he lost the election by a considerable majority, though the favours of the Crown were now showered on that University.[1]

The Methodists endeavoured to draw notice to themselves, but were disappointed. Lord Baltimore was prosecuted for a rape on a loose girl, who had staid in his house for some days under many opportunities of escaping, but was acquitted on his trial, notwithstanding the hypocrites had much incensed the populace against him.[2] Six young methodists were expelled from Oxford, but their party could raise no clamour on this supposed persecution.[3] Whitfield, their archpriest, attending one Gibson, who was hanged for forgery, to the gallows, and preaching his funeral sermon, assured the audience that he was gone to heaven ; and that a fellow executed at the same time was probably in the same paradise, having had the happiness of touching Gibson's garment.[4] But these impieties and

---

[1] Charles Jenkinson [afterwards First Earl of Liverpool] had also a powerful family interest in Oxfordshire, being the eldest son of Colonel Charles Jenkinson, whose father and brother, each a Sir Robert Jenkinson, had in turn represented the county for many years.   His introduction to public life has been always ascribed to the zealous and effectual support he gave to Lord Parker and Sir Edward Turner in the famous contest for the county, in 1754, when many successful poetical squibs came from his pen.   Sir Edward Turner or his friend Lord Harcourt, the chief of the Oxfordshire Tories, certainly obtained for him the post of private secretary to Lord Bute.—L. M.

[2] Lord Baltimore was properly acquitted, but the trial brought before the public such disgusting instances of his profligacy as to render the intervention of the Methodists to direct the indignation of the people against him quite superfluous.   He soon after went abroad, and died at Naples in 1771, and having left no issue by his wife, a daughter of the Duke of Bridgewater, his title became extinct.—(*George Selwyn and his Contemporaries*, vol. ii. pp. 205, 266, 269-72.)—He published in 1767 *A Tour to the East in the Year 1763 and* 1764, etc.   It was reprinted in 1768, and has since become very rare.   A curious account of it and of its author is given in the *Bibliothèque des Voyages*, vol. ii. p. 79.—L. M.

[3] For a fuller account of the expulsion of these Methodists from St. Edmund Hall, Oxford, see *Gentlemen's Magazine* for 1768, pp. 225-6, 410-12, and Tyerman's *Life of the Rev. George Whitefield*, (1876-7) vol. ii. pp. 542-4.—E.

[4] James Gibson, a solicitor, was executed at Tyburn on 23rd March 1768. Whitefield in the following year started on his seventh missionary visit to America, where he died on 30th September 1770.—E.

martyrdoms were drowned in the lustre of St. Wilkes's glory, and for once the barefaced libertine carried away the vulgar from the holy knaves.

It is true that half the success of Wilkes was owing to the supineness of the Ministers. Lord Chatham would take no part in business. The Duke of Grafton neglected everything, and whenever pressed to be active, threatened to resign. The Chancellor, placed between two such untractable friends, with whom he was equally discontent, avoided dipping himself further. Conway, no longer in the Duke's confidence, and who was more hurt at neglect than pleased with power, stood in the same predicament. Lord Gower thought of nothing but ingratiating himself at St. James's, and though what little business was done, Lord Weymouth executed, it required all Wood's violence and animosity to Wilkes to spur him up to any activity. Wood indeed said that if the King should pardon Wilkes, Lord Weymouth would not sign the pardon. The Scots complained grievously of this want of spirit; and the Lord Mayor consulting the Chancellor on what he should do if Wilkes should stand for the City, and being answered that he must consult the Recorder,[1] Harley sharply replied, ' I consulted your Lordship as a minister; I do not want to be told my duty.' Some of the sheriff's officers, too, not having dared to apprehend Wilkes, though a *capias* had been issued for that purpose, the Lord Mayor insisted on their being turned out of their places.

Previous to his surrender Wilkes went to Bath, but met with neither honours nor notice. A subscription had been opened for him, and went on but heavily. His enemies served him better. Lord Mansfield tried every subterfuge of the law, not so much to crush Wilkes as to shift the odium of the prosecution on any other shoulders; and as the law is never defective in furnishing expedients to meanness and chicanery, and as the lowest quibbles appeared like armour to the eyes of Lord Mansfield's

---

[1] James Eyre, who was Recorder of London from 1763 to 1772. (See *infra.*)—E.

cowardice, it is scarce credible what stores of rusty nonsense were brought forth on this occasion, to the equal disgrace of the Chief Justice and the practice.

On the 20th, Wilkes, according to his promise, appeared to his outlawry in the King's Bench. He did not avow himself for author of the *North Briton*, though he owned he had written the forty-fifth number, and approved every word of it. When he recollected the *Essay on Woman* he confessed he blushed ; yet pleaded that it would not have been published unless stolen from him. He complained of the usage he had received, and of the alteration of the record. Lord Mansfield palliated the latter charge ; and then pronounced that Wilkes was not before the court, as nobody had taken out the writ *capias utlegatum*, which he affirmed the Attorney-General ought to have done. This implied that an outlaw could not surrender himself voluntarily, though he might get anybody to take out that writ. The judges, Yates and Willes, agreed to this jargon, having been induced by Mansfield to cast the blame on the Attorney.[1] On this curious reasoning was Wilkes dismissed. His speech had been received with little applause, and he retired without riot. He had, indeed, advertised a request to the people to make no disturbance ; yet the Government had been so much alarmed that a

---

[1] The report of these proceedings by Sir James Burrow would in some measure justify this observation of Walpole, for there seems from it to have been much coquetting between the Bench and the Attorney-General (De Grey), and an apparent desire by each to shift the responsibility upon the shoulders of the other. In delivering judgment upon the two cross motions then before the Court, viz., that of the Attorney-General for Wilkes's committal, and that of Serjeant Glynn that Wilkes should be admitted to bail, Lord Mansfield makes this remarkable admission :—' I have no doubt but that we *might* take notice of him upon his voluntary appearance as the person outlawed and commit or bail him, but we are not absolutely *bound* to do it without *some reason* to excuse the going out of the regular course.' And in reference to the conduct of the Attorney-General Mr. Justice Willes thus expresses himself : ' I don't see why the Attorney-General should demand of the *Court* to commit the defendant upon this outlawry, when he himself has long suffered him to go at large without any attempt to take him up, or even issuing process against him.'—(Rex *v.* Wilkes, *Burrow's Reports*, vol. iv. pp. 2529-2535.)—L. M.

field-day had been appointed in the Park, that troops might be at hand to quell any tumult.

It appeared from this mock scene that an outlawry cannot be set aside but by a process to show there is a flaw in it. Accordingly the profession who love to accumulate absurdities[1] rather than to correct a ridiculous maxim, always take care to prepare a flaw in an outlawry. Wilkes had demanded from the Attorney-General a writ of error, and he had promised it, but was dissuaded on the 19th by the Master of the Rolls, and on the 20th the Attorney came into court without it. He would have taken it out then, but by some other rule it was then too late, or Wilkes should have surrendered to the sheriff. It was on these informalities that Lord Mansfield had argued that Wilkes was not before the court, for, being an outlaw, the law knew no such person; yet this nonentity his Lordship had suffered to revile him to his face on the seat of magistracy.

In the mean time the Parliament was chosen to the content of the Court, though by the inactivity of the Duke of Grafton, and the unpopularity of their chief friends, the majority was not greater than in the last assembly. Sir James Lowther, the Favourite's son-in-law, was beaten at Carlisle and in the counties of Westmoreland and Cumberland, though he was returned (I think) for the latter against a majority of thirty-four.[2] The Duke of Portland ravished those provinces from him in which he had been paramount, at the expense of forty thousand pounds and to the great damage of his fortune; nor were Sir James's disbursements less considerable, to which the

---

[1] The reason assigned for these voluntary errors is, that the punishment of outlawry is greater than the crime on which it is inflicted—but is it more sensible to facilitate the defeat of an outlawry than to lessen too rigorous a punishment?

[2] The poll for Cumberland was :—Henry Curwen (Whig), 2139 : Sir James Lowther (Tory), 1977 : Henry Fletcher (Whig), 1975 : Humphrey Senhouse (Tory), 1891. Lowther was unseated on petition in December 1768, and on 6th April 1769 Sir Gilfred Lawson, the High Sheriff of the county, was committed to the custody of the Serjeant-at-Arms for having acted 'partially and illegally' at the election, which was said to have cost close upon £100,000.—E.

odious act of ravishing the Duke's estate from him for an election purpose added signal disrepute. The county of York thanked Sir George Savile for having introduced the bill against *nullum tempus,* and the Duke of Portland published his case. It displayed the partial and unhandsome conduct of the Treasury, though the Duke could not prove that the lands wrenched from him had not been encroachments of his family. Lord Spencer had not been less profuse in a contest for the town of Nottingham.[1] The immense wealth that had flowed into the country from the war and the East Indies, bore down all barriers of economy, and introduced a luxury of expense unknown to empires of vaster extent. At the same time the incapacity of the Court, which had first provoked the nation by arbitrary attempts, had now sunk the government to a state of contempt ; and Wilkes's triumph having manifested the pusillanimity and want of vigour both in Ministers and magistrates, almost every class of the lower orders thought it a moment for setting up new pretensions in defiance of authority.

At Peterborough the mob rose and demolished Mr. Sutton's new hospital for inoculation.[2] The coal-heavers committed great violences on the river and in Wapping ; and by the meeting of Parliament the metropolis was a theatre of tumults and anarchy :—but of these presently. Nor was the press idle ; satires swarmed against the Court, and the authoress of all those calamities was the object at which the most envenomed arrows were shot. In a frontispiece to a number of Almon's *Political Register*[3] she and Lord Bute were represented in her bedchamber ; and lest the personages should be dubious, the royal arms in a widow's lozenge were pictured over the bed.

[1] This is probably a mistake for Northampton, in the contest for which and the ensuing petition Lord Spencer expended at least £70,000.—L. M. (See *supra,* vol. i. p. 34, note 8.)

[2] The opinion of the King's physicians and surgeons on Daniel Sutton's system of inoculation is printed at length in the *Gentleman's Magazine* for 1768, p. 75.—E.

[3] For April 1768.—E.

On the 27th, Wilkes was carried by a *capias* to the King's Bench. Great bail was offered by Humphrey Cotes, but rejected by the court; and the prisoner was committed to the King's Bench. When he left the court, the people stopped his coach on Westminster Bridge, took off the horses, and drew him themselves to a tavern in Cornhill,[1] dismissing the tipstaves that guarded him, and insisting that he should not go to prison. He persuaded the mob, however, to disperse, and, slipping out by a back door, went immediately and surrendered himself at the King's Bench Prison.

The Cabinet-Council, in the mean time, were strangely irresolute and uncertain how to act.[2] The King, the Princess, and the Scots, could not bear the idea of Wilkes's triumph, nor would hear of his being suffered to enjoy a seat in Parliament.[3] The Chancellor was all moderation; Conway, as usual, fluctuated between both opinions. The Lords Gower and Weymouth were for extremities. Yet the total inaction of Lord Chatham, and the sullen negligence of Grafton encouraging no violence, it was determined not to expel Wilkes in the very short session that was soon to meet to give substance to the Parliament, since, no proclamation having been issued to summon this meeting for business, it might be thought too precipitate rigour. The Ministers, it was decided, should only lay in their claim against his admission, unless the House should be much fuller than was expected in so late and short a session, and the voice of the meeting should be loud for expulsion. The measure was neither equitable nor politic, and betrayed a want of firmness. It would give time, if

---

[1] Walpole is not quite accurate here. Wilkes appears to have been dragged to the 'Three Tuns' in Spitalfields. See the *Annual Register* for 1768, p. 100.—E.

[2] The Duke of Grafton says in his *Memoirs*, that at the first Cabinet no one contemplated the difficulties which afterwards arose out of Wilkes's case. Many persons, among whom was Walpole himself, considered that Parliament was the very place where Wilkes would do least hurt.—(See Walpole's *Letters*, vol. v. p. 93.)—L. M.

[3] See the King's letter of the 25th of April 1768.—*Correspondence of George III. with Lord North* (1867), vol. i. p. 2.—E.

the flame of faction should spread, for counties and boroughs to instruct their members to oppose expulsion, and presented an opportunity to France of blowing up the embers. Great numbers of French had resorted hither at that time and to Ireland; and though the carelessness of the Ministers was so great as to neglect scrutinizing into it, there were grounds for suspecting that Wilkes was privately encouraged by the Court of France.[1] The Comte du Châtelet, their new Ambassador, had certainly had communication with him at Paris, though Châtelet strenuously denied it; and several Frenchmen of quality had sat with Wilkes on the hustings during the election for London, and were protected by him there and at Brentford; though without such protection, a Frenchman at an election would at any time have a risk of being ill-treated by the mob. They visited him in prison; and one of their agents, to my own knowledge, had intimate connection with him. This was one Kendal, an Irishman, who, though of distinguished service in his profession—the army,—had skulked here obscurely for a year, and when he did appear the second winter at M. du Châtelet's, it was rarely but at very private hours. He had passed himself for a Frenchman that could speak no English, yet having accidentally and unawares discovered his knowledge of our tongue, he afterwards conversed in it fluently. It happened that going one evening to M. du Châtelet's, I found them perusing an English book. I looked over Kendal's shoulder, and saw the name of John Wilkes written in the particular character of his own hand, which was something womanish. Kendal hurried the book into his pocket with some confusion—yet I had time to observe

[1] His daughter returning from France at the time of the Dauphin's wedding, when all post-horses were stopped for the service and relays of the Dauphiness, who was expected from Vienna, Miss Wilkes was regularly furnished with post-horses to Calais. [There is no confirmation of this statement in Wilkes's *Correspondence*, nor is it reconcilable with the fact that he was at that period in great distress for even small sums. The suspicion, however, was very general. Lacretelle says, ' Wilkes, en agitant sa patrie, servit si bien les desseins du Duc de Choiseul que quelques Anglais le regardèrent comme son agent secret.'—*Histoire de France*, vol. iv. p. 174.—L. M.]

the title. It was Sir James Porter's *Letters on the Turks*,[1]
—a work published after the sale of Wilkes's library, and
consequently showed it was borrowed from himself.
Though wishing well to Wilkes's cause against prerogative, I should blush to myself if I concealed the ill I
thought of the man. This story has led me from my
argument ; I meant to add that to allow Wilkes to retain
his seat for six months, and deprive him of it afterwards,
was heaping injustice upon oppression.

His outlawry was argued in the meantime at the
King's Bench by Serjeant Glynn, as erroneous, and maintained by Thurloe. Lord Mansfield said the court was
to take time to consider the respective arguments (though
it was known that a flaw was purposely inserted), and put
off the decision to the next term—a delay which detained
Wilkes in prison and prevented his taking his seat in
Parliament. His appearance there was dreaded by the
Administration, especially as it was whispered that he
intended to move for an augmentation of the pay of the
army, on pretence of the dearness of provisions. Could
he shake the loyalty of the guards the Government would
have had little to trust to—so great was its weakness and
unpopularity. Nor did the Ministers depend on being
able to carry his expulsion. Beckford from factious views,
Hussey from integrity, and Lord Granby from candour,
declared against so rigorous a measure. Nor were all
men satisfied of the propriety of the time, many doubts
having arisen whether the Parliament could transact
business, as such intention had not been mentioned in the
proclamation,—an informality soon passed over, it being
necessary to renew the Militia and Corn Bills, which
had been granted only to the end of the next session.
In truth, some exertion—at least, some appearance
of authority—was become of absolute necessity, the

---

[1] Sir James Porter was Ambassador to Turkey for fifteen years. He was
subsequently Minister at Brussels, and died on 9th December 1776. His
Observations on the Religion, Law, Government and Manners of the Turks
appeared in 1768.—E.

mutinous spirit of the people and the contempt in which the Government was held, carrying various classes of men into most dangerous excesses. The town of Boston, in America, had invited the other colonies to unite against taxation. The Irish were as warm against receiving an augmentation of troops ; and the Irish country gentlemen, though apprehending for their property from the designs of France, did not dare to declare for a larger army, as the new octennial election was approaching.

But it was in the metropolis itself that the flame of riot burst out with most violence. Before the King's Bench prison, where lay the people's idol, were constant tumults. The sailors aboard the merchantmen in the river mutinied for increase of wages, rose to the number of four thousand men, and stopped all outward-bound ships from sailing. The watermen on the Thames, and even the journeymen hatters set up equal pretensions, thinking the season favourable to their demands, and excited by the reigning scarcity and by the agents of Wilkes. Harley, the Lord Mayor, alone behaved with spirit, and seized some of the rioters, and bade the rest draw up a petition to Parliament, if they wanted, or had pretensions to redress.

During this ferment the new Parliament met on May the 10th, and was opened by commission, the King making no speech, as the session was to be so short. A great mob assembled round the Houses clamouring for Wilkes and liberty. Lord Hillsborough complained of this to the Lords, and the Chancellor moved that the constables should be ordered to disperse the people. Lord Sandwich proposed to send and inquire if the riot had ceased. The Duke of Richmond laughed at their fears and said it was nothing. The Duke of Grafton asked with much warmth if it was nothing when the mob joined the name of Wilkes, who had been committed to prison on the addresses of both Houses, with the sacred sound of liberty ? —but Grafton's warmth was burning stubble, that easily blazed and was easily extinguished. The House of Commons elected Sir John Cust, their former speaker.

A worse tumult happened the same day at the King's Bench prison, whence the mob attempted to deliver Wilkes, and carry him to the House of Commons. The riot act being read and the guards sent for, a skirmish ensued, and one Allen, a young man of fair character, who, some said, had been merely a spectator, was pursued and murdered inhumanly by a Scotch soldier as he fled. The tumult was quashed, but Allen's death only served to exasperate the people. His dead body was borne about the streets with signal lamentation, and interred with parade. Handbills had been previously dispersed among the soldiers, entreating them not to fire on their countrymen, but the third regiment of guards being employed, who were all Scots, the soldiers had carried the handbills to their officers, nor had been seduced by Wilkes's promise of obtaining for them increase of pay. The circumstance of Scots being employed in this massacre, as it was denominated, greatly increased the discontents; and the officious folly of Lord Barrington, who wrote a letter as Secretary at War, to thank the regiment for their behaviour as if they had gained a victory, shocked even those who were not factious.[1] Gillam, the Justice of Peace who had ordered the soldiers to fire, was tried for murder and acquitted. Whitfield, who had a mind to be tampering in these commotions, prayed for Wilkes before his sermon. Another mob burned a new invented sawing-mill belonging to one Dingley.[2]

On the 11th a vast body of sailors attended the Houses,[3]

---

[1] Lord Barrington's injudicious letter will be found in Woodfall's *Junius*, vol. iii. p. 57, note. The inscription on William Allen's monument in the churchyard of St. Mary's, Newington, describes him as having been 'inhumanly murdered near St. George's Fields . . . by Scottish detachments from the army.' Several persons, besides Allen, were killed in this riot. An account of Gillam's trial is given in the *Annual Register* for 1768, pp. 227-34.—E.   [2] See p. 31, note 1, *supra.*—E.

[3] Lord Mansfield, sitting by the Duke of Bedford in the House of Lords, said, if something vigorous was not done immediately, there would be a revolution in ten days, and the Government overturned,—yet when a motion was made against the riot, that dastardly magistrate sat still and did not utter a syllable.

but in a modest manner, and desiring only to have their grievances considered, with promise of acquiescing to the determination of Parliament. They declared their attachment to the King, and meeting Wilkes's mob attacked and dispersed it. Yet notwithstanding this respectful behaviour, the Privy Council, weighing the damage occasioned to the merchants, issued out a proclamation against the sailors. The same day an account came that the proposed augmentation of the army in Ireland had been rejected by that Parliament.

On the 12th the Earl of Suffolk moved the Lords to address the King to confer some mark of distinction on the Lord Mayor Harley for his activity and spirit. The Duke of Grafton said his Majesty intended it, and was considering what honour to bestow on him. As Lord Suffolk was attached to Grenville, his motion marked that Grenville's high spirit could not digest the pusillanimity of Government, though no longer Minister himself, and that he was glad to point out that pusillanimity.

At night a great meeting was held at Lord North's on the subject of Wilkes, but determined nothing. Lord Barrington, Lord Clare, and Sir Gilbert Elliot were for expelling him; Conway, unwilling to contradict his former behaviour, was for staying till the next winter.[1] Lord Granby was firm against expulsion. To his natural lenity had been added the address of Calcraft, who, having been treated with haughtiness and contempt by the Duke of Grafton on a late election, had seduced Granby from his attachment to the Court with art worthy of his master, Lord Holland. Lord Granby was in his power by the

[1] The Duke of Grafton states in his MS. Memoirs, on the authority of Mr. Bradshaw, who was present at the meeting, that with one exception the company 'were for expelling Wilkes on the double ground of outlawry and conviction. Mr. Conway declared as much before he came away. The single exception was Mr. Hussey, who expressed himself strongly against a second expulsion for the same offence in being the author of a political libel, for he said that Wilkes's conviction for the poem could not be thought of in the House of Commons without coupling it with the means used to obtain evidence against him.'—L. M.

money Calcraft had lent him ; and none of the enemies
the Duke of Grafton raised every day, proved a sharper
thorn than Calcraft. Nor was Conway himself, though less
irascible, much less offended with the Duke. From having
been his intimate friend and associate in administration,
Grafton had coarsely shuffled him out of the Secretary's
office to make room for Lord Weymouth ; and now, on
the opening of the Parliament, had deputed Lord North,
the Chancellor of the Exchequer, to read the King's speech
to the members at the Cockpit, without a word of apology
to Conway, who had officiated the last time ; nor could
his loss of place excuse such coldness in a friend.

On the 13th died the Princess Louisa, the youngest of
the King's sisters, except the Queen of Denmark. She
had long languished under the family complaint, and seemed
to be but a child of twelve years old.[1] This was the third
of her children the Princess of Wales lost in two years.

The same motion that had been made to the Lords in
favour of Mr. Harley, was carried unanimously in the
Commons. Grenville painted the supineness of the Ministers in strong colours.[2] Wood[3] defended them with heat
and sharpness. Burke and Lord John Cavendish proposed
a longer session, and dropped reflections on dissolution of
connections, which Conway took up as levelled at him.
Not a word was said on Wilkes. The Chancellor and
Lord Shelburne, the former from opposition to the
Bedfords, the latter from enmity both to them and
Grafton, declared earnestly against the expulsion : yet the

---

[1] She died of consumption, aged nineteen.—E.

[2] The debate is reported in Cavendish's *Parliamentary Debates*, vol. i.
pp. 4-17. The disunion that prevailed among the Opposition, some treating
the riots as most alarming, others as comparatively unimportant, gave the
Government great advantage in the discussion. It may be inferred from
the Duke of Grafton's MS. Memoirs that the Government had been taken
by surprise. He says, 'It was extraordinary that this combination of the
seamen was not foreseen by the merchants in a case wherein they were so
much interested ; for if the slightest information had reached the Admiralty,
a few frigates and light vessels brought up the river would have easily supported the civil power in preventing any outrage.'—L. M.

[3] 'Palmyra' Wood, Lord Weymouth's Secretary.—E.

Rockingham party did not discover that the Chancellor was hostile to the Bedfords, nor would have joined him if they had, so inveterate were they both to him and Lord Chatham ; nor did they find out that Conway was out of humour, for they found out nothing. Harley was soon afterwards made a privy councillor, and had a lucrative contract.[1]

The riots continuing, and the journeymen tailors taking advantage of them and of the mourning for Princess Louisa, rose in a great body, and went to petition Parliament for increase of wages, but were prevailed on by Justice Fielding to behave with decency. Lord Barrington on this occasion moved to enable the King to embody the militia on emergencies—the first experiment for enlarging the power of the Crown with that accession of strength. But Sir George Savile, and even Lord Strange and other courtiers, opposed the motion so ardently, that it was dropped ; though Grenville, on the other hand, declared for the proposition.[2] The sailors

---

[1] The Hon. Thomas Harley was the fourth son of Edward, third Earl of Oxford. He had been bred a merchant, his father having succeeded to the title late in life through a collateral limitation on the death of the second Earl without male issue. His success in business, and his personal worth, and perhaps still more, his birth, made him a considerable person in the City. As a politician he seems to have given an unvarying and indiscriminate support to almost every Administration. In 1776 he had the good fortune to extricate himself from City politics by being elected Member for Herefordshire, where he had a large estate, and he continued to represent the county almost till the time of his death, at an advanced age, in 1804.—L. M. [Harley's case is the sole instance of the Mayoralty being held by the son of a Peer. He was admitted to the Privy Council on 27th May 1768, an honour which had not been conferred upon a Lord Mayor of London since Sir William Walworth, and which has not been conferred upon any Lord Mayor since Harley.—E.]

[2] See Cavendish, vol. i. pp. 21-26. After Lord Barrington, as Secretary at War, had moved for leave to bring in the bill, Lord North said that he did not know whether he should or should not oppose the motion ! On the second discussion, when the measure was virtually dropped, Lord Barrington assured the House that the bill did not proceed from any consultation of the Ministers, but from himself as a Minister of the Crown, and on that ground he protested against the Opposition claiming a triumph from its withdrawal, —a declaration that enabled Mr. Burke to say fairly enough that there could be no triumph over such weak and broken troops. If, however, the statement

were appeased by the merchants agreeing to enlarge their pay.

The new Parliament produced many new speakers, of whom the most eminent was Dunning, the Solicitor-General, but whose fame did not rise then in proportion to the celebrity he had attained at the bar. The others, of far less note, were, Mr. Cornwall, a sensible lawyer,[1] Mr. Phipps, son of Lord Mulgrave, a young man whose application forced him at last into notice, and who, though a seaman, was so addicted to the study of the law, that he got the appellation of *the Marine Lawyer* ;[2] a young Mr. Cavendish,[3] hot-headed and odd ; a Colonel Lutterel,[4]

made by Lord Barrington was correct, it strengthens the suspicion elsewhere expressed in these notes that he acted on this as on other occasions at the King's instigation.—L. M.

[1] Charles Wolfran Cornwall, brother-in-law of Charles Jenkinson, afterwards first Earl of Liverpool, sat for Grampound for 1768 to 1774. He subsequently represented Winchelsea and Rye, and was a Lord of the Treasury from 1774 to 1780, when he was elected Speaker in succession to Sir Fletcher Norton. He died in office 2nd January 1789, aged fifty-three. He is laughed at in the *Rolliad* (1799), p. 65, for his habit of drinking porter during the debates and for other peculiarities. See also Wraxall's *Historical and Posthumous Memoirs* (1884), vol. i. pp. 259-61 ; vol. iii. p. 385 ; vol. iv. p. 269 ; vol. v. pp. 244, 246.—E.

[2] Captain the Hon. Constantine Phipps, R.N., M.P. for Lincoln, succeeded his father as second Baron Mulgrave in September 1775. He filled various official posts, and was created Baron Mulgrave in the peerage of Great Britain on 13th August 1790. He died on 10th October 1792. He is one of the principal butts of the *Rolliad* (1799), the authors of which sarcastically allude to his ' tried integrity and worth ' (p. 24), his ungainly figure (p. 14), and his inharmonious voice (p. 8). He was a man of talents and application. In 1773 he took part in a Polar expedition of which he afterwards published a valuable account. A collection of his speeches in the House of Lords was published after his death.—E.

[3] Henry Cavendish, M.P. for Lostwithiel, was the elder son of Sir Henry Cavendish, Bart., of Doveridge Hall, Derbyshire, whom he succeeded in the Baronetcy in May 1776. It is to him that we are indebted for the interesting accounts of the debates of this otherwise ' unreported Parliament ' now preserved in the British Museum, a portion of which was published by Joseph Wright (London, 1841-3, 8vo). Sir Henry Cavendish died on the 3rd August 1804, aged seventy-one.—E.

[4] Eldest son of Simon, Lord Irnham, who had two other sons—Temple, who was a poet, and had parts, but proved a tedious orator ; and the third, who was a seaman, and had most parts of the three. He had also two daughters, of whom Anne, the elder, then married to a Mr. Horton, was very

more absurd and impudent; and James Townshend and Sawbridge, who will be often mentioned, though not for their eloquence.   Lutterel had a personal enmity to Wilkes, and had declared that he would force the House into some resolution on Wilkes's case.   Accordingly, he moved that the proper officer should acquaint the House why Wilkes had not been taken into custody sooner. Lord North said the motion was so absurdly worded, that he could not think himself pointed at; but he alleged that everything had been left to due course of law.   This was confirmed by the Attorney-General; and young Mr. Lyttelton, only son of Lord Lyttelton, urging with decency that the time was not proper while the case was depending in the courts below, the previous question was put and carried: yet not a word was uttered in Wilkes's favour. Mr. Lyttelton, who soon after lost his seat, his election being contested, had parts and knowledge, and conciliated much favour by that first essay; but his character was uncommonly odious and profligate, and his life a grievous course of mortification to his father.   More will be said of him hereafter.[1]

So spiritless an Administration, whose measures were not planned, but started indigested out of the daily occurrences, was not likely to give serious attention to remote situations.   They endeavoured to doze over all thoughts of the Continent; and yet the enterprising

engaging, and rose afterwards to a very extraordinary rank.   [Lord Irnham, who was subsequently created the Earl of Carhampton, had *five* sons and *three* daughters.   The eldest son, Henry Lawes Luttrell, famous as the ministerial nominee for Middlesex and afterwards for his rigour as Commander-in-Chief in Ireland (1796-7) was at this time M.P. for Bossiney. The marriage of his sister Anne with the Duke of Cumberland, brother of George III., on 2nd October 1771, gave rise to one of Junius's bitterest letters. —(Woodfall's *Junius*, vol. iii. pp. 415-418.)—E.]

[1] The Hon. Thomas Lyttelton had been returned for Bewdley at the General Election, but was unseated on petition in January 1769.   He succeeded his father in August 1773, and died the 27th November 1779, when the peerage became extinct.   For the celebrated ghost story connected with his death, see *Notes and Queries*, second series, vol. iii. pp. 270, 339; vol. v. p. 165; vol. vi. p. 153; third series, vol. ii. p. 107; fifth series, vol. ii. pp. 401, 508; vol. v. pp. 341, 379.—E.

activity of the Duc de Choiseul now and then interrupted their slumbers, though it could not dispel them entirely. Stung with our victories in the last war, and aware of our supineness, that ambitious man was meditating new wars, impatient to indemnify his master for some of their losses by new usurpations. The poor Corsicans were the first victims of his politics. He had for some months been preparing a mighty invasion of their island. Sixteen battalions were destined to the conquest, which was sheltered under a pretended purchase from the Genoese. De Sorbe, their agent at Paris, and born there while his father exercised the same function, had suggested the idea. Pride, impotence, and revenge had operated to induce the Genoese to sell their title to a more formidable usurper,—the liberty of others appearing a marketable commodity to a republic composed only of nobles, who are ever ready to be subordinate tyrants. The object was too considerable to be indifferent to us : Corsica, in the hands of France, might essentially affect our Mediterranean trade during a war. To suffer the conquest were a disgrace, and would imply timidity. Generosity towards a free nation, who had struggled so long and successfully for their liberty, and had sought our protection, the poor Corsicans could not venture to expect. One of the few acts of Lord Bute's monarchic[1] and dastardly Administration had been to forbid our sending succours to the Corsican rebels, as he called them—a sentence that betrayed his heart, not his sense. What right had the little republic of Genoa to tyrannise over the freemen of Corsica? Genoa had acted throughout the late war with as much partiality to France[2] as she

[1] This was very like his pitiful countryman, James the First, who had disclaimed his own son-in-law, the King of Bohemia, when elected for their Prince by an oppressed nation.

[2] It is true Lord Granville had provoked the Genoese in the year 1743 by the treaty of Worms, in which he had proposed to force Final from the Genoese, and give it to the King of Sardinia. France had rescued Genoa from the Austrians. Still, there was no moral or political reason for our taking part for the Genoese against the Corsicans. The despotic principles of Lord Bute suggested that preference.

dared, and was rewarded by our proscribing her enemies.
On the other hand, our interference now might light up
another war; and though the finances of France were in
at least as bad a situation as our own, we could ill have
supported the burthen, and were in too distracted a
situation at home to make war advisable. The Council
assembled on the point. Parliament might blame them
for taking a part, or for taking none—the latter half of
the dilemma suited their natures best, and no resolution
was then taken. Yet procrastination produced no repose;
alarms thickened from every quarter: the mutinous spirit
of the people broke out, whether the occasion was political
or private. A butcher, murdered in a brothel at Dublin,
had raised such a flame, that forty houses were pulled
down by the mob, and several persons killed.

At such a crisis the Ministers would not venture dismissing the Parliament to a distant period, but on the
20th of May adjourned it only for a fortnight, intending,
by short prorogations, to keep it in readiness to meet.[1]

Of all the tumults, the fiercest and most memorable
was the following. A dispute having arisen between the
coalworkers and the coalheavers, the latter of whom were
chiefly Irish—nay, some of them Whiteboys, an Act of
Parliament had passed the last year, subjecting the coalheavers to the jurisdiction of the alderman of the ward;
an office had been erected, and one Green, who kept an
alehouse, had been constituted their agent. Houston, a
man who wanted to supplant Green, had incensed the
coalheavers against him, and they threatened his destruction. Apprised of their design, he every night removed
his wife and children out of his house. One evening he
received notice that the coalheavers were coming to
attack him. He had nobody with him but a maid-servant
and a sailor, who by accident was drinking in the house.
Green asked the sailor if he would assist him? 'Yes,'
answered the generous tar, 'I will defend any man in

---

[1] The debate on the Adjournment is reported in Cavendish, vol. i.
pp. 28-30. It turned chiefly on the disturbances among sailors.—L. M.

distress.' At eight the rioters appeared, and fired on the house, lodging in one room above two hundred bullets; and when their ammunition was spent, they bought pewter pots, cut them to pieces, and fired them as ball. At length with an axe they broke out the bottom of the door; but that breach the sailor defended singly; while Green and his maid kept up a constant fire, and killed eighteen of the besiegers. Their powder and ball being at last wasted, Green said he must make his escape: 'for you,' said he to the friendly sailor, 'they will not hurt you.' Green, retiring from the back room of his house, got into a carpenter's yard, and was concealed in a saw-pit, over which the mob passed in their pursuit of him, being told he was gone forwards. I should scarce have ventured this narrative, had not all the circumstances been proved in a court of justice. Yet how many reflections must the whole story create in minds not conversant in a vast capital—free, ungoverned, unpoliced, and indifferent to everything but its pleasures and factions! Who will believe that such a scene of outrage could happen in the residence of Government?—that the siege lasted nine hours, and that no Guards were sent to the relief of the besieged till five in the morning? Who will believe that while such anarchy reigned at one end of the Metropolis, it made so little impression at the Court end that it was scarce mentioned? Though in London myself, all I heard was, that a man had been attacked in his house, and had killed three of the rioters. Nor were the circumstances attended to, till the trial of Green for murder, of which he was honourably acquitted, divulged his, his maid's, and the sailor's heroism. Yet did not the fury of the colliers cease, though seven of them were taken and executed. Green was forced to conceal himself from their rage; but his sister, giving a supper to her friends for joy of her brother's safety, her house was attacked by those assassins, their faces covered with black crape, who tore her into the street, and murdered her. Yet, perhaps, of all the circumstances of this tragedy, not one was so singular, from the display of so great a mind, as the indifference of the sailor, who never owned himself, never claimed honour or recompense for his generous gallantry.   As brave as the Cocles of fabulous Rome, his virtue was satisfied with defending a man oppressed ; and he knew not that an Alexander deserved less fame than he, who seemed not to think that he deserved any.

The Bedford faction, who had got almost entire possession of the Duke of Grafton, began to perceive how little security there was in that tenure.   They found that every disgust inspired him with thoughts of resigning. They saw the immediate necessity of strengthening themselves lest some sudden caprice should hurry him to resign, and leave them weak at Court, or exposed to the dislike of the next Minister, whoever it should be. Rigby in particular had not attained the paymastership which Grafton had engaged to him on the first opportunity, and was sure of being the first victim if Grenville, whom he had sacrificed, should return to power.   With as little decency as he had abandoned him, Rigby now made secret offers to Grenville to support him, if the Duke of Grafton should quit—but they were rejected, both from the haughtiness of Grenville's nature, and by the positive injunction of Lord Temple, who sent Calcraft to Lord Hertford with an account of that transaction ; adding, that his Lordship had sworn to his brother, that should he ever join the Bedfords, he (Lord Temple) would persecute him to the last hour of his life.   This Lord Hertford was desired to communicate to the King, with offers from Lord Temple to serve his Majesty whenever he should be wanted.   This mine failing, Rigby pushed the Lords Gower and Weymouth to unite with him in insisting with the Duke of Grafton on the removal of Lord Shelburne, who, they said, betrayed them, and opposed all their measures in Council.   The accusation did not want truth ; nor was its purport unwelcome either to the Duke or to the King.   The former hated him for enjoying Lord Chatham's favour; and the King had not forgotten the tricks that Shelburne had played Lord Bute. To make the proposal still palatable, the Cabal offered to his Majesty the choice of the Duke of Northumberland or Lord Egmont, his own creatures, of Lord Holderness, anybody's creature, or of Lord Sandwich, their own friend, to replace Lord Shelburne. Willing as he was to give up the last, the King had adopted a rule of turning out no single man, both from pusillanimity, and from never being sorry to embarrass Ministers, whom he had not taken from inclination. Thus was Shelburne saved for some months longer. In his chief point Rigby had very soon better success.

On the 2nd of June the Parliament met, and was again adjourned for three weeks. On the 8th Wilkes's outlawry was debated in the King's Bench. The Judges of that Court had agreed with their chief, Lord Mansfield, to reverse it; yet the latter now maintained it in a fine oration, but in the conclusion pronounced it void from a flaw; which, he said, had not been noticed by the prisoner's counsel. This curious error was, that the proceedings were stated *at the County Court for the County of Middlesex*; when lo! the form ought to have been *at the County Court of Middlesex, for the County of Middlesex*—a form of words, said that oracle of law, absolutely necessary. It was said that Serjeant Glynn, Wilkes's counsel, had made the same notable discovery two months before in his pleading; and thus the Chief Justice had not even the honour of the chicanery he boasted. It was still more ridiculously, and with as little truth, that he vapoured on his own firmness. He knew, he said, in what danger he held his life, but he was past sixty, and valued not the remnant of being. He would act boldly; *fiat justitia, et ruat cœlum*—prodigious danger when he was doing what was an act of popularity, and which probably he would not have done but from timidity![1] The reversion of the

---

[1] In a letter on these proceedings written shortly before the judgment reversing the outlawry, Walpole says, 'In short, my dear sir, I am trying to

outlawry having an appearance of being favourable to the prisoner, the mob huzzaed, though he was remanded to prison till he should receive sentence.

In the meantime a new calamity befel the Court. Cooke, the other member for Middlesex, died, and Serjeant Glynn, as the champion of Wilkes, was set up by the popular party for Middlesex. Cooke was Joint-Paymaster with the younger Thomas Townshend, a friend of the Duke of Grafton, who, to gratify Rigby with the whole employment, offered to make Townshend one of the Vice-Treasurers of Ireland. Townshend refused it with warmth, saying, he would not be turned backwards and forwards

explain to you what I literally do not understand.'—(*Letters*, vol. v. p. 103.) That he was not better informed at the date of these Memoirs is proved by the statement in the text. It was, however, no disgrace to be ignorant of the absurd technicalities by which Lord Mansfield's very able judgment is defaced ; nor should they attach any stain to the memory of a judge who had to expound the law and not to make it. Lord Mansfield's love of the prerogative did not in this instance lead him into the slightest injustice. Following the order which the form of the proceedings naturally suggested, he commenced with an elaborate and lucid examination of all the arguments which the ingenuity of the defendant's counsel, arguing from the reversal of the outlawry, had most ably urged ; and after carefully reviewing and combating each *seriatim*, he disposes of them in these words : ' These are the errors which have been objected, and *this* the manner and form in which they are assigned. For the reasons I have given, I cannot allow any of them.' After a spirited vindication of his character, and a bold declaration of the utter indifference in which he held all the menaces by which he had been publicly and privately assailed, he proceeds to advert to a technical error in the *Writ of Exigent*, which by a series of precedents and cases he shows to be fatal to the writ, and on *that* ground decides that the outlawry could not stand, adding at the conclusion of his judgment, ' I beg to be understood that I ground my opinion *singly upon the authority of the cases adjudged*, which as they are on the *favourable* side, in a *criminal* case *highly penal*, I think ought not to be departed from.'—Burrow's *Reports*, vol. iv. p. 2549.

The error upon which the reversal proceeded was, that after the words ' at the County Court ' the writ altogether omitted to state ' of the County of Middlesex,' a ground obviously different from that which Walpole here suggests. It is observable, also, that the discovery of this error had *not*, as Walpole states, been made by Serjeant Glynn ' two months before in his pleading ; ' it is probable, however, that Walpole may have confounded this with another error relied on by the Serjeant, but overruled by the court,— namely, that the averment ' Brook Street *near* Holborn in the County of Middlesex ' was not a sufficient averment that Brook Street was in Middlesex. A clear account of these proceedings is given in the Life of Lord Mansfield

every six months ; and resigning, joined the Opposition.[1] On the 10th, Rigby kissed the King's hand as Paymaster. He was succeeded as Vice-Treasurer of Ireland by Lord Clare. Lord Hillsborough returned to the Board of Trade, with the superintendence of the Colonies, in which function his conduct will be long remembered.

The Bourbon Courts, who had not been able to persuade the Pope to dissolve the Order of the Jesuits, proceeded to extremities. The King of Naples seized Benevento ; and France, possessing herself of Avignon, declared it unalienable from the Crown, and with reason.[2] It was not with the same foundation that she went on with hostilities against Corsica. Monsieur Francis, their Secretary here, said that, if we asked with the decency due to a great nation, France would tell us she did not mean to retain the possession—if we menaced, Monsieur de Choiseul would declare war. Their having no intention of keeping Corsica was false ; and it was believed afterwards, that if we had spoken in a high tone, they would have desisted from the

(No. IX. of the *Law Magazine*), in an able and yet not servile defence of that eminent lawyer, who, with all his defects of character, will always be regarded as one of the brightest ornaments of British jurisprudence. It was written by Mr. Plunkett, the author of a history of the Roman law, who has since died, a Puisne Judge of St. Lucia.—L. M.

[1] Thomas Townshend, the 'Tommy Townshend' of Goldsmith's *Retaliation*, was grandson of the second Viscount Townshend, and M.P. for Whitchurch. He seems to have been badly used on this occasion (Walpole's *Letters*, vol. v. p. 106). He was afterwards twice Secretary of State—under Lord Shelburne and William Pitt, whose brother married Townshend's daughter. In 1783 he was created Baron, and in 1789 Viscount Sydney, and died at Chiselhurst on the 13th June 1800, aged sixty-seven.—E.

[2] The Pope published a most satisfactory refutation of the claim of the French Government, but the French troops retained their conquest. A body of French troops under the Marquis de Rochecourt took possession of Avignon on the 11th of June. No resistance was offered by the papal authorities, the Legate only making a protest, accompanied by a declaration that the invaders had subjected themselves to the ecclesiastical penalties enumerated in the Bull *In Cœnâ Domini*. The plea set up by the French was the invalidity of the original alienation of Avignon to the Pope by Jeanne of Naples in 1348. The Pope published a reply, which was thought conclusive by all but the French, who retained possession of the territory they had seized, until it suited their interests to resign it.—L. M.

enterprise.   The brave resistance of the natives, if supported by us, would soon have put the matter out of
dispute.   The French did not taste the project, nor could
Choiseul lead the King so easily into a war as he desired.[1]

On the 18th, sentence was pronounced on Wilkes.   For
the *North Briton*, No. XLV., he was condemned to pay a
fine of £500 and to suffer imprisonment for ten months.
For the Essay on Woman, £500 more, and imprisonment
for twelve months, to be computed from the expiration of
the first ten.   He was to find security for his good behaviour for seven years, himself being bound in £1000,
and two sureties in £500 each.   Rigorous as the sentence
was, the Court had not dared to enforce it with its usual
severity ;[2] the pillory was for the first time omitted in a

---

[1] The Duke of Grafton states in his MS. Memoirs that Lord Rochford's
instructions only stopped short of a declaration of war.   'At one time Lord
Rochford was confident that he should have succeeded, and wrote over that
the Duc de Choiseul's language had so much softened, that he had every
hope that the French Ambassador would not risk the attempt.   In the
audience of the next week, he found to his great surprise the former tone
taken up ; and in a private letter to me, he attributed the strange change in
the Duc to the imprudent declaration of a great law Lord (Lord Mansfield),
then at Paris, at one of the Minister's tables, that the English Ministry were
too weak, and the nation too wise, to support them in entering into a
war for the sake of Corsica.'   The remonstrances thus made by Lord Rochford having failed, the Duke of Grafton despatched Captain Dunant, a Gene-
vese officer, who had served with distinction in the Swiss troops of the King
of Sardinia, to Corsica, with the view of learning how far assistance could be
surreptitiously afforded to Paoli by the English Government, and the result
of the mission was, that the Corsicans obtained several thousand stand of
arms from the stock at the Tower.   Lord Camden seems to have been ready
to have gone further.   The Duke of Grafton saw no necessity for an immediate decision, being under the impression that the Corsicans might still
hold out ; and the events which followed, and will be mentioned hereafter,
took him completely by surprise.—(Duke of Grafton's MS. Memoirs.)—L.M.

[2] Almon says the sentence was condemned by everybody as unjustifiably
severe.—(*Memoirs of Wilkes*, 1805, vol. iii. p. 272.)   On the other hand, Mr.
Grenville, in his celebrated speech against Lord Barrington's motion for
Wilkes's expulsion, comments on it as very lenient, and contrasts it with Dr.
Shebbeare's, who for his *Sixth Letter to the People of England* was sentenced
to be fined, to stand in the pillory, to be imprisoned for three years, and to
give security for good behaviour for seven years.   This, too, was whilst Mr.
Pratt (afterwards Lord Camden) was Attorney-General.—(Cavendish, vol. i.
p. 160.)—L.M.

case of libel and blasphemy, and Wilkes triumphed by this manifestation of their terror.   Anet, a poor honest priest, had been pilloried in this reign for writing against Moses.[1]   Some imputed his prosecution to Archbishop Secker,[2] who charged it on Lord Bute.   Lord Bute denied it.   Whoever was the prosecutor, Lord Mansfield had willingly executed the inquisitorial power.

The night before the publication of Wilkes's sentence, he dispersed handbills to excite the mob to sedition; but so many late tumults had so terrified the citizens that they took little notice of him, and even were not averse to being protected by the Guards.   After sentence, he published a violent advertisement against Lord Halifax, and bound himself never to accept place or pension.   The paper which contained that declaration was so eagerly bought up, that by eight in the evening it was sold for half-a-crown.   Lord Halifax stood in a worse predicament: it depended on a jury to give Wilkes what damages they should please against the Earl.   No limits were set to them by law, nor could King or Parliament remit the fine,

---

[1] Peter Annet, who was a coarse but forcible writer, is said to have been born at Liverpool in 1693.   For attempting to prove in the *Free Enquirer* that 'the prophet Moses was an imposter,' he was convicted in November 1762 of blasphemous libel, and sentenced to a month's imprisonment in Newgate, to stand twice in the pillory, to a year's hard labour in Bridewell, to pay a fine of 6s. 8d., and to give securities for good behaviour during the rest of his life.   After his release, Annet kept a small school at Lambeth. He does not appear to have been in orders.   He died on 18th January 1769.—E.

[2] The Archbishop could with little propriety have set on foot such a prose-cution, having in the early part of his life exceeded Anet in the latitude of his irreligion.   Whether he incited it or not, I do not know.   It is justice to his character to say that he privately allowed Anet £50 a year to support him in prison, where he died.   [This charge against the Archbishop also made by Walpole elsewhere, has been repeatedly refuted.   It appears to rest on the very slender foundation of a foolish story told by some superannuated com-panion of Secker's at Leyden, where the latter, in the fulness of his passion for metaphysics, probably indulged in paradoxes by way of argumentative exercises, which it would be very unjust to regard as his real opinion.   Bishop Watson, when a student at Trinity, wrote a paper to refute Clarke's main argument to prove the existence of God, yet no one ever thought of calling him an atheist.—L. M.

as it instantly became the property of the injured person. Faction might rate his injuries at a hundred thousand pounds. It was computed that the expenses attending the prosecution of Wilkes had already cost the Crown no less a sum.

The Bostonians were not more peaceable than the populace of London. A ship arriving there, and the custom-house officers, according to the direction of the late Act of Parliament, proceeding to visit it, the mob rose, drove the officers out of the town, forced them to take refuge in a frigate in the harbour, and pillaged their houses. Two regiments were ordered thither, the Cabinet-Council being unanimous in that opinion, except Lord Shelburne, who adhered to his former principle, that England had no right to tax America, unless represented. The Chancellor Camden excused his own change of opinion, which, he said, had been only speculation ; now an Act of the Legislature had affirmed the right of taxation. Lord Bottetort, a very courtier, who was ruined in his fortune, was sent Governor to Virginia, where resided some of the ablest of the American patriots ; yet in the two years that he lived to govern them, his soothing flattering manners had so wrought on the province, that his death was bewailed with the most general and affectionate concern.

CHAPTER VIII

Family of Lord Bute.—Death of Archbishop Secker.—Trial of a Soldier for Murder in a Riot.—Arrival of Christian the Seventh of Denmark.—Removal of Sir Jeffrey Amherst from Virginia.—Contemplated Disgrace of Lord Shelburne.—Resignation of Lord Chatham.—Lord Rochford made Secretary of State,—Privy Seal given to Lord Bristol.—State of the Country.—Meeting of Parliament.—Meditated Expulsion of Wilkes.

1768

ON the 2nd of August, the favourite Earl of Bute, whom foolish conduct, and the odium attending it, had thrown into a real, imaginary, or pretended ill state of health, set out for the waters of Barege. His mortifications were, in truth, sufficient to break a firmer spirit ; nor had his fortune or wealth contributed but to his unhappiness, his domestic griefs being as poignant as his unpopularity. His eldest daughter, an amiable woman, was wedded to Sir James Lowther. His third daughter, whom the Northumberlands had obtained for their son, was discontent with her husband, and was confined by his family to the country under pretence of a gallant disposition, though the world suspected that the fall of her father had made the Duke and Duchess wish to get rid of the daughter.[1] Lord Bute's second son, the heir of his mother's vast riches, had married ill, grew to hate his wife for having drawn him into marriage, and would not live with her, though his father forgave her, and solicited their reconciliation.[2] It

---

[1] Lady Anne Stuart married Earl Percy on the 2nd July 1764, from whom she was divorced on the 16th March 1779.—E.

[2] The Honourable James Archibald Stuart, who, on inheriting the estates of his mother and uncle, took the additional names of Wortley and Mackenzie respectively, married in May 1767, Margaret, daughter of Sir David Cunynghame, Bart. His eldest surviving son was created Baron Wharncliffe in 1826.—E.

was perhaps not the least of the Earl's sorrows, that
though, by the interest of the Princess, Lord Bute and
his Cabal retained the chief power in the secret counsels,
the King was not sorry to be delivered from the thraldom
in which the Earl had held him :—at least, it was known
that his Majesty dreaded of being suspected of retaining
too great partiality to the Favourite, though he had
resolution enough to avow or discountenance him entirely.

On the 3rd died Secker, Archbishop of Canterbury,
whose character I have given at large before. His early
life had shown his versatility ; his latter time, his ambition ; but hypocrisy not being parts, he rose in the Church
without ever making a figure in the State.[1] Dr. Frederic
Cornwallis, Bishop of Lichfield and Coventry, a prelate of
inconsiderable talents, but a most amiable, gentle, and
humane man,[2] was preferred to the primacy by the Duke
of Grafton, who had a friendship for the Bishop's nephew,
Earl Cornwallis.   Terrick of London, the most time-

[1] See *supra*, vol. i. p. 16, and vol. iii. *infra*. If Dr. Secker had not been
the intimate friend of the Duke of Newcastle and Lord Chancellor Hardwicke,
his character would no doubt have obtained the warm praise instead of the
constant abuse of Walpole. Bishop Hurd, who did not love him, says that
he was a wise man, an edifying preacher, and an exemplary bishop.—
(Warburton's *Works*, 1811, vol. i. p. 69.) He was very young when he left
the Dissenters to join the Church, and the Dissenters never questioned the
honesty of his change of opinions. Some of their most eminent writers have
recorded their respect for him. The purity of his life brought on him the
charge of hypocrisy from those alone who did not care to practise the same
irtues. After enjoying for ten years the rich revenues of the primacy,
he left an insignificant fortune, and his distribution of his patronage was
equally disinterested. He was the last of the learned divines who have filled
the highest dignities of the Church.—(*Life* by Porteus, also *Memoirs of Mrs.
Carter*, 1808, vol. i. pp. 402-5.)—L. M.

[2] He was the seventh son of Charles, fourth Baron Cornwallis. While at
Cambridge, 'he had the misfortune,' says Cole, 'to have a stroke of the
palsy, which took away the use of his right hand, and obliged him to write
with his left, which he did very expeditiously ; and I have often had the
honour to play at cards with him, when it was wonderful to see how
dexterously he would shuffle and play them.'—(Add. MSS., British Museum,
5866, p. 214.) As Archbishop, he was much respected and beloved for his
courtesy and hospitality. He died at Lambeth on the 19th March 1783,
aged seventy.—E.

serving of the clergy, was sorely disappointed in missing
the first mitre of England.

On the 9th came on at Guilford the trial of a soldier
for the murder of young Allen, in St. George's Fields.
Wilkes, impatient to signalize himself, and by his presence
to excite a tumult, procured to be subpœnaed as a witness;
though it was notorious that, being in prison at the time,
he could have distinguished nothing from his window.
The real murderer had been conveyed away by the Government, and the man tried not being the true criminal, was
acquitted. No bill was found against the commanding
officer of the party; and Wilkes returned to his gaol without having occasioned any disturbance.

In the midst of these disorders arrived Christian the
Seventh, King of Denmark, his Majesty's brother-in-law.
This young Prince had left his dominions some months
before, intending to visit the chief nations of Europe;
and having great curiosity to see England, had proposed
this visit. The English Monarch, who had no taste for
show or amusements, and who every day sank more and
more into privacy and lifeless solitude, had waived the
offer on pretence of the national confusions; but Christian,
who had both the obstinacy and caprices of youth and
royalty, had persisted, and came. Not a single nobleman
—not a single equipage was sent on the road to receive,
escort, or convey the Danish King. He arrived at St.
James's in a hired carriage. The only attention paid to
him was, that an apartment was new furnished, gilt plate
brought from the Tower, and an expensive table kept for
him and his suite. Neither the King nor Queen were at
St. James's to receive him; and the King even arrived
there to his levée an hour later than usual. He then saw
his Ministers; and the King of Denmark was at dinner
before King George would admit Lord Hertford, his own
Lord Chamberlain, who brought a message from the Dane,
who had had the attention of ordering his own lords to
wait on the King at his levée. It is scarce to be credited
that though Christian was in his palace, he neither went

to him nor received him there, but coldly sent him word he would see him at the Queen's palace at half-an-hour after five. When common decency was thus neglected, it is not wonderful that national interest was forgotten. Christian, at that time, was a pensioner of France, and it imported us to win him out of their hands. When he afterwards went to Paris, he found every mark of respect, every instance of magnificence and liberality that a great Court, attentive to its interest or glory, knew how to bestow.

This Danish King was, in truth, an insipid boy ; and there appeared no cause for his expensive ramble, though to support it he had laid a tax on all his placemen and pensioners. He took notice of nothing, took pleasure in nothing, and hurried post through most parts of England without attention, dining and supping at seats on the road, without giving himself time enough to remark so much of their beauties as would flatter the great lords who treated him. This indifference was excused in a whisper by Bernsdorffe,[1] his Prime Minister, who attributed it to his Majesty's extreme short sight, which Bernsdorffe confessed was the great secret of the State. Yet the King's manner was very civil ; and though his person was diminutive and delicate, he did not want graceful dignity. He had taken an early dislike to his Queen, and had disgraced his cousin, the Prince of Hesse, for espousing her interest. Himself was then influenced by the Russians, Bernsdorffe and the Russian Minister governing him entirely ; the latter even with rudeness to the Queen. But the King had a favourite, who had still more power over him, Baron Holke, a handsome young man, who attended him in his travels.

---

[1] Count Jean Hartwig Ernest de Bernsdorffe, a man of considerable reputation and influence, had been Foreign Minister to Frederick V. On the occasion of this visit, Walpole describes him as 'a decent, sensible man,' but 'bowing and cringing' to the King 'at every word in the face of a new and free nation' !—(*Letters*, vol. v. pp. 118-120.) He died in 1772, aged fifty-nine. His nephew, Count André de Bernsdorffe, was Prime Minister of Denmark from 1784 to his death, on 21st January 1797.—E.

Princess Amelie, who felt the dishonourable treatment of her nephew, and who did not dislike to mark it to the public, made a ball and great entertainment for him at Gunnersbury. The King and the Princess Dowager then paid him the same civilities ; but to show how much they disliked the precedent, left Princess Amelie out of their entertainments. In France, whither he went next, the literati cried up this young Monarch as a pattern of a patriot King : and it was probably from their praises he imbibed so much merit that at his return to his kingdom he granted to his subjects free liberty of the press.[1] The idea was certainly not instilled into him here by the King or the Princess Dowager.

The promotion of Lord Bottetort to the Government of Virginia had started a new difficulty. Sir Jeffery Amherst was their Governor. His eminent services and the rank of Commander-in-chief, which he had held in the American war, had placed him too high for residence in a single province. Yet the mutinous spirit of that Colony in particular required the presence of a Governor. Lord Hillsborough had hinted this necessity to Sir Jeffery, adding that if he did not choose to go thither, the King would give him a pension equal to that of Governor. Amherst had ever behaved with as much coolness and modesty as sense. His honour started at the word pension—yet not so fiercely but it was thought he would acquiesce ; at least Lord Hillsborough, who had not so much delicacy, too lightly conceived the bargain struck, and too officiously to make his court, as Lord Bottetort was a favourite, named him Governor. The event was unfortunate to Amherst, whose wounded pride drew him into discovering too full a fund of vanity, self-interest, and vehement obstinacy. His first step was to resign his regiment. The next, on the Duke of Grafton's trying to

---

[1] This piece of flattery was abruptly crushed. The poor King became on his return a mere phantom of royalty, first in the hands of his wife, next of the Queen Dowager. In 1784 his son was raised to the Regency, and succeeded to the Crown on his death, in 1808.—L. M.

soften him, was to demand a peerage, a grant of the coal mines in America (which it was thought might produce thirty thousand pounds a year more) and an American peerage, if any were bestowed. To the last the Duke replied at once, that the King had forbidden his naming a peerage for any man.

Sir Jeffery's intrinsic merit, the removal of him in favour of a Court tool, and his scorn of the pension, immediately presented him as a beloved victim to the Opposition. Lord Hillsborough in particular was acrimoniously pursued by the younger Burke in many publications. General Conway, a friend of Amherst, and who felt for him, undertook to reconcile the breach, and at last prevailed on him to accept as reparation a promise of the first vacant regiment, and a peerage when any peers should be made. Amherst stickled for having his brother included in the patent, but could not obtain it. At first he acquiesced and suffered Mr. Conway to acquaint the King with his acceptance of the terms; but in three days flew off again and insisted on his brother being in the patent. Conway urged that his own last words to him had been 'Sir Jeffery, take notice your brother is not included in the peerage,' and showed him the impropriety of the pretension, the younger Amherst having neither services nor an estate to entitle him to such distinction. He now asked both an American and English peerage for himself and his brother, and it was not till after many conferences and fluctuations, that he at last submitted to the terms Conway had proposed.[1] Even before the affair was finally concluded, Conway

[1] The Duke of Grafton's Memoirs confirm Walpole's account of this transaction, and he adds that 'the Cabinet were unanimous in their resolution for the removal of Sir Jeffrey Amherst.' It was in the manner of filling up the vacancy that they laid themselves open to the suspicion of having accommodated a private job under the pretence of reforming a public abuse, and people said, with some plausibility, 'It was not Virginia that wanted a governor, but a Court favourite that wanted the salary.' (See the clever letters in Woodfall's *Junius*, vol. iii. pp. 80-155.) Lord Bottetort's being a follower and friend of Lord Bute, increased the cry against him.—L. M.

himself was on the point of quitting the Court with equal
disgust. The Duke of Grafton told him that it was not
an absolute promise of a peerage, and that the King had
only said that when any peers should be made, his
Majesty would consider Sir Edward Hawke and Sir
Jeffery Amherst.[1] Conway, who had received the positive
promise from the King, was hurt beyond measure, and
the more as the King now affirmed that the promise had
only been provisional. I discovered the cause of this
variation. Rigby had seduced Sir Laurence Dundas, the
rich Scotch Commissary, who chose nine members into
Parliament, from George Grenville, and had offered to carry
him and his suite to Court, if the King would promise Sir
Laurence a peerage. The King, who had involved himself in so many like promises that he had tied his hands
from making any, refused to comply with the demand.[2]
Rigby resented the denial in the warmest terms—said
that Mr. Conway could make peers when he could not,
and was the effective Minister; and he fired the Duke of
Grafton's jealousy by telling him that Lord Hertford,
Mr. Conway, and I, had done this without his Grace: to
others he said, that I had drawn the Duke to acquiesce,
by telling him that the Bedfords would some day or other
betray him. I had told him when his Grace betrayed
Mr. Conway to them; since that time I had not ex-
changed a word with him, and utterly avoided him.
Rigby only suspected this, because he knew how much
reason I had to think so; and the event proved that I
knew them well. I did not doubt but Rigby had sent
General Fitzwilliam,[3] the first mover, to Conway to advise

[1] Both Sir Edward Hawke and Sir Jeffery Amherst were raised to the
peerage in May 1776.—E.

[2] Sir Laurence Dundas, who represented the Linlithgow burghs, 1747-48,
Newcastle-under-Lyme, 1762-68, and the City of Edinburgh, 1768-81, started
in life as a woollen draper in Edinburgh. He was created a Baronet in
November 1762, and died on the 21st September 1781. His only son was
created Baron Dundas. See more of him *infra*.—E.

[3] The Hon. General John Fitzwilliam, had been Groom of the Bedchamber
to William, Duke of Cumberland, when Mr. Conway was in the same post
about his Royal Highness, and had long been intimate with Rigby. [He

him to undertake Amherst's reconciliation. If it succeeded, Amherst would be saved to the Court; if it failed, Conway was likely to be involved in the quarrel. Conway, however, laboured the point so earnestly, that he satisfied Amherst, or would have resigned his own regiment and preferments and meddled no more. This new charge, however, contributed to exasperate the Duke of Grafton's alienation from Conway, and the Bedfords neglected nothing to inflame it. As the first year of a Parliament is chiefly engrossed by contested elections, there were two that nearly interested the Duke—one for his friend, Lord Spencer, the other for Sir James Lowther, against the Duke of Portland.[1] It happened that Conway, who was chosen for Thetford by Grafton himself, was engaged on opposite sides in both. In the first, Sir George Rodney was antagonist to Colonel Howe, Lord Spencer's member. Rodney had offered himself as evidence for Conway on the miscarriage at Rochford, and therefore had not been examined by the opposite side. This was a debt of gratitude, and Conway remembered it. For the Duke of Portland he had been engaged by the Cavendishes, and to Conway that family was the law and the prophets. Though I did not, whatever the Bedfords thought, wish to make a breach between Conway and the Duke of Grafton, yet I was desirous that both they and the Duke should feel the want of him. At the same time, seeing how strict that connection grew, I thought it prudent for Conway to leave a door open between him and the Rockingham faction : I therefore urged him to stay away on Elections, and take no active part in Parliament. This was particularly adapted to my views of preventing a hearty junction of that party with Grenville. Should Conway sit silent, whom Grenville always selected to

died in 1789, and left his fortune to one of his servants. He was uncle to Viscount Fitzwilliam (of Ireland), who founded the noble museum that bears his name at Cambridge ; and on the death of whose brother the title became extinct.—L. M.

[1] The elections for the borough of Northampton and the county of Cumberland. See *supra*, p. 136.—E.

attack on American affairs, I knew his rage on the Stamp Act would hurry him into the indiscretion of falling foul of that part of his allies who had contributed to its repeal —and indeed Grenville seldom failed of confirming my conjecture, but there is little merit in such sagacity. *The passions of men*, to those who are much conversant with them, *write a very legible hand.* I proved as little mistaken in what I foretold of the treachery of the Bedfords to Grafton. The consequences to him will show the necessity of these details. No account of *public* measures would explain his conduct. It must be remembered that his mind, as Lord Camden said of it, was capable of embracing but one single object. The machine of Government was too complicated to occupy it at all. The Bedfords were so much the reverse, that when they had no point of cunning to carry, they still thought it cunning to do something, and thus often made their situation worse. At this moment to disgust Shelburne, whom they had not yet removed, they prevailed on the King to name Mr. Lynch,[1] one of their friends, Minister to Turin. Though this was in Shelburne's department, he would not resent it openly.

But though the King would not comply with the Faction, they had got such entire possession of the Duke of Grafton, that Shelburne's removal [2] was determined, and at last ex-

---

[1] Afterwards the Right Hon. Sir William Lynch, K.B. He was the eldest son of Dr. Lynch, Dean of Canterbury, by the youngest daughter of Archbishop Wake. His family had long been settled at Groves, near Canterbury, and he represented that city from 1768 to 1774. He usually resided at Groves, where he had greatly embellished the house and park, and collected some fine pictures. He died abroad in 1785, leaving a widow, but no issue. —L. M.

[2] Lord Shelburne had been on very cold terms with the Duke of Grafton since the commencement of Lord Chatham's illness. This coldness at length grew into absolute hostility; but it was at the instigation of the King, not less than of the Bedford party, that Lord Shelburne was removed; and such, indeed, was his alienation from his colleagues, that even the Chancellor acquiesced in the necessity of his removal, and, as the following letter shows, did not much regret it. 'It does behove his Lordship (Lord Shelburne) either to be cordially reconciled or to resign, for it is neither just nor honourable to confound, much less to betray, an Administration while he remains

torted from his Majesty—a measure that produced an event of much great *éclat*, and little apprehended.   Lord Chatham, who had remained in voluntary confinement, unheard of and unthought of, scarce any man knowing the situation of his mind or intellects, offended at the meditated disgrace of Shelburne, or thinking the reigning confusions a proper opportunity of regaining his popularity and importance, wrote a letter to the King on the 12th of October, couched in terms of deplorable petition, begging mercy, begging leave to resign, begging to be delivered from his misery.   His health, he said, would not permit him to serve, and he feared it never would.   The King, with his own hand, answered his letter, and entreated him to keep his place.[1]

To the Duke of Grafton, Lord Chatham wrote the next day in a different style, complaining of the disgrace of Lord Shelburne, and of the treatment of Sir Jeffery Amherst.   This was sufficiently explicit, and the moment of timing his resignation but a month before the meeting of Parliament announced the projects brooding in his breast, and his hopes of distressing by a short warning.

a member of it.   I should wish the first on many accounts, and yet I fear that can hardly be expected, considering what has passed, especially the last affront in setting aside his Lordship's nomination to Turin.'—(Letter from Lord Camden to Duke of Grafton, MS.)   I can find no confirmation of the insinuation in Mr. Burke's *Thoughts on the Cause of the Present Discontents*, that Lord Shelburne's removal was a punishment for the warmth of his representations to the French Court on the subject of Corsica.   These representations, indeed, appear to have been fully sanctioned by the Duke of Grafton, and had they been disapproved by the Cabinet, Lord Rochford who so warmly urged them on the Duc de Choiseul would certainly not have been Lord Shelburne's successor.—L. M.   [See Lord Edmund Fitzmaurice's *Life of the Earl of Shelburne*, vol. ii. pp. 118-164, where the events which led to Shelburne's resignation on the 19th of October are fully discussed.—E.]

[1] Walpole does not here quite accurately represent the course of events. On the 12th and 13th October, Chatham wrote two letters to Grafton complaining of the treatment of Amherst and Shelburne, and asking the Duke to convey his resignation to the King, who, in an autograph letter of the 14th, refused to accept it.   In answer to which Chatham wrote to the King on the same day : ' I supplicate again on my knees your Majesty's mercy, and most humbly implore your Majesty's royal permission to resign.'—(*Chatham Correspondence*, iii. 338-44.)—E.

A war had given him his consequence, a war must restore it. America, even Corsica, presented hopes of war. Lord Shelburne, I knew from Sir Horace Mann, had been tampering with Paoli, the Corsican general; and, from one of Lord Chatham's messengers, when I was three years before in France, I had learned his directions of inquiry into the state of their ports—a meritorious attention, and not common to him with any other of our Ministers.

Resign he did. Yet the Court, though embarrassed at first, felt no inconvenience from losing him. The Duke of Grafton, as the King trusted he would, was so earnest on procuring a divorce, that he would not risk being defeated by parting with the power of influencing the Parliament in his favour. Nor, whatever were his obligations to Lord Chatham, did they call on him to take the same step. Lord Chatham had designed him for a mere tool of office, and had not only not consulted him, but, totally excluding him from his sight, had left him exposed to all the difficulties into which a state of feigned or actual frenzy had thrown the Government. Possessed of a Premier, the Court easily kept the machine together, and with but small inconvenience filled up the vacancies; for Shelburne, to avoid dismission, resigned on the pretext of following Lord Chatham.

As the latter had to the King pleaded no disgust, and publicly professed none, the Court affected to suppose he had none; and accordingly acted as if they believed he had no hostile intentions, by distinguishing his few remaining friends. Lord Camden, the Chancellor, was requested to keep the Seals, and consented. The Privy Seal was given to Lord Bristol, as a particular compliment to Lord Chatham. Lord Rochford was made Secretary of State, and was succeeded by Lord Harcourt, as Ambassador to France. Mr. Thomas Walpole, my cousin, who was much connected with La Borde, the banker of the French Court, arrived soon after from Paris, and told me that Lord Weymouth had been, on this change, transferred to the southern province, at Choiseul's

desire, who hated Lord Rochford. It had seemed extraordinary that Lord Rochford, just returned from the
French embassy, should not be employed in a department
he was conversant in.   It was still more extraordinary,
that the Minister of France could influence the destination
of our Secretaries of State.   It was most shameful, that
Lord Rochford should be so *misapplied* in compliment to
Choiseul, when the cause of the latter's hatred to him,
was the spirit with which Lord Rochford had behaved,
particularly with regard to the affair of Corsica, against
which he had remonstrated, with more warmth than he
had been encouraged to do from home ; and had he, as he
told me himself, been authorised to hold a firm language,
France would not have ventured to proceed in that conquest.   Lord Rochford was a man of no abilities, and of
as little knowledge, except in the routine of office ; but he
meant honestly, behaved plausibly, was pliant enough to
take whatever was offered to him, and too inoffensive to
give alarm or jealousy to any party.[1] Lord Bristol was
not so fortunate : Lord Chatham disavowed him, and
Lord Temple published that disavowal, with every appendix of abuse.[2] Yet though, no doubt, Lord Bristol
had catched with alacrity at the offer of the Privy Seal,
he had had the prudence to sanctify his acceptance with
Lord Chatham's consent.   The transaction, as I received
it from his own mouth, stood thus :—the Chancellor sent
him the offer in the King's name, and added, that no man
would be so agreeable to Lord Chatham for a successor.
Lord Bristol begged delay, and wrote to Lord Chatham,
enclosing the Chancellor's note.   Lord Chatham in his

---

[1] William Henry Nassau Zulestein, fourth Earl of Rochford.   See *supra*,
vol. i. p. 10.   He was Ambassador at Madrid from 1763 to 1766, and at
Paris from 1766 to 1768.   He succeeded Shelburne as Secretary of State for
the Southern Department on 21st October 1768, but was transferred to the
Northern Department on 19th December 1770.   He resigned office in
November 1775, and died on 28th September 1781.   In spite of the un-
qualified praise bestowed upon him in Letter 49 (Woodfall's *Junius*, 1814,
vol. iii. p. 177), Rochford appears to have been a man of but little ability. — E.

[2] See *Grenville Papers*, vol. iv. pp. 405-6 and note.—E.

reply, written by his wife, said, that being out of place himself, it did not become him to give advice, but wished his Lordship success in his Majesty's service. No disavowal of the Chancellor's note being made, and the letter being signed by Lord Chatham, *with respect, esteem, and attachment,* if it was equivocal, Lord Bristol had certainly no reason to interpret it in an adverse sense ; at least, he was as justifiable in misunderstanding, as the other could be in equivocating. In political chicanery, decorum has the better cause.[1] The Chancellor's conduct was less reducible to a standard. It was not known whether his friendship with Lord Chatham was at high or low water mark. He had given many hints of his friend's frenzy, and in the resignation did not seem to have been consulted. But it was sufficient to throw some blemish into his character, that the public had any doubts on his conduct. It did not clear up as he proceeded, but was clouded with shades of interest and irresolution ; and when it veered most to public spirit, was subject to squalls of time-serving, as by the Court it was taxed with treacherous ambiguity. He hurt the Court often, rarely served it to its satisfaction, but hurt himself most by halting now and then in the career of his services to the public. To Lord Chatham it could but be mortifying to be deserted by three men he had so highly elevated as the Chancellor, the Duke of Grafton, and Lord Bristol—the last two with so little merit on their parts ; and, if he was just enough to reflect on the little confidence he had placed in the two first, it could not soften that mortification.[2]

Imperceptible almost as was the sensation occasioned

---

[1] This correspondence between Lord Chatham and Lord Bristol has been published in the *Chatham Correspondence* (vol. iii. p. 347). Walpole's personal dislike of Lord Bristol, which is little disguised in these Memoirs, could alone have made him regard that nobleman's conduct in this transaction as in the slightest degree objectionable.—L. M.

[2] Instead of being deserted by these noblemen, it would be more fair to say that Lord Chatham had deserted them. There is no excuse for his conduct to Lord Bristol. His relation to Lord Camden was of a different character, for the latter was under deep obligations to him ; but all intercourse between them had long been suspended, and their friendship had,

by Lord Chatham's resignation, his dreaded name still struck other courts with awe.   Both Spain and France apprehended that his every step announced war.   Mr. H. Walpole[1] told me, that when the news arrived at Paris, Fuentes, the Spanish Ambassador, took him aside, and adjured him, as his father and uncle (my father) had been lovers of peace, that he too would do his utmost to preserve it.   Fuentes owned too, that *he hoped we should master our Colonies, or theirs too would catch the flame, and throw off the yoke in like manner.*

I now return to the other events of the year.   The ill temper of the Colonies increased.   Every mail threatened

from Lord Chatham's fault alone, withered into a mere loose political connection.   Still, the severance of that tie alarmed Lord Camden; and his letters to the Duke of Grafton, on receiving the first intelligence of Lord Chatham's resignation, betray deep anxiety.   He writes from Bath on the 14th of October, after expressing a faint hope that Lord Chatham's resolution may not be final : 'Your Grace and I feel for each other.   To me I fear the blow is fatal, yet I shall come to no determination.   If I can find out what is fit for me to do in this most distressed situation, that I must do ; but the difficulty lies in forming a true judgment. . . . I do assure your Grace that my mind is at present in too great an agitation to be soon settled, and therefore I do not give myself leave to form an opinion concerning my own conduct.'   On the 16th, he writes in the same strain : 'Nothing could give me so much satisfaction as to join with your Grace in one line of conduct, and yet I plainly see that our situations are different, and the same honour, duty to the King, regard to the public, operating upon two minds equally aiming at the same end, may draw us different ways, but I daresay your Grace will believe me in all events and circumstances what I really am, with all respect and unfeigned attachment,' etc.   The regard expressed in this note for the Duke of Grafton was perfectly sincere, and when they met in London Lord Camden yielded to the Duke's solicitations.   Various considerations united to bring him to this decision.   He was not insensible to the advantages of office.   He had made no provision for children whom he tenderly loved.   One of these children happened at the time to be alarmingly ill.   The King pressed him to remain.   The country, whose welfare he identified with the political principles he professed, might suffer from his resignation.   It was an error of judgment, for with the name of Lord Chatham the Cabinet lost the distinction that attached to Lord Chatham's policy; and the small minority in which Lord Camden found himself, lingered on for a while, suspected by the country, thwarted by their colleagues, and discountenanced by the King, until the resignation to which they were driven had become a matter of comparative indifference to the different parties in the State.—L. M.

[1] This is a slip of the pen.   Mr. Thomas Walpole was no doubt the author's informant.—E.

nearer union between them. Boston took the lead in all violences, and Virginia imitated their remonstrances ; and being governed by able and independent men, these memorials were boldly and sensibly drawn. Two regiments had been ordered to Boston in the last August ; and in November, advice came of their being landed without opposition, of their being quartered there, and of their having ordered the inhabitants to deliver up their arms, with which the people had quietly complied. However unwelcome this force was to the mutinous, a great number, who had been awed into concurrence with the predominant spirit of the factions, were rejoiced at daring to be peaceable ; and even some few other towns had previously declared against the Opponents. This intelligence, the reconciliation of Sir Jeffery Amherst, and the miscarriages of the French in Corsica, who had been thrice beaten there, were of seasonable advantage to the resettled Administration, and enabled them to face the opening of the session with confidence. There had been a riot, indeed, on Wilkes's birthday, and the Duke of Northumberland's windows had been broken for the part he took on the Middlesex election ; but, as that great Duke was now on ill terms with the house of Bute, the Court did not take to heart his being insulted. A fresher instance of his Grace's meanness and ingratitude broke forth : Rigby had obtained a regiment for his brother-in-law ;[1] the Duke insisted on it for Earl Percy, his son, and told the Duke of Grafton aloud at Court, that if it was not granted, himself would resign the Lieutenancy of Middlesex, and do all the hurt he could on the election. The King was enraged, but was forced to comply ; but both Duke and Duchess were so ill received thereafter by both King and Queen, that they resigned their post the next year.

On the 8th of November the Parliament met. The King's speech was blustering and empty. Lord Chatham

---

[1] Colonel Bernard Hale, who became a General in the army on 25th October 1793, and died on 13th March 1798.—E.

did not appear, and Lord Temple was absent too.   In the
Commons, though they talked on the general state of
affairs till eleven at night, there was no division. Grenville
spoke with acrimony against Lord Chatham, who, he said,
was the source of the troubles in America by his declaration in favour of their pretension of not being taxed; but
he was a poor man, now past everything, and therefore he
would say no more of him.   But what excuse could be
made for the First Magistrate (Lord Camden), who had
held the same doctrine—at least, such a speech had been
printed as his; if it was not genuine, why was it not
disavowed?   The Chancellor was defended by Dunning,
who was prolix without brightness.   Colonel Barré, who
had resigned with his protector, Lord Shelburne, made a
better figure, as usual, in Opposition; Dowdeswell was
dull and opinionative; Burke shone, particularly on our
inattention to Corsica; but the House seemed to take no
interest in that cause.   Sir Edward Hawke and Admiral
Saunders disputed long on the importance of that island
—if it could be called a dispute, when both wanted words
to express very indistinct ideas.   For the Administration
the day was very favourable.[1]

But the great question of the time, *whether Wilkes
should be allowed to be a Member*, wore a less prosperous
aspect.   The King, with emotion, told Lord Hertford how
much he was hurt that Wilkes must continue to sit; for
Lord Granby, Sir Edward Hawke, and General Conway,
had told the Duke of Grafton that they would oppose his
expulsion: that Lord North was willing to undertake the
service, but that it could not be attempted against three
such men—who were, in truth, three of the most respected
characters in the House.   The question was of great importance, and lay between the dignity of Parliament and
the right of the freeholders to elect whom they pleased for
their representative—a fatal separation of interests that
ought never to be separated; and one of those questions
which the rashness and weakness of the Reign had

---

[1] For a full report of this debate see Cavendish, vol. i. pp. 32-46.—E.

Hamilton, Pinxt   HoustonMezzo.

Colonel Barré.

brought into discussion from behind the veil of venerable uncertainty. That Parliament should not have power to reject from their body a most disgraceful member, whom a former Parliament had ejected for crimes of serious dye; that it should be obliged to receive so profligate a man, and one actually in prison and under sentence for a libel, seemed a compulsion to which few societies would or are obliged to submit. On the other hand, no law of the land or of Parliament disqualified such a man from being chosen. The rule is marked to freeholders, whom they may or may not elect. The whole body of the House of Commons is but an aggregate of the representatives of the several counties or boroughs; and what right had other counties or boroughs to prescribe to the County of Middlesex whom it should or should not elect? Are not the freeholders the best judges with whom they shall trust their interests? Parliament was never supposed to have a right of revision but on contested elections. Still less is it proper or safe that a majority should have authority to expel a member duly chosen. If extended, that idea would go to a predominant party purging the House of all that are disagreeable to them. The danger to the Constitution is augmented when it is notorious that the majority is, of late years, almost always sold to the Court. There would be an end of Opposition, and consequently of liberty, if the Crown might garble the House of Commons at will. The difficulty increased to the Court on the present question, in that there was no one precedent directly in point. All that could be found, after the most intense search, were strained to make them depose in favour of expulsion. The case of my father, Sir Robert Walpole, in the reign of Queen Anne, came the nearest to that of Wilkes. He was expelled and imprisoned. The town of Lynn re-elected him, and he was again expelled—but then it was by the same Parliament, and not by a new one.[1] It was

---

[1] As Wilkes was elected into the succeeding Parliament, and was allowed to sit, his expulsion at this time cannot be deemed a precedent to justify the

the more unfavourable, this precedent, that the persecution of my father was carried on in the days of, and by, a Jacobite Administration. Was that a precedent the House of Hanover ought to have adopted? It was not, however, the only precedent of a Stuart reign that was copied into the code of George the Third—nor the least obnoxious precedent that the present Court and its ductile House of Commons established on the present question; another being engrafted on it far less defensible, and of very dangerous example. But the reader must be conducted by regular steps to that strange proceeding, which, like other measures of the Reign, engendered more vexation to the Court than was compensated by its success.[1]

On the day for fixing hearings of contested elections, Sir George Maccartney, who was returned from Russia, and had married Lord Bute's second daughter, spoke for the first time, and with very bad success, though his parts had been much cried up. He was a young and handsome Irishman, attached to Lord Holland, with whose eldest son he had travelled as a kind of governor. He was an amiable man, with various knowledge, and singular memory, but no other extraordinary talents. He was now Secretary to the Lord-Lieutenant of Ireland, in the room of Lord Frederic Campbell, than whom there were few men who had more grievously offended the King; but the humiliations which his Majesty had brought on himself, obliged him at one time or other to employ or reward those most obnoxious to him.

On the 14th, Sir Joseph Mawbey, formerly in Opposition, and made a baronet by the Whigs, presented a petition from Wilkes, complaining of the hard usage he had received, and couched in warm and offensive terms. Mawbey declared he had been enjoined by his con-

---

expulsion of any man because he had been expelled by a former Parliament. No part of his expulsion can be turned into a precedent, unless on the argument that he was then a prisoner under sentence.

[1] The arguments for and against the expulsion of Wilkes are stated with neatness and force by Mr. Burke in the *Annual Register* for 1769, pp. 68*-73*.—L. M.

stituents of Southwark to present the petition, intimating that his delivery of it was not a voluntary act. The man was vain, noisy, and foolish, and soon grew a hearty partisan of his client.[1] The House ordered the petition to lie on the table—a mark of dislike; and Lord Strange called for the record to show the commitment of Wilkes had been just. The step in his favour was thought injudicious, and likely to advance his expulsion.[2] Grenville, who by Lord Temple's injunction was to be against that expulsion, knew not how to digest the petition; while the Opposition, with more reason, were for rescinding the iniquitous vote that had taken away Wilkes's privilege.

[1] See *supra*, vol. i. p. 285, note 2.—E.
[2] See the debate in Cavendish, vol. i. pp. 46-49.—L. M.

CHAPTER IX

War between Russia and Turkey.—The King of France's new Mistress.—
Death of the Duke of Newcastle.—Affairs of Corsica.—Quarrel between
the Duke of Grafton and Lord Hertford.—Commencement of the Debate
on Wilkes's Case.—Ayliffe, a Solicitor, sent to Prison by the Lords.—
Dispute concerning the Appearance of three Lords as Witnesses for
Wilkes.—Riots at the Middlesex Election.—Characters of James Towns-
hend, Sawbridge, and Colonel Onslow.—Publication of a Letter of Lord
Weymouth.—Resolution Passed by the Lords on American Affairs.—The
Cumberland Election.—Wilkes demands to be heard at the Bar of the
House of Lords.—Ridiculous Importance given to this Person.

1768

IT was at this period that advice came of the Grand
Signor having declared war against Russia, in consequence
of the intrigues of the Duc de Choiseul at the Porte.
France and the Czarina had long been on ill terms.   She
had thwarted the influence of that Court over the Northern
Crowns, and mutual haughtiness had begotten mutual
hatred.   Choiseul, who, with the ambition of Richelieu,
wanted his coolness and some of his art,—and who, though
greater than the Cardinal by disdaining little revenge,
thought great revenge spoke a great Minister, had conjured
up this tempest, and soon had cause to lament his own
work.[1]   The arms of the Czarina, who had two hundred

---

[1] It has been supposed that the great object of the Duc de Choiseul in
encouraging Turkey to engage in war with Russia, was to procure the
possession of Egypt for France as a reward for her interference.   The Count
de Vergennes had from the first predicted the issue of this unequal conflict.
He in vain laid before the Duc the military incapacity of the Sultan Mustapha,
the apathy of the Ministers, and the inefficiency of the Turkish levies.
'J'armerai les Turcs contre la Russie,' he said, 'aussitôt qu'il vous conviendra,
mais je vous préviens qu'ils seront battus.'—(Lacretelle, *Histoire de France,*

thousand of the best-disciplined troops in Europe, ample provision of military stores, and a yearly saving of a fifth of her revenues, were not unlikely to miscarry against an unwieldy, shattered empire, sunk in sloth and ignorance, and new to war from long disuse. It was not luxurious Bachas, the sudden weeds which shoot up to power in a seraglio, that Richelieu let loose on the Empire : it was Gustavus and his hardy Swedes. The event in both cases was suitable to the concoction. Catherine triumphed over the star of Choiseul, as Mr. Pitt had done. Even the rocks of little Corsica for some time kept at bay the armies of France. A still more contemptible enemy was undermining that enterprising Minister. Old Marshal Richelieu, who had preserved none of his faculties but that last talent of a decayed Frenchman—a spirit of backstairs intrigue, had contrived to give to his master at near sixty, what at twenty the King would not take from his recommendation, —a new mistress. On the death of Madame de Pompadour, his Majesty had declared that he was grown too old to expect love to his person, and therefore would have no more a favourite sultana. But, as if men only declare they know what is sensible in order to mark their folly in stronger colours, he now ran headlong into an amour that every circumstance attending it stamped with ridicule. The nymph was past twenty-six, and her charms, which were not striking, had lost more than their bloom. Nor had she ever risen to any distinction in her profession, but ranked with those wretched women who are the sport of the loosest debauchees, and the objects of the most casual amours. She had been entertained, not for his own pleasure, but to draw to his house young travelling Englishmen, by a Comte du Barry, who kept a gaming table, and who had exercised the same laudable industry in taverns here. Mademoiselle Lange was pitched upon by the Cabal of Choiseul's enemies as the instrument of

vol. iv. p. 212.)—L. M. [The ostensible cause of the war was Catherine's refusal to withdraw her troops from Poland, the Sultan declaring that their presence there lead to encroachments on Turkish territory.—E.]

their plot, and of his downfall. To dignify this Helen with a title [1]—for Du Barry was a man of quality—his brother was ordered to marry her; and the other, from having been a pimp to Richelieu, ascended to be his associate in politics. Belle, first valet-de-chambre to the King, and who exercised the same function for his master as Du Barry for Richelieu, was prevailed on or bribed to present the new Countess to the Monarch.

On the 17th of November died the Duke of Newcastle at the age of seventy-five. He had had a stroke of palsy some months before; and then, and not till then, had totally abandoned politics. His life had been a proof that even in a free country great abilities are not necessary to govern it. Industry, perseverance, and intrigue, gave him that duration of power which shining talents and the favour of the Crown could not secure to Lord Granville, nor the first rank in eloquence and the most brilliant services to Lord Chatham. Adventitious cunning repaired Newcastle's folly, rashness overset Lord Granville's parts, and presumptuous impracticability Lord Chatham.

The same day Mr. Seymour moved for *all* papers that had passed between this Court and whatever other Power, relating to Corsica—a proposal so absurd, that he was forced to correct and restrict it to our correspondence with France on that subject: yet even thus it was little tasted. Grenville himself supported the motion coldly, and owned, that if he was pressed to decide, he should disapprove a war, if Corsica alone were the object.[2] Burke said, many would subscribe to the support of the Corsicans, if the Ministers would recall the proclamation issued when Lord

[1] It is deemed an etiquette in France (which must make other nations smile) that the most Christian King's mistress must be a married woman.

[2] He also said maliciously enough, ' I would not put in threats of a war on purpose to make the funds fall, nor would I fight a duel on every the slightest affront; but I do not care to receive one affront after another, lest I should be obliged to fight at last. . . . In private life a man who seems doubtful about fighting is more likely to fight than any other.' The most interesting part of the debate is the discussion between Mr. Stanley and Mr. Grenville on the expediency of producing papers on a negotiation still pending.— (Cavendish, vol. i. pp. 52-61.)—L. M.

Bute was at the head of affairs, to prohibit any aid being
sent to those *rebels*—for so that unhappy people had been
denominated by another free island! The young Duke
of Devonshire, at that time at Florence, had given £400,
and with the other English there had raised a sum of
£2000, and sent it to Paoli.[1] But at home, the tone of
monarchy prevailed in the senate. The Tories retired or
voted with the Court; and by ten at night, the motion
was rejected by 230 to 84—a day of fortunate omen to
the Court at the opening of Parliament, and equally
propitious to the Duc de Choiseul; but humiliating to this
country, and fatal to the Corsicans! It was telling
France we did not dare to interfere with her usurpations.
Remarkable too it was, that the King seldom obtained a
Parliamentary triumph that did not disgrace his Crown.

Yet was this confirmation of his power on the point of
being overset by the moody and capricious temper of
Grafton himself. The very next day, as I was going
through Pall Mall, I met that Duke, driving rapidly to
St. James's. As he passed my chariot, he threw himself
almost out of his own, with a countenance so inflamed
with rage, that I thought him distracted, as I knew of no
offence I had given to him. In the evening, going to
inquire after the Queen, who lay in, Lady Hertford, then
in waiting to give answers to the company, ran up to me
in the utmost disorder of tears and consternation, and
begged I would that instant go to her lord, as she did not
know what might happen between him and her nephew.
This was more and more mysterious to me; but, after
she had told me a few words on the subject, and I had
prevailed on her to compose herself a little in so public a
place, I went to Lord Hertford, and learned the whole
story. Their son, Lord Beauchamp, who was ambitious
of establishing a great power in his family, both by

---

[1] The same attachment to liberty made him, in after years, the warm
friend and supporter of Mr. Fox. He was indolent and reserved, or he
might have played a great part in politics, for he possessed no common
talents. He died in 1811.—L. M.

income and parliamentary interest, had by a favourable opportunity secured, as he thought, the borough of Coventry, where the late Duke of Grafton, Lady Hertford's father, had had the principal weight.   The present Duke had beheld that progress with uneasiness, and was not without jealousy of Lord Hertford's favour with the King, and even of his aspiring to the Treasury.   A vacancy happening, the Duke had rudely refused his interest (for the Crown has much influence there) to Lord Hertford for a Mr. Nash, whom the latter supported against Sir Richard Glynn ; the Earl, who had one son already member there, declining, from fear of envy, to set up another of his family.   At the same time that he asked the Duke of Grafton's interest, he had solicited the Secretary at War, Lord Barrington, Sir Edward Hawke, First Lord of the Admiralty, and General Howard, Governor of Chelsea College, to influence some soldiers and sailors, who had votes at Coventry, in favour of Mr. Nash.   Rigby had learned this detail from Mr. Bradshaw or Sir Richard Glynn, who had purchased the interest of one Waring[1] in that place, the latter of whom had been ill-used by Lord Beauchamp, and had married a natural daughter of Ranby the surgeon, one of the flatterers of Mrs. Haughton.[2]   She and Rigby inflamed the Duke against Lord Hertford, representing it as an attack on the Treasury, and had painted me as the adviser, though no man living had so rooted an aversion to electioneering ; nor did I, till the quarrel broke out, know one syllable of the detail, nor even who were the parties concerned.   But what was my astonishment when Lord Hertford told me, that that very morning, when I met the Duke in his raging fever, he had gone to the King, and told him he would resign !   He had declared the same intention to Lord

[1] Walter Waring had been an unsuccessful candidate for Coventry at the general election in 1768.   He was M.P. for that city from January 1773 until his death in February 1780.—E.

[2] Nancy Parsons, the Duke of Grafton's mistress, had originally lived with one Haughton (or Horton) a West Indian slave-merchant.   She married Charles, second Viscount Maynard in 1776.—E.

Granby, and had sought the Chancellor to notify it to him likewise. From thence, with unparalleled insolence, he had repaired to Lord Hertford, and charged him with assuming the powers of the Minister. Lord Hertford allowed he had been in the wrong in soliciting the interest of the Crown, without his Grace's approbation; but offered to repair all, by releasing the votes he had obtained of that sort. No; this would not satisfy. Sir Richard Glynn must also be satisfied; must declare he did not think the Duke, who had promised him his interest, had broken his word. So outrageous was the Duke's behaviour, that Lady Hertford, who was present, at last broke out, and told him, she would not hear her husband thus injuriously treated by her nephew. Mr. Conway, too, interposed; and the King writing a very obliging letter to the Earl, reminding him of the fable of the bundle of sticks, and Lord Hertford quitting all pretensions to the vacant seat,[1] though with hearty discontent on his part, and with greater reluctance on his son's, a plausible pacification ensued, and the wayward chief consented to resume the reins. As I laughed at his frowardness, and had had no hand in the measure, I took care not to be included in the treaty, though I had advised the Earl not to push it to a rupture (which I needed not to fear he would), as he had not been strictly regular in the formality of proceeding. The story were not worth remembering, if it did not exemplify the Duke's touchy humour, which converted trifles into tempests, and his Administration into a scene of private animosities.

This passion was no sooner subsided than the Duke declared himself candidate, to succeed the Duke of Newcastle as Chancellor of Cambridge, and was chosen; Lord Hardwicke, who had had thoughts of canvassing for it, withdrawing his pretensions.

The Opposition, in the meantime, was split into smaller factions. Grenville had written a bulky pamphlet on the

---

[1] Sir Richard Glynn polled 525 votes and his opponent Thomas Nash 512.—E.

state of the nation,[1] in which he had kept no terms with
the Rockingham party.   They determined to reply to
it ; and, as will be mentioned hereafter, hurt themselves
much more than Grenville had hurt them.   The Duke of
Richmond, who had too much sense not to perceive the
want of it in his friends, was sick of their conduct ;   nor
were they so blind as not to see how much they had
prejudiced their affairs by so total a proscription of Lord
Bute and his creatures,—an error they endeavoured to
repair in their answer to Grenville, but which they managed
so awkwardly, by dropping sight of him, and speaking
but obscurely of his tools, that they made no court to the
King, left the Cabal equally offended, and yet scarce
marked out to the people any objects of unpopularity :[2]
but the Court was now so far from wanting their assistance,
that the operations of the private Cabal all tended to
exclude their new allies from entering too intimately into
their secrets.   Lord Harcourt's embassy to France had
left open the post of Master of the Horse to the Queen.
Lord Delawar, her Chamberlain, and a favourite, would
not take it ; on which the Bedford faction asked it for
Lord Waldegrave ;[3] but the King and Queen prevailed
on the Duke of Beaufort [4] to accept it, who was a converted
Jacobite, and more fit for their purpose.[5]

On the 23rd of November, report was made to the
House on Wilkes's case.   Beckford treated the last Parliament and its corruption in severe terms.   Sir Gilbert

---

[1] *The Present State of the Nation*, etc. (Dublin, 1768, 8vo.)   It was written
by William Knox under Grenville's supervision.   Burke's answer, *Observations on a late publication intituled The Present State of the Nation* is printed
in his *Works* (1815), vol. ii. pp. 7-24.   See *infra*.—E.

[2] This will be explained more fully hereafter.

[3] John, third Earl Waldegrave.   He had married a sister of the Duchess
of Bedford.   [4] Henry Somerset, Duke of Beaufort.

[5] There is some confusion here.   John West, second Earl Delawarr, had
been Master of the Horse to the Queen from 1766 to 1768 when he was appointed Chamberlain in succession to Lord Harcourt, and retained the post
till his death on 22nd November 1777.   His appointment as Chamberlain left
open the Mastership of the Horse, which was conferred on the Duke of
Beaufort.—E.

Elliot took this up with great warmth, and said it was an instruction to the Committee of Privileges not to hear a former Parliament abused. There was an instance, he said, upon the Journals, of a member expelled for attacking a former Parliament. This doctrine was received, as it deserved, with much indignation. Grenville said, he would not abuse the last Parliament; but, to be sure, it had been much given to rescinding its own acts. Barré commended it ironically for submitting to let officers be cashiered for their parliamentary conduct : they had, no doubt, been thought cowards!—(He had been one of the dismissed.) Conway said, whoever had turned *him* out, he forgave them. The Ministers were glad to let Sir Gilbert's assertion be passed off, under a sort of acknowledgment that preceding Parliaments ought to be mentioned with decency. Much was said on rescinding the vote on privilege, and Chauncey Townshend promised to move for it. Barré said, such a motion ought to come from the Treasury Bench, for the sacrifice of privilege had passed against the opinion of the present Chancellor (Camden); and, in the other House, the present head of the Treasury (Grafton), and the present head of the Church (Cornwallis), had strongly protested against it. The Ministers at last agreed that Wilkes should be heard to his petition in person or by counsel; and appointed the hearing three days before the approaching new election for Middlesex. Conway said it were better to let his petition lie on the table without notice. Sir Joseph Mawbey, then mentioning Lord Barrington's letter of thanks to the 3rd Regiment of Guards, for the execution in St. George's Fields, as if they had conquered a foreign enemy, his lordship, with that steady confidence with which he always defended any particular servility in his conduct, said, he had not regarded what had been said against him without doors, but now would satisfy the House on what he had done. This vindication consisted in avowing that *he* had advised the King to thank the soldiers ; *he* had added the postscript of his own accord ; *he* had promised the accused soldier support ; *he* had supplied him with public money ; *he* had protected and maintained him since—and, if any man would move for his letter, *he* would second it. Sir William Meredith did move for his letter, and Lord Barrington seconded ; but the Ministers' tender of *such conscious and modest innocence,* interposed ; and though they commended his alacrity in justifying himself, they declared, they could not in prudence let the measures of Government be called thus intemperately in question ; and the Opposition, finding it vain to contest, gave it up without a division.[1]

An Opposition so distracted and disunited, called for recruits—at least, for something that might sound creditable in the ears of the public, and keep up a spirit. Calcraft, who had the best head for intrigue in the whole party, contrived a reconciliation between Lord Temple and Lord Chatham, as a prelude to the re-appearance of the latter ; and Lady Chatham was made to say, that her lord had got an efficacious fit of the gout, which was to imply that his head was quite clear. Still this coalition in that family had no other effect than to alarm the Bedfords, who, concluding, according to a prevailing notion at that time, that nothing could withstand the union of the three brothers, and forgetting how lately they had deserted Grenville, or rather, remembering it with fear, thought the best method of securing themselves was to add another treachery, and betray the Duke of Grafton. On this they determined in a meeting at Rigby's, and sent to offer themselves to Grenville—and were, as they deserved, rejected.

Calcraft's next step was to try, through me, to connect Mr. Conway with the Grenvilles. Nothing was further from my wishes than to see Grenville restored. However,

---

[1] Cavendish, vol. i. pp. 61-73. Lord Barrington evidently wanted a vote of approbation to countenance his very injudicious letter ; and judging from the tenor of his public life, as well as from the course pursued by the Ministers on this occasion, there is strong ground for suspecting that Lord Barrington had written the letter to please the King, or even at his Majesty's instigation.—L. M.

having so lately experienced how intent Rigby was to sow division between the Duke of Grafton and his old friends, and how easily that could be effected, I was not sorry to keep on fair terms with the Grenvilles, in order to widen the breach between them and the Bedfords ; and with that view I received Calcraft's overtures with ready civility, while my inclination was to re-unite Conway and his old allies—but, in truth, all the several factions were so indifferent to me, that I entered heartily into the views of none, nor ever intended more to enlist with any.

On the 28th, Sir Joseph Mawbey moved, at the request of Wilkes, that the Lords should be desired to allow Lord Temple to appear in the House of Commons as a necessary witness for him. This was easily granted ; but though this was all that was notified, the House had no sooner consented, than Mawbey demanded the same leave to be asked for Lord Sandwich and Lord March, whom Wilkes desired to examine. This step was singularly artful, nor could the House make a distinction, when it had complied on Lord Temple. The hope of Wilkes was, either that the House of Lords would refuse to let the three lords attend the summons, or that the two latter lords themselves, who must see to what an insolent scrutiny they would be exposed, would refuse to appear ; and thence a breach might happen between the two Houses. But a new House of Commons, so recently chosen, and at such enormous expense to great part of the Members, was not likely to quarrel on punctilios, and hazard a dissolution. Besides the three lords, Wilkes desired to summon the Solictor-General Dunning, Hopkins, a friend of the Duke of Grafton,[1] a common barber, and some other persons. Mawbey also moved for an account of all moneys issued from the Treasury to Carteret Webbe their solicitor, to carry on prosecutions ; but this the Ministers would not

[1] Richard Hopkins, of Oving House, near Aylesbury, Clerk Comptroller of the Green Cloth. He was a Lord of the Admiralty, 1782-3, 1784-91, and a Lord of the Treasury, 1791-7. He represented Dartmouth, 1766-80 and 1784-90, Thetford, 1780-4; Queenborough, 1790-6, and Harwich from 1796 to his death on 18th March 1799.—E.

assent to. Grenville said, that everybody must be sensible, that in his situation, he could not object to the demand —but then, and in all his conduct, he marked how strongly his sentiments went with the Administration, though his rage at being out of place carried him against them.   To have lost his power, and to be driven to abet Wilkes—it was a Dominican friar, reduced to fling open the gates of the Inquisition.   Rigby happened not to come into the House till the votes had passed for Lord Temple and Lord Sandwich : he did oppose that for Lord March, but in vain.[1]

If the Lords Sandwich and March were apprehensive of the torture which Wilkes meditated for them, there were two other men no less embarrassed at their own situation ; these were the Duke of Grafton and the Chancellor.   The part each took was consonant to his character : Grafton dashed into violence against his former principles ; Lord Camden leaned to popularity.   The first declared he would be guided by Lord North, his Chancellor of the Exchequer and Minister of the House of Commons, who offered to carry on the war vigorously against Wilkes, contrary to the sentiments of Mr. Conway.   This last was consulted by the Chancellor, and both agreed in recommending moderation.   An opportunity was soon given to the Chancellor of avowing his opinion, which he did, as the Court thought, even with hostile intentions.   During the tumults at the end of the last session, one Hesse, a justice of peace, had taken up a rioter eight days before the Houses rose, and by different accidents had been prevented from carrying his prisoner before the Lords, and then dismissed him.   Hesse was then sued for false imprisonment ; and one Ayliffe, a solicitor, notified the prosecution to the Solicitor of the Treasury.   The Treasury supported the justice ; and just before the re-meeting of Parliament, Ayliffe had offered to compound the suit, which the justice refused.   The Earl of Egmont com-

---

[1] Cavendish states that Rigby opposed the motion for the attendance of Lord Sandwich.   See *Parliamentary Debates*, vol. i. p. 75.—E.

plained to the Lords of that prosecution as a breach of privilege, and made a warm and able speech against riots, and on the licentiousness of the people. The Government, he said, was at the eve of destruction. He had found that no man would set his face against the evil, and therefore he would, though he might be stoned as he returned to his own house. He professed he was of no party, nor attached to any : he saw that all was faction. The people were destoying themselves by their own licentious conduct. The Lords alone could save the country ; their *dictatorial power* could and had authority to do it. The Lex and Consuetudo Parliamenti was on their side, of which he quoted precedents from the time of Richard the Second. He said he would move four re-solutions, and then call witnesses to prove his assertions. The first resolution was, that no inferior court could meddle in any case that was before the House of Lords. This was assented to with applause and unanimity. The second went further in the same sense. Lord Mansfield highly approved Lord Egmont's intentions, but thought his second resolution went too far, and might involve them in difficulties and want explanations ; and he held that the first resolution was sufficient. Lord Egmont said he had done his duty, and would leave what he had thrown out with the House. On this the first resolution alone passed—but not without Lord Lyttelton's censuring the high-flown expression of *dictatorial power*. This the other explained and softened. The Chancellor was dis-pleased with the whole proceeding, and thought the prosecution of the justice a mere case of common law. The offenders, Ayliffe and Biggs the rioter, were then examined. The latter proved to be a tool of Wilkes, under direction not to answer ; yet from ignorance he was brought to answer enough that was censurable. Ayliffe, though far more artful, prevaricated so shamefully, that it was moved to commit him to Newgate. The Chancellor tried to explain that the case did not relate to the Lords, and proposed only to reprimand Ayliffe ; but the Duke of

Grafton firmly resisting, and the Chancellor dividing the House, had only four other lords of his opinion,—Lord Lyttelton, Lord Rockingham, Lord Abingdon, and Lord Milton, against fifty-one; so Ayliffe was committed to prison, and Biggs, as a low creature, reprimanded; which reprimand was pronounced by the Chancellor, with this mark, 'As the Lords have *now* declared this a breach of privilege,' etc. Lord Temple was not present, though it had been expected that the demand for the three lords would be discussed; but instead of showing any desire to obey the summons of Wilkes, he declared he should go into the country till after Christmas. This was regarded as an intimation that he had no longer any connection with Wilkes. When the House of Commons sent to make the demand, the Lords replied they would send an answer by their own messengers; and though the demand was made on the first of December, they put off the consideration to the fifth. At the same time the ministerial party in the Commons, on pretence that Carteret Webbe wanted more time, and that Jenkinson was ill in his bed, put off the appearance of Wilkes to the twelfth. On that the Lords determined to adjourn their committee on that business *sine die*, and to send no answer, having found no precedent on the journals for sending the three lords. On the contrary, usage bore that Wilkes should have applied first to the three lords themselves, who might have gone voluntarily before the Commons, as the Earls of Westmoreland and Morton[1] had done in the last reign—or if the three lords had refused to appear, the Commons then might have sent to demand them, which probably would have been refused. When Lord Somers had appeared before the Commons, and an extravagant question had been put to him, he said he hoped nobody thought him absurd enough to answer such a question, put on his hat and walked out. Lord

---

[1] The Earl of Westmorland obtained leave to appear before a committee of the House of Commons on 30th May 1758, the Earl of Morton on 25th February 1765.—(*Journals of the House of Lords*, xxix. 343; xxxi. 50.)—E.

Sandwich told the Lords that as an individual he was ready to appear before the other House, but desired their Lordships to consider that he had been Secretary of State in the heat of Wilkes's affair, and that he should not answer to any improper question. Sir Joseph Mawbey moved to have the Lords requested to send the three lords on the day appointed for Wilkes's appearance; but this was rejected. The next day (the 6th) he moved to demand the three lords that they might give an account of what they knew of a subornation of perjury procured by public money, meaning the transactions of Webbe and Kidgel against Wilkes. Grenville said, he would answer that one of the three (Lord Temple) would not appear willingly against him, his brother, nor could he have known anything of the disposal of public money. On this Lord Temple's appearance was waived. This motion was renewed the next day for the two others and sent to the Lords. The Peers flamed at a charge for subornation of perjury against two of their members. Lord Marchmont took it up with most warmth. Lord Sandwich said, he defied the aspersion, desired to be sifted, knew he had been called Jemmy Twitcher, and had despised it; but this charge was too offensive to be borne. The Lords demanded an instant conference. The Commons replied, they had sent them four different messages that day; they desired to know on which they demanded a conference? That being explained, they met, when the Lords made their complaint. The Commons put off the consideration to the next day, when, to show disrespect by delay, Beckford moved for all patent papers relative to America, which, though rejected by 122 to 77,[1] detained the House so late that they could not enter on the business of the conference.

With regard to America, a Council was held on the 6th, at which the Duke of Grafton produced a plan for re-settling it. Conway found it very hazardous and objected

---

[1] Beckford's motion was rejected by 127 to 72 votes.—(*Journals of the House of Commons,* xxxii. 93.—E.)

to it. The Duke was wroth, said he had drawn it himself, and had not slept for thinking of it. He had, he owned, communicated it to Dyson—and then foolishly produced a letter which showed that he had sent his plan to Dyson, who had rejected it, and given him the other. Conway would not bend, but said, as long as he came to Council he would speak his opinion freely; and the Chancellor justified his conduct.

The Commons determined to be firm in their answer to the lords; to deny that they meant to charge the two lords as guilty of subornation of perjury, for then they must have accused them directly; but to assert their right of demanding their appearance; and a Committee was appointed to draw up this answer. Rigby told them, that, if desired privately, both Sandwich and March would be ready to come before them, but the House would not commission any private man to make the request. On the contrary, on the morrow the committee drew up a resolute answer; but the Court, dreading a rupture of the two Houses, secretly prevailed on the Lords to acquiesce and be content with the answer. The two Earls offered to go before the Commons; and their House allowed them.[1]

On the 8th of December came on, at Brentford, the poll for electing a knight of the shire for Middlesex, in the room of Mr. Cooke, who had died since his election. The Court again set up Sir William Beauchamp Proctor. Wilkes recommended his counsel, Serjeant Glynn, a man of unexceptionable character. Till past two in the afternoon everything was quiet; but then arose an outrageous tumult, begun, as was generally believed, by Sir William's mob, who had been intended only for defence. Whichever side was the aggressor, an almost general engagement ensued, in which, though a man was killed on Glynn's side, his faction was victorious. They knocked

---

[1] For Cavendish's account of these proceedings, see his *Parliamentary Debates*, vol. i. pp. 75, 77-83, 93-5, 99-100, 131. Lord Sandwich and March gave evidence on 31st January 1769.—E.

down several that presented themselves to vote, seized the books of the poll, and drove away the sheriffs. The House of Commons was hearing the contested election for Cumberland (of which more hereafter) when at nine at night James Townshend and Sawbridge arrived from Brentford in their boots, and gave an inflammatory account of the riot. They were followed by the sheriffs, who, at Calcraft's instigation, came and demanded how they were to proceed. Artfully as this interlude was conceived, the House behaved with prudence and temper, avoiding to enter into any party consideration, nor inquiring which side had given the provocation. On the contrary, they only ordered the sheriffs to proceed to the election the next morning, and, if impeded, to apply to the House. All the books of the poll, except one, it was thought would be recovered.[1]

James Townshend and Sawbridge becoming considerable actors in the scenes that followed, it is necessary to give some brief account of them. The father[2] of the former had been all his life attached to the Court. The son, inheriting an easy fortune from a relation, and being of a fiery constitution, and not void of parts, had entered into the politics and following of the Earl of Shelburne, and had a mind assorted to violent and determined counsels. Sawbridge was brother of the celebrated historian, Mrs. Macaulay. He had quitted the army on

---

[1] Cavendish, vol. i. pp. 95-9.—E.

[2] Chauncey Townshend. They were not related to Lord Townshend's family. [Mr. James Townsend was at this time M.P. for West Looe. Lord Shelburne brought him in for Calne on Mr. Dunning's elevation to the peerage, and he represented that borough till his death in 1787. He spoke at times with considerable effect in the House of Commons. One quality very requisite to the success of a popular leader he certainly possessed,—and that was, resolution ; he showed it on all occasions. I have heard, on good authority, that a highway robbery having once been committed in his neighbourhood, he disguised himself as a countryman, and with his friend, the late Mr. Parker of Munden, in Hertfordshire, set out in search of the offender, and succeeded in overpowering and apprehending him. Mr. Parker used to dwell on the man's ludicrous astonishment in discovering that his captors were gentlemen.—L. M.

marrying a lady[1] of large fortune. Independence and
his sister's republicanism had thrown him into enthusiastic attachment to liberty. His soul was all integrity,
and his private virtues all great and amiable. His
capacity, thought not deficient, was not bright, nor his
eloquence adapted to popularity. Consequently he was
more respected in his party, than followed, his honesty
restraining the dictates of his zeal, and his bigotry being
founded on principle, not on doctrines and creeds.[2]

A man differently constituted began now to distinguish
himself on the other side. This was Colonel George
Onslow, nephew of the late Speaker. He had been
known as one of those burlesque orators who are favoured
in all public assemblies, and to whom one or two happy
sallies of impudence secure a constant attention, though
their voice and manner are often their only patents, and
who, by being laughed at for absurdity as frequently as
for humour, obtain a licence for saying what they please.
This man, who was short, round, quick, successful in jokes,
and of a bold and resolute nature, had gone warmly into
Opposition, with Lord Rockingham and the old Whigs;
but now with his cousin, the elder George Onslow, had
enlisted under the Duke of Grafton, and followed the
banners of the Court; incensed particularly at Wilkes for
exposing the correspondence of his cousin, lately one of
Wilkes's passionate admirers.[3] The Colonel seeing a man
in the street, pasting up a speech of Oliver Cromwell,
ordering the people to pull the members out of the

---

[1] Daughter of Sir Orlando Bridgman, who died a few weeks after her
marriage. His second wife was Miss Stephenson.—L. M.

[2] John Sawbridge was at this time M.P. for Hythe. He afterwards sat for
the City of London. He acted as Sheriff with Townshend during Beckford's
celebrated Mayoralty, 1769-70, and was himself Lord Mayor, 1775-6. ' He was
a stern republican in his principles, almost hideous in his aspect ; . . . of a
coarse figure, and still coarser manners ; but possessing an ample fortune, and a
strong understanding.' He was also 'the greatest proficient at the game of whist,
who was then to be found among the clubs in St. James's Street.'—(Wraxall's
Memoirs (1884), vol. iii. p. 423.) He died on 21st February 1795.—E.

[3] This correspondence will be found in Woodfall's *Junius*, vol. iii.
pp. 229-233.—E.

House, Onslow seized the fellow in spite of the mob, and complained of him to the House. This act was applauded, and the prisoner ordered to attend. He accused a milkman of having incited him, and the latter was committed to Newgate.[1] An exploit of greater rashness and much more memorable consequence, about two years afterwards, will confirm what I have said of this Colonel.[2]

Ayliffe, the other state prisoner, petitioned for release. Lord Sandwich proposed he should be enlarged, provided he would inform against others of his accomplices. This inquisitorial measure was treated severely, as it deserved, by the Duke of Richmond—and Ayliffe was discharged. At the same time Wilkes brought three writs of error into the House of Lords, on Lord Mansfield's alteration of the Record, and on the double punishment of imprisonment for ten months and twelve months inflicted on him for the *Essay on Woman*, and the *North Briton*.

On the 10th, the books of the poll being recovered, the House of Commons ordered the sheriffs to examine them, and then to renew the poll on the 14th. Rigby moved to put off the appearance of Wilkes to the 17th, Jenkinson, a material witness for Carteret Webbe, having had a relapse. Sir Edward Deering[3] said angrily, he saw nothing was meant but delay—why did not the Ministers put it off at once?—and then himself moved in scorn to adjourn that appearance till January the 27th. The Ministers gladly caught at the offer, and it passed.

A letter of Lord Weymouth previous to the murder of Allen in St. George's Fields, and couched in imprudent terms,[4] had been printed in the *St. James's Chronicle.*

---

[1] Cavendish's *Parliamentary Debates*, vol. i. p. 100.—L. M.

[2] He was the eldest son of Lieutenant-General Richard Onslow, a younger brother of the Speaker, by Miss Walton, the niece and heiress of the gallant Admiral Sir George Walton. He succeeded his father as Member for Guilford in 1760, and continued to represent it until 1784. He died in 1792. —L. M.

[3] Sir Edward Deering, Bart., of Surrenden Deering in Kent, M.P. for New Romney, 1761-87. He died on 8th December 1798, aged sixty-six.—E.

[4] It was to excite the magistrates to do their duty against riots, promising them protection. It was interpreted as preparatory to a massacre.

Lord Pomfret was desirous of complaining of it, but the Duke of Grafton insisted on making the complaint himself, and did with extraordinary heat, and the Lords ordered Baldwin the printer to be taken up. The letter had been accompanied by a very daring comment. Baldwin at the bar of the Lords said he had received the papers from one Swan a printer, who appeared likewise. He was a plain, honest man ; confessed he had been alarmed at the seizure of Baldwin, yet had been determined to sacrifice himself, his wife, and children, rather than betray any man. He had therefore applied to Mr. Wilkes, to whom he had gone three times a week for letters to be printed in the newspapers, and had asked him what he should do? Mr. Wilkes had answered, ' Declare you received all those papers from me.' This hardiness threw the Lords into a rage ; but the Duke of Grafton, checked by Wilkes's boldness, proposed to defer the consideration till the morrow. The Duke of Bolton professed to detest Wilkes, and wondered their Lordships could hesitate a moment ; but the Minister, perceiving the new difficulty into which he had plunged, Wilkes being as yet a member of the other House, and willing to take advice, persisted in deferring the consideration.

On the 14th, Serjeant Glynn was returned for Middlesex by a majority of 264 votes ; but though the City and the Strand were illuminated on that occasion, Wilkes, to prevent complaints and to display his authority, had issued such strict orders to his partisans, that not a man appeared in the streets—such was his influence even from his prison !

The Lords then passed six or seven resolutions on American affairs ; of which the only strong one was, to address the Crown to prosecute in England all who had been engaged in treasonable practices in the Colonies. Lord Temple, who had not appeared till then during the session, said all this was doing nothing, and went away. Lord Shelburne professed himself an American, but declared he would wait for a better opportunity of speaking his thoughts. The Duke of Richmond called on the Ministers to acquaint the House with what sums had been received from the new duties. The Duke of Grafton answered, Nothing had been received, for the Commissioners had been imprisoned by the mob : but he would go further ; he believed nothing had been received from any part of America ;—but another of the Ministers, more prudent, interrupted him, and said the Duke of Richmond's question was nothing to the point before them. The resolutions passed.

The other House had been engaged in hearing the contested election for Cumberland, which, under the names of the candidates, comprehended the great rival-ship between the Duke of Portland and Sir James Lowther. The Duke was a proud, though bashful, man, but of an unexceptionable character, which was illuminated by the hard measure he had so recently received from the Treasury, who had wrested an estate from him in favour of Sir James for the purposes of this very election. To the unpopularity of being son-in-law of the Favourite, Sir James united many odious arbitrary qualities, and was equally unamiable in public and private.[1] The countenance of the Crown itself could not serve him against these prejudices. Even in *that* House of Commons

[1] He was called with reason the petty tyrant of the North, and the stories still related of his pride, caprice, and cruelty in Westmoreland and Cumberland, are almost incredible. If he possessed a virtue, it was as Peter Pindar said, in his well-known epistle to him, ' A farthing candle 'midst a world of shade ' (*Works*, 1812, vol. iii. p 12). His eccentricities were such as to cast doubts on the sanity of his intellect. He fought several duels for causes ludicrously inadequate. This did not prevent his making an impassioned appeal to the House of Commons in 1780, on the duel of Lord Shelburne and Colonel Fullarton, against the impropriety of duels arising out of language in the House of Commons, as interrupting the freedom of debate (*Parliamentary History*, vol. xxi. 319-327). Mr. Pitt owed to him his first introduction into public life—as his first seat was for Sir James's borough of Appleby,—a favour amply returned, by Sir James being raised in 1784 to the Earldom of Lonsdale. He was more useful than creditable as a political adherent. No man of his day spent such large sums in election contests, or obtained greater success in them, notwithstanding his extreme personal unpopularity. It is said that above seven thousand guineas were found in his

he lost his cause by 247 to 95, the Scots, the Princess's Cabal, and a few more, alone supporting him.   The Duke of Grafton, affecting candour to repair the injury he had done to the Duke of Portland, took no part till the two last days, and then, though acting zeal for Sir James, sent only the two Secretaries of the Treasury to his assistance. The Bedfords, resenting the disappointment of Lord Waldegrave by the promotion of the Duke of Beaufort, deserted Sir James Lowther, though professing to wish well to his cause, some of them staying away, others voting against him in compliment to Lord Weymouth, who had married the Duke of Portland's sister; and Lord George Sackville, who had hung so long on Lord Bute to no purpose, spoke strongly against Sir James, to show his discontent; on which Sir James said to him, ' My lord, you ought to have remembered that you have been on your trial too :'—nor was Sir James satisfied with this rebuke, as will be seen hereafter.

Baldwin, the printer, being the same day discharged and reprimanded by the Lords, and the Chancellor, in delivering their reproof, having distinguished between the liberty and the licentiousness of the press, Lord Sandwich moved the House to desire him to print his reprimand, which the other felt as it was meant.

Wilkes demanded to be heard at the bar of the Lords, to justify his writings.   They dreaded his appearance; and, to shift it off from themselves, desired a conference with the Commons, in which they communicated a vote they had passed, in which they pronounced the censure on Lord Weymouth's letter an infamous and scandalous libel, and desired the Commons to agree with them.   To this they added the evidence.   Lord North, at his return from the conference, moved to concur with the Lords; but Grenville said they must first hear the evidence.

cassette at his death in 1802, destined for the approaching general election,— ' a vast sum to collect in gold at a time when even at the Queen's commerce- table guineas were very rarely staked, and when specie could scarcely be procured even by men of the largest fortune.'—(See more of him in Wraxall's *Historical and Posthumous Memoirs*, 1884, vol. iii. pp. 537-560.)—L. M.

Seymour and others reflected on Lord Weymouth's letter; and Macleane,[1] a creature of Shelburne, said, if Wilkes's preface to the letter was conceived in gall, the letter itself was written in blood. It was determined to hear the evidence on the 19th, and Wilkes himself on the 20th. Wilkes, no ways intimidated, spread handbills, in which he avowed the publication both of Lord Barrington's and Lord Weymouth's letters. Lord North, at a previous meeting of the chief members of the House, had almost pledged himself to go into the examination of Wilkes; but Conway pleaded for moderation, and told them he meant to propose to send back to the Lords to leave him to the law. It was agreed Mr. Conway should throw this out, and see how it was tasted. But the Ministers again changed their minds (probably by orders from Court), and resolved to go into the examination after the holidays. James Townshend, Phipps, and Lord John Cavendish proposed to do nothing, which Conway approved; but others, desirous of hearing the evidence, brought it on, heard it, and then moved to hear Wilkes's defence on the 27th, which was agreed to.[2]

Wilkes, on the same day, humbly petitioned the Lords to allow him to be present on the 21st, at the hearing of his writs of error, and produced a precedent for it in 1764. The Chancellor said the cases were not parallel, the precedent regarding an appeal, not a writ of error, and that it would not be allowed in the courts below; yet he proposed to search the journals for a precedent, and, as there was none, this would have been the least exceptionable manner of denying his request; but the warmer Lords calling out, 'Reject! reject!' the petition was rejected, and Wilkes was left to complain of a new hardship.

The Duke of Grafton, growing alarmed at finding that he had driven from himself every friend, and rested only on the Bedfords, cast about for reunion with Lord Hertford

---

[1] Lauchlin Macleane, M.P. for Arundel.—E.
[2] See Cavendish's *Parliamentary Debates*, vol. i. pp. 106-115.—E.

and his brother; and to raise their jealousy, told the former that Lord North was uneasy at his situation, and he apprehended would resign, Mr. Conway not supporting him; in which case, the power of the House of Commons must fall to Mr. Grenville, as Mr. Conway would not undertake it; and the only other person fit for it, Sir Gilbert Elliot, being too obnoxious as a Scot. Lord Hertford told him frankly that though Mr. Conway had supported Lord North, his Grace must remember how he himself had used the family; that Mr. Conway had adhered to his Grace against the Rockinghams, had consented to stay in the Cabinet for his sake; and yet, so far from being trusted or consulted, was never admitted within his Grace's door. The Duke professed how glad he always was of seeing Conway—and there the re-union rested, till the Duke had new complaints to make of others.

On the 21st, Wilkes petitioned the Lords to put off the hearing his writs of error; as Serjeant Glynn, his counsel, was confined with the gout, having once only (on his election) been brought down to the House of Commons. That impetuous and unfeeling man, the Earl of March-mont, proposed to name counsel for him, and hear him directly; but the Chancellor, objecting to such violence, and applauding Glynn for defending Wilkes *since his misfortunes*, the Lords adjourned the hearing till after the holidays. Both Houses then adjourned; and Wilkes terminated the year by declaring himself candidate for the ward of Farringdon Without, whose alderman, Sir Francis Gosling, was just dead.[1]

I have been as brief as possible on the several stages of Wilkes's history, detailed in so many publications; yet the subject must be tedious to future readers not interested in so ridiculous a war. Yet, were the steps omitted, who could conceive how the affairs of a great nation could stand still, while all the attention of the nation and of

---

[1] Sir Francis Gosling was an eminent banker in Fleet Street, where his descendants still carry on business.—L. M.

the public hung on such a motley character? He was dignified by the asperity of the Court; but not the vengeance of the Princess, the connivance—nay, and passion[1] of the King, or the rancour of the Scotch, could raise his importance so high, as to excuse or palliate their employing their thoughts, time, and power, to crush a personage that was fitter to be the merry Andrew than the martyr of one of the most formidable Courts in Europe.

[1] The *Grenville Papers* and the *Correspondence of George III. with Lord North* contain ample proof how deeply the King was interested in the success of the various prosecutions against Wilkes.—E.

CHAPTER X

Douglas Peerage Claim.—Andrew Stuart.—Trial of Macquirk and Balf.—
Discussions concerning Wilkes.—Resolutions on America.—Wilkes
appears before the House of Commons.—Censure on him passed.—His
Expulsion carried.—Republican Party in England.—Grenville's *State of
the Nation.*—Burke's Reply.

1769

ON the 2nd of January Wilkes was chosen alderman of
the ward of Farringdon Without.   Bromwich, a merchant
of paper for furniture, stood against him, but soon gave
up the contest, Wilkes polling thirteen out of fifteen
hundred ; and thence the latter became a magistrate of
the Metropolis, while yet a criminal of State, and a
prisoner!   At the same time the outrageous abuse, for
which he had been sentenced, was continued in *North
Britons*[1] (though no longer written by him) and in other
public papers.   Even the constables of the City, were
almost to a man, devoted to Wilkes.

On the 13th, at a ballot at the East India House, the
agreement with the Government was rejected by 248
proprietors against 207.

The next day two of the rioters at Brentford, on the
side of the Court, were tried at the Old Bailey, and
convicted of the murder of George Clarke ; but their
counsel, urging that there was a flaw in the indictment,
judgment was stayed till the point could be argued, when
that plea was overruled, and the criminals were ordered
for execution on the 17th, the King not daring to interfere
with a pardon.

[1] The *North Briton*, which had been suspended at the time of Wilkes's
arrest, was resumed on the 10th May 1768, and was continued weekly till
the 11th May 1771, when it was incorporated with *Bingley's Journal.*—E.

The 16th, the House of Lords meeting after the adjournment, Wilkes's writs of error were argued before them by his counsel, Glynn, and Davenport; on the side of the Crown by the Attorney-General, De Grey, and Thurloe—Dunning, the Solicitor-General, not choosing to act, as he had been so much employed in behalf of Wilkes. Wilmot, Lord Chief Justice of the Common Pleas, in the name of the other judges (Lord Mansfield, and the judges of the King's Bench, not being present as parties), gave a full opinion against Wilkes, and the verdicts were confirmed without one peer saying a syllable against them, but suffering themselves to be directed by the judges.[1]

About this time was heard decisively the great cause between the Houses of Douglas and Hamilton, by appeal to the Lords,—a cause as singular and as ambiguous as perhaps ever came before a court of judicature. The last Duke of Douglas,[2] a kind of lunatic, had at various periods made different wills; at first in favour of the Hamiltons, the nearest males of his race; but latterly he had substituted as his heir the son of his sister, who having offended him by marrying a poor, elderly gentleman,[3] had retired to France, and there, though herself past fifty, had been, or pretended to have been, delivered of two boys,[4] of whom one only survived. A cloud of circumstances concurred to make the Hamiltons suspect that both children were supposititious, and purchased of different peasants. The

---

[1] See *Journals of the House of Lords*, xxxii. 222-3.—E.

[2] He had murdered a man in his own castle, where he always lived, and the affair had been winked at on supposition of his insanity, and perhaps from the difficulty of bringing to justice or of getting evidence against so great a lord in the centre of his dependants, and in so remote a country.

[3] Colonel, afterwards Sir John Stewart, Bart., of Grandtully. The marriage took place on the 4th of August 1746. He died in 1764. It appears from the pleadings that when he married Lady Jane Douglas he was reduced in health, spirit, and circumstances, but was a man naturally of an ardent temperament, and had led a bustling, dissipated life.—L. M.

[4] She was delivered of twins on the 10th of July 1748, at Paris, in the house of Madame le Brun, in the Faubourg St. Germains, according to the evidence in the cause.—L. M.

Duchess of Douglas, a woman of bold and masculine spirit, and herself a Douglas, who had artfully procured to get married to the Duke after the death of his sister, whom she had never seen, espoused the cause of Lady Jane's children, and prevailed on the Duke, in his last days, to restore the inheritance to his rejected nephew.   The widow Duchess of Hamilton, one of the beautiful Gunnings, and of a spirit equally proud and pertinacious, though of the most delicate frame and form and outward softness, as obstinately defended the cause of her sons, particularly of the youngest, who had been named the former heir ; and being incited by one Andrew Stuart, a very able young man, and one of the trustees of her children, she, at immense expense to the Duke, her son, had pursued the disquisition into the births of Lady Jane's children ; and, by the books of the police at Paris, had, at the distance of near twenty years, and by the industry of Stuart, collected such a mass of circumstantial evidence, that it seemed to many men to prove that Lady Jane had never been with child, nor ever resided long enough in one place to give even an air of probability that she had lain in ; to which should be added, that Lady Jane could never fix on any consistent account of the person in whose house, or of the house in which she had been delivered, and in which she allowed she had not stayed above three or four days. Much proof appeared of Lady Jane's art and hypocrisy : on the other side, little or none that she had acted like a mother, having neglected the younger child entirely for a year ;[1] and the survivor proving to have all probable appearance of a swarthy French peasant,[2] and no ways resembling his pretended parents, who were fair and sandy, like most Scots.   The Duke, Lady Jane's brother, had, till

---

[1] It should be observed, however, that in the judgments they delivered in the House of Lords, both Lord Camden and Lord Mansfield argue very strongly from Lady Jane's conduct to her children that she was their mother.—L. M.

[2] This was the general impression.   Lord Mansfield, on the contrary, was satisfied that the children in every way resembled Sir John Stewart and Lady Jane,—'the one, the finished model of himself, and the other the exact picture in miniature of Lady Jane.'—(*Parliamentary History*, xvi. 531.)—L. M.

near his death, been persuaded of the imposture; and the cause coming before the Lords of Session in Scotland, had, after the fullest discussion, been determined in favour of the Hamiltons.[1] Mankind grew wonderfully divided in their opinions, when the cause was now brought before the English Peers. Though the cheat, if one, had its foundation, and almost its detection, in France, the French inclined to the legitimacy of the children; so did the generality in Scotland: and, above all, the compassion excited in favour of infants avowed by both parents, though, in truth, very equivocally by Lady Jane on her death-bed, carried the current in favour of young Douglas. He was not less eagerly patronised by the Duke and Duchess of Queensberry: the Duke was his guardian; and the Duchess, no less celebrated formerly by Prior, Pope, and Swift, than the Duchess of Hamilton, in the times of which I write, was still, more singular and persevering than the two other dames of the same rank,—circumstances that contributed powerfully to attract the attention of the public. Much perjury appeared on both sides—certain proof on neither; the want of which decided the suit, at last, in favour of the compassionate part of the question.

After a hearing of many and long days, with an attendance scarce ever known there on a cause, the House of Lords reversed the decree in favour of the Hamiltons, and restored the Douglas. The Lord Advocate Montgomery[1] spoke for thirteen hours in three days, and with applause. Mr. Charles Yorke was the least admired. The Duchess Douglas thought she had retained him; but hearing he was gone over to the other side, sent for him, and questioned him home. He could not deny that he had engaged himself for the House of Hamilton—'Then, sir,'

---

[1] The Douglas cause occupied the Court of Session at intervals from 1762 to 1767, and was decided by the casting vote of Lord President Dundas, the judges being equally divided in opinion.—E.

[2] James Montgomery, M.P. for Peeblesshire, was Lord Advocate, 1766-75, when he was appointed Lord Chief Baron of Scotland. He was created a Baronet on 16th July 1801 and died on the 2nd April 1803.—E.

said she, '*in the next world whose will you be, for we have all had you?*' Mr. Alexander Wedderburne (for the Hamiltons, too), spoke with greater applause than was almost ever known. Dunning, on the same side, and Norton for the Douglas, made no great figure. The Duke of Bedford, Lord Sandwich, and Lord Gower,[1] were the most zealous for the Hamiltons. Lord Mansfield, it had long been discovered, favoured the Douglas; but the Chancellor Camden, with dignity and decency, had concealed his opinion to the very day of the decision. The debate was opened by the Duke of Newcastle, and very poorly. He was answered by Lord Sandwich, who spoke for three hours with much humour, and scandalised the bishops, having, with his usual industry, studied even the midwifery of the case, which he retailed with very little decency. The Chancellor then rose, and with becoming authority and infinite applause, told the Lords that he must now declare, that he thought the whole plea of the Hamiltons a tissue of perjury, woven by Mr. Andrew Stuart; and that were he sitting as judge in any other court, he would order the jury to find for Mr. Douglas; and what that jury ought to do on their oaths, their Lordships ought to do on their honours. He then went through the heads of the whole case, and without notes recapitulated even the dates of so involved a story; adding, that he was sorry to bear hard on Mr. Stuart, but justice obliged him. This speech, in which it was allowed he outshone Lord Mansfield, had the most decisive effect. The latter, with still more personal severity to Stuart, spoke till he fainted with the heat and fatigue; and, at ten at night, the decree was reversed without a division,[2]—a

---

[1] Lady Susan Stuart, daughter of the Earl of Galloway, and third wife of Earl Gower, was the intimate friend of the Duchess of Hamilton, and governing her in all other points, was very zealous for her in this cause, and had engaged the Bedford connection to support it.

[2] The speeches of Lord Mansfield and Lord Camden are to be found in the *Collectanea Juridica*, vol. ii. p. 386, and *Parliamentary History*, vol. xvi. 518. It is scarcely possible that the report of Lord Mansfield's can be correct. It is equally poor both in composition and in argument; the main

sentence, I think, comformable to equity, as the child was owned by both parents, and the imposture not absolutely proved; yet, in my opinion, not awarded in favour of truth—a declaration I should not be so arrogant as to make, if many very able men were not as much persuaded as I am of the child being supposititious. Nor was the cause terminated at last without a duel between Andrew Stuart and Thurloe, who had poured out torrents of abuse on his antagonist in the course of the pleadings; but no mischief was done. This curious trial was set forth by each party in such ample volumes, that it is unnecessary to give a larger detail of it here; but a few concomitant and subsequent circumstances require a place.

The Duke of Bedford, the Earls of Sandwich, Bristol, and Dunmore, and Lord Milton, protested against the decision in favour of Mr. Douglas, for that he was not proved to be the son of Lady Jane, and for that they thought it had been proved that he was not so. The next morning Mr. Andrew Stuart found on his table a bond for four hundred pounds a year for his life, a present from Mr. Johnstone Pulteney,[1] his friend, in consideration of

argument, indeed, being that a woman of Lady Jane's illustrious descent could not be guilty of a fraud. The report contains none of the invectives against Andrew Stuart to which the text refers,—an omission which has been attributed to Lord Mansfield's extreme caution or timidity,—and had no other effect than to encourage Mr. Stuart to attack him afterwards with greater fierceness; whilst against Lord Camden, whose speech was at least equally severe, he made no assault whatever.—(Lord Brougham's *Historical Sketches*, vol. iii. pp. 164-5.) Lord Camden's speech has been reported with unusual care, and is no doubt a fine specimen of judicial eloquence. Still, it does not fairly grapple with the difficulties of the case, and some of the strongest objections, too, in the way of the Douglas claim are left entirely untouched.—L. M. [Sir George Hardinge, who was present, has left an interesting account of the delivery of Lord Camden's speech. See Campbell's *Lives of the Chancellors* (1846), v. 363-4.—E.]

[1] William Pulteney (formerly Johnstone), M.P. for Cromarty, 1768-74 and for Shrewsbury, 1774-1805, married first, on 10th November 1760, Frances Pulteney, who inherited the property of the Earl of Bath, and secondly, on 5th January 1804, Margaret, widow of his friend Andrew Stuart of Castlemilk and Torrance. He succeeded to the Baronetcy on the death of his brother, Sir James Johnstone of Westerhall, in September, 1794, and died on 30th May 1805, aged seventy-six. He was supposed to be the richest commoner in the

the cruel treatment he had met with. When the news
arrived at Edinburgh that the Douglas had carried his
cause, the mob rose and almost killed the President of
the Session who had been against him. They broke into
Holyrood House, plundered the apartments of the Hamiltons, and made it dangerous for their friends to remain in
the town. The sedition lasted two days, nor was put an
end to but by the guards. Mr. Andrew Stuart, some
considerable time after, printed and gave away a tract on
the case, and more particularly in his own defence against
Lord Mansfield. It was a prodigy of abilities, reasoning,
and severity, yet observing a show of tenderness and
decorum that did not abate the edge of the satire.[1] Some
circumstances too, corroborating the question he supported,
had abated since the trial ; and at last the principal evidence for the Douglas was convicted of perjury in another
cause in France.[2] Lord Mansfield, agreeably to his
cowardice and implacable character, answered the book
only by preventing Stuart from being sent to India in a
very lucrative employment.

Kingdom. His habits were extremely economical, and Wraxall compared
his dress and figure to those of Pope's Sir John Cutler.—(*Historical and
Posthumous Memoirs*, 1884, v. 268.). His only daughter by his first wife
was created Countess of Bath in 1803.—E.

[1] These *Letters to the Right Honourable Lord Mansfield* were published in
1773 (London 8vo). Their author, Andrew Stuart, was admitted a Writer to
the Signet on 10th August 1759. He represented Lanarkshire from 1774 to
1784, and Weymouth from 1790 until his death on 18th May 1801. Stuart
was keeper of the Signet, 1777-9, and a Commissioner for Trade and Planta-
tions, 1779-82.—E.

[2] Without examining the records of France this fact cannot safely be
altogether denied; but after many inquiries both among Scotch and English
lawyers, the authenticity of it seems to rest with Walpole alone. Had it
happened before Mr. Stuart's *Letters* were published in 1773, of course he
would never have omitted so important a fact ; but neither in his *Letters*, nor
in a French account of the Douglas cause published in 1786, nor in any
other publication that has fallen in the editor's way, is there the least notice
of any such thing : besides this, nobody remembers even to have heard of it ;
and it is not a story likely to be forgotten, had it ever been mentioned.—L. M.
[The decision of the House of Lords in the Douglas cause is now generally
considered to have been right. See Lord Campbell's *Lives of the Lord
Chancellors* (1846), vol. v. p. 290, note.—E.]

Another trial intervened and divided the notice of the public—at least, of the people. Macquirk and Balf, the persons condemned for murder at the election at Brentford, were Irish chairmen, and had notoriously been hired with other mob on the side of the Court candidate. When they were pronounced guilty, the populace gave a shout —a shocking indecency, very properly reproved by the Recorder. Execution was decreed on the 17th. However, on the eve of their appointed fate, the Ministers took courage and reprieved them *pro tempore*, on these considerations—one Allen, the prosecutor, finding himself in the midst of the adverse mob at Brentford, had been protected and his life saved by Macquirk. Allen thence carried Macquirk to an ale-house, and there the ungrateful villain wormed out of his benefactor many circumstances that proved Macquirk had been engaged in the riot, though he had not struck the deceased. The wretch was so heated by party, that he turned informer against Macquirk, though when condemned, Allen did intercede in his favour, but the Judge told him he had made that intercession vain. Macquirk behaved with great decency, only desiring three or four days to prepare for death. Balf, though dipped in the riot, had clearly had no hand in the murder, yet was found guilty of constructive murder, which induced the Court to recommend him to mercy.

The glaring cruelty of putting two men to death, who had neither committed the deed nor meditated it, made such an impression on Mr. Boyle Walsingham,[1] a seaman and man of quality, that though warm in party, his good nature was revolted, and on the 20th he declared in the House of Commons that he wished to see the chairmen pardoned, and though he knew not in what manner it might be proper to apply for mercy, he should be happy to see it extended to those unfortunate men. Sir William

---

[1] He was the fifth son of the Earl of Shannon, [and M.P. for Knaresborough. He went out to the West Indies some years afterwards as Commodore, in the 'Thunderer,' seventy-four, and perished with all his crew in the celebrated hurricane of 1779. He had married one of the daughters and co-heiresses of Sir Charles Hanbury Williams.—L. M.

Meredith, a man remarkably averse to punishments that reached the lives of criminals, joined in the same humane sentiments. Lord North said it would not be necessary to make a motion, for he was persuaded his Majesty would be ready to grant his pardon the moment he should know it was the sense of the House of Commons. This application coming from two gentlemen of fair characters, and both in Opposition, was very fortunate for the Court, who were embarrassed how to act, the people being savagely inflamed against the chairmen, and instigated by a virulent *North Briton* to clamour for the execution; but in the House of Commons there was not a dissenting voice against pardon; and the criminals were accordingly respited during pleasure, the Ministers fearing that entire pardon at once would but more enrage the populace.[1]

In the meantime the Court of Aldermen having discovered that the election of Wilkes into their body had been irregular by the poll being closed on the withdrawing of Bromwich without making the proper notification, the election was declared void. Wilkes, in strong terms advertised his protest against the vacating his election, and exhorted the citizens to oppose that step. The electors at Westminster also instructed their members to support his right of election for the county of Middlesex, and enjoined them never to cease endeavouring to obtain redress of the illegal measures pursued against him, and vindicating the rights of the people who had chosen him their representative. Martin, a banker of a very fair character,[1] who had voted against him at all the late elections, was so shocked at the resolution of the House of Commons,—which, though having voted that writing and publishing a libel was not within the case of privilege, had yet gone further than even that vote of their own, and had censured Wilkes, who had only republished

---

[1] See the *Gentleman's Magazine* for 1768, p. 587; 1769, pp. 51-53, 108. Certainly the execution of these men would have been an act of gross injustice.—L. M.

[2] Joseph Martin, M.P. for Gatton and subsequently for Tewkesbury. He died on the 29th April 1776.—E.

the *North Briton*, and had not been *proved* to have written it,—that he moved a new resolution, that Wilkes did not come within the description of that resolution, which seemed to make both writing and publishing necessary ; and which being very penal, ought to be interpreted in the mildest sense. This Lord North opposed ; and even George Grenville voted against Martin's motion, which, if just, would seem to make the House trifle in its resolution. Much was said for and against Wilkes. Colonel Lutterel was particularly severe on him, and both Lord Granby and Conway voted against the motion, which towards eight o'clock was rejected by above one hundred and sixty to seventy-one. [1]

Conway was in one of his difficult situations. A Council had been held during the holidays on Wilkes, in which it was determined to bring on his affair. Rigby the next day prevailed to have that resolution changed without acquainting Conway ; and then the Bedford faction told the King there was no acting with Conway, who always in the House adhered to his own opinion, and would not acquiesce in what was determined in Council. This, which was often true, was false now ; but Lord Ligonier was dying, and the Bedfords wished to procure the Blues for Lord Waldegrave. The Duke of Grafton, however, told them that the Blues were engaged to Conway ; yet the Duke and the King too complained to Lord Hertford of his brother's impracticability. Conway justified himself to the King on the falsehood of the present charge, at the same time avowing his own delicacies. The King received his declaration but coolly. Lord Hertford (I believe by his Majesty's order) spoke to me on his brother's future behaviour on Wilkes, fearing he would ruin himself should he oppose Wilkes's expulsion. I told him, as was true, that I had avoided talking to Mr. Conway on that subject, as I would neither take upon me to advise Mr. Conway again to the prejudice of his fortune, nor on the other hand would counsel him to counteract his former

[1] See Cavendish's *Parliamentary Debates*, vol. i. pp. 115-120.—E.

behaviour.   Indeed, I saw great confusion arising.   The
House of Commons acted without justice or decency : the
other party were no less violent, and were setting up juries
against the judges.   The latter were generally inculpable ;
and though juries ought to be still more sacred, yet in the
hands of a Middlesex jury at that time, no man's life was
safe.   Integrity could not attach itself to either party.
Captain Walsingham, Martin the banker, and Sir William
Meredith, were proofs on different sides that conscientious
men condemned the excesses of their own parties.   Though
the Court relaxed nothing of its animosity to Wilkes, yet
it had received too many mortifications not to be cautious
how it ventured on any further strides of power.   Still, I
would not make my court by trying to influence Mr.
Conway to countenance their plans ; nor, though I began
to fear the consequences of Wilkes's unprincipled rashness
and despair, would I suffer any interested motive to fix
the balance of my opinions.

On the 25th the resolutions on America were considered
in the House of Commons.   Beckford offered a petition
from persons calling themselves a majority of the Assembly
of Boston, praying a repeal of the late taxes; but that
Assembly being dissolved, Lord North objected to the
reception of their petition ;[1] yet, as petitioning the Parliament was the most decent and desirable mode of com-
promising the heats, many wished to accept it, and Dyson
proposed words to qualify that acceptance.   Lord North,
after some irresolution, yielded, and the further consideration of the resolutions was postponed to the next day,
when they passed by a great majority.[2]   Colonel Barré,

[1] The Petition was from 'the major part of the Council of the Province of
Massachusets Bay,' signed by Samuel Danforth the President of the Council.
Lord North contended that by the constitution of the colony the Council
could not act separate from the Government except in their legislative
capacity, and in that case the Governor was President of the Council.   Owing
to the recent dissolution, they could no longer act in their legislative capacity.
The President, therefore, had no authority to sign in that character.—(Cavendish's *Parliamentary Debates*, vol. i. p. 185.)—L. M.

[2] This debate and another on the same subject on the 8th of February are
reported in Cavendish, vol. i. pp. 191-225.—E.

in the debate, drew ridiculous portraits of the several Ministers.

On the 27th Wilkes was once more chosen Alderman of Farringdon Ward, without opposition. The same day he was carried before the House of Commons, attended by a great concourse of people, who, however, by his order soon dispersed, or behaved with singular decency. His committees too, who had regimented the mobs of London and Westminster, conducted them with composure and regularity. Lord Barrington moved that Wilkes might be confined to speak only to the two allegations of his complaint,—the alteration of the writ, and the subornation of witnesses.[1] The Opposition objected to the restrictions, and combated them till ten at night. Serjeant Glynn pleaded for Wilkes, and spoke with a clearness, argument, decency, and propriety, that was applauded by both sides; and though attacked by Norton and the Attorney-General, who called him *Wilkes's representative*,[2] he defended himself with a modesty that conciliated much favour. The debate turned chiefly on general warrants and libels: George Grenville defended the former, and himself, and the Lords Egremont and Halifax :—on the latter, to pay his court, he said that libels against Ministers were not to be regarded, but against the King were serious. Dyson, as usual, was shrewd, and, as usual, ill-treated by the Opposition; Colonel Barré, the day before, having baptized him by the name of *Mungo*, a black slave in a new farce called *The Padlock*,[3] who is described as employed by everybody in all jobs and servile offices. Burke ridiculed the Ministers as he had done the day before with greater applause; and Barré, repeating his attacks, was called to order by Rigby, whom he had described as a jolly, eating, drinking fellow, who finding himself now in a comfortable situation, seldom spoke. Being provoked at the interrup-

---

[1] This motion was made by Lord North. It was supported by Lord Barrington. See Cavendish, vol. i. pp. 120-1.—E.

[2] The Speaker decided this to be an improper expression.—L.M.

[3] *The Padlock* : a comic opera by Isaac Bickerstaffe was produced at Drury Lane in 1768.—E.

tion, Barré rejoined surlily, 'The gentleman denies being a Minister, and calls me to order; but I have not done with him yet.   Whether Minister or not, he lies in a bed[1] to himself; I do not envy him, nor would I have his principles to lie in his bed.'   This unpleasant attack thunderstruck Rigby, who coloured, and not choosing to have the last sentence explained, made no reply.   The House then divided, and the restrictions were carried by 278 to 131, Grenville and his friends being in the majority, as were Lord Granby, Sir Edward Hawke, and Conway.

Wilkes was then called in, seemed abashed, and behaved with great respect to the House.   He demanded to be admitted and to take the oaths as a member, which after some debate was refused on his being a prisoner.   His counsel were then called in, and were informed that they must confine themselves to the two points of his allegation; but it being then near midnight, the House adjourned to the 31st.[2]   The next day Conway told me, he and Lord Granby had agreed to stay away on the expulsion : having declared against violent measures, they would not concur in it ; and disapproving Wilkes's attacks on the Government, they would not defend him.

Wilkes appeared again before the House on the 31st. He complained that his character had been aspersed in the printed votes, which accused him of blasphemy, though he had not been convicted of it ; and demanded reparation. The case was this :—some time before, when the House, at the motion of Lord Clare, had sent for the roll of his conviction on the *North Briton* and *Essay on Woman*, it appeared that the clerk had forgotten to indorse them ; on which he had been ordered to indorse them as they ought to have been ; on which he wrote there the titles of *seditious libel* and *blasphemy*.   Dyson, who adjusted the votes for the Speaker, had (probably by design) inserted these titles in the votes.   When Martin the banker had

---

[1] Alluding to the Paymaster's place, which had been split into two, but was again given to Rigby alone.

[2] This debate is reported in Cavendish, vol. i. pp. 120-8.—L. M.

lately moved to admit Wilkes, and the House had refused on account of his condemnation for those libels, they were going to renew those words ; but Beckford objecting to the word *blasphemy*, the House had acquiesced, and intituled the piece *a profane and impious libel.* Norton now endeavoured to prove that he had been convicted of *blasphemy*, because it being in the charge, and he being brought in guilty of the premises, Norton inferred that he was convicted of it ; but Serjeant Glynn showed that in all indictments charges are ridiculously exaggerated, and though a man may be brought in guilty of a crime, half the articles of a charge are never attempted to be proved. Sir George Savile and Sir Joseph Mawbey stiffly maintained the same argument. Lord North, Dyson, and the Ministerial party as obstinately supported the contrary ground, till General Conway showed the injustice of the tenet, and that it was at most *constructive blasphemy* ; on which Sir George Savile joining him, and the House applauding, Dyson was forced to insert other palliating words—a great point gained to Wilkes, to have gotten rid of the actual condemnation for blasphemy. He then proceeded on his defence, and brought Curry, a printer, to prove the manner in which the *Essay on Woman* had been stolen from Wilkes by the means of Carteret Webbe, who had sent Curry to Carrington, the messenger to be paid for the theft. Curry showed and owned himself an infamous rogue ; and having first sold Wilkes, was now in his pay. Men were shocked at the treachery used towards Wilkes, and thence he again gained ground. The two Earls were then brought before the House. Wilkes only asked Lord Sandwich (the projector of the plot) if he knew of Curry being bribed by the Ministry, and being promised a place? The Earl answered, that he had promised him all proper protection, but had nothing to do with the disposition of public money. Lord March said, Kidgell had shown him the fragment of the *Essay on Woman,* and he had advised him to complain of it ; but had never seen Carteret Webbe till within the last four days. Webbe, now blind, sat there at the bar, and was grievously abused by Davenport, Wilkes's counsel.[1] At two in the morning the House adjourned the further consideration till the next day.[2]

Amongst these notorious personages, notice must be taken of Sir Fletcher Norton. He had been purchased for this business (for even his attachment to Lord Mansfield and the Court were not sufficient to secure his zeal, though the cause was so bad) by the place of Chief Justice in Eyre and a pension of £3000 a year. It was stipulated that Norton should quit the law, and be chief manager in the House of Commons; but no sooner was the bargain struck and the pension secured, than Norton, not caring to give up £7000 a year, which he got by his profession, pleaded that he could not *in honour* abandon his clients. His next *point of honour* was trying to prove by construction that Wilkes had been condemned of more than he had been condemned. Another acquisition to the Court was Sir Laurence Dundas, the rich commissary, a friend of Grenville, and now seduced from him by Rigby, another late friend of Grenville. Dundas commanded the votes of nine members. He demanded a peerage for himself, having acquired above eight hundred thousand pounds in less than four years of the late war—so far fairly that he had executed the commission on cheaper terms than any one else had offered. He was, besides, nobly generous; yet it would have been gross indeed to have raised him to the peerage on no other foundation than the money he had gained from the public. It was known too, that Prince Ferdinand had been on the point of hanging him on part of his contract not being furnished so soon as he had engaged it should be.[3]

---

[1] See *supra*, vol. i. p. 219, note 2. Webbe had been Member for Haslemere, 1754-68, but was now out of Parliament.—E.

[2] Norton does not appear to have taken part in this debate. The arguments ascribed to him by Walpole were used by Blackstone. See Cavendish, vol. i. pp. 128-131.—E.

[3] This surely was more disgraceful to the Prince than to Sir Laurence Dundas; but the Prince would no doubt have hanged, and with more reason,

Carteret Webbe's counsel was then heard in his defence, and to move compassion, pleaded before his face that he was decayed both in eyesight and understanding. Wilkes's counsel replied. Dr. Blackstone[1] then moved a long, obscure question, setting forth that Wilkes's complaint against Lord Mansfield was frivolous and trifling; and as the Courts below had pronounced that alteration of writs was not unusual, the charge was scandalous, as tending to calumniate the Chief Justice, and lessen the respect of the people for the law and the judges. He was seconded by a young Mr. Payne,[2] who spoke for the first time with much applause, though his language was wonderfully verbose. He was connected with Lord Mansfield, and as his speech was interlarded with law anecdotes, the person in whose behalf it was uttered was supposed to have assisted in the composition. Payne was a good figure and possessed himself well, having been accustomed to act plays in a private set; but his usual dialect being as turgid as Othello's when he recounts his

Lord George Sackville, if he had dared, and this did not obstruct that nobleman's promotion.—L. M. [A somewhat similar story is told of General Craufurd in the Peninsular War. He threatened to hang a commissary if certain rations were not ready at a given time. The commissary complained to Wellington, who replied : ' Then I should strongly advise you to get the rations ready; for if General Craufurd said he would hang you, by God, he 'll do it.—E.]

[1] Author of the *Commentaries on the Law*. He was a very uninteresting speaker, and was afterwards made a judge. [His principles being strongly Tory, drove him into a line of conduct on Wilkes's affair unlike the rest of his life, for in other respects he showed himself an honest, able, and amiable man. He probably regretted his subserviency to the directions of the Ministers, for he refused the office of Solicitor on Dunning's retirement, and was delighted to be raised on the following month to a seat on the Bench, which he held till his death, in 1780. An interesting life of him is prefixed to his Reports.—L. M.]

[2] Ralph Payne was at this time M.P. for Shaftesbury. He subsequently represented Camelford, Plympton, and Woodstock. In 1772 he was made a Knight of the Bath, and in 1795 raised to the Irish peerage as Baron Lavington. His manners were pompous and his political principles unstable, but he and his wife, the Saxon Baroness de Kelbel, enjoyed great social popularity both in England and Antigua, where he had property, and of which he was twice Governor. He died there on the 1st August 1807, when his title became extinct.—E.

conquest of Desdemona, he became the jest of his companions and the surfeit of the House of Commons. Serjeant Glynn showed the injustice of the motion, for as it was clear and allowed that the writ had been altered, had not the prisoner a right to plead that alteration in his own defence? Norton and the Crown lawyers were warm on the other side; on which Barré called them the heavy artillery of the Court; or rather, said he, they resemble the elephants in Eastern armies, which fall back upon and put their own troops in confusion. The Ministers maintained their point till very late at night, though the House gave many signs of disgust at the violence of their proceedings. At last George Grenville, with attention to Lord Mansfield, and yet disapproving the question, wished some middle and temperate method could be hit upon. The House loudly agreed with him, but Lord North and Norton stuck firm, and the latter declared he would divide the House, though he should be alone. The Ministerial party then cried out as loudly on that side; till Conway rose, and taking notice that a minute before everybody had roared for moderation, and now were again for violence, proposed that, instead of harsh words, they should correct the motion, and say, that the alteration of writs not being unprecedented, the charge against Lord Mansfield should be declared groundless. Grenville approved this, and even Norton, and that amendment was accepted without a division. Thurlow then, at past one in the morning, moved that Wilkes had not made out his charge against Webbe (though a letter had been produced from him to Curry and three other printers, bidding them take care to be uniform in their evidence, and though Curry had been subsisted at the expense of the Government), and that the charge was frivolous and groundless. If these last words, he said, were disputed, the debate must be adjourned to another day. The Opposition, weakly or fatigued, objected only to the latter words, and offered to acquiesce in the former part of the vote, if the censure was promised to be omitted;

with which Thurlow complied, and then carried the rest of his motion.[1]

On the 2nd, Wilkes was again heard; owned his preface to Lord Weymouth's letter, said he gloried in it, and only wished he had made it stronger. The Attorney-General moved to vote that preface a scandalous and seditious libel, tending to subvert all order and government. Sir George Savile moved the previous question. Grenville, and even Dr. Blackstone, opposed the Attorney's motion, as Wilkes ought to be tried for a libel at common law, and not by the Houses of Lords and Commons. Dyson reminded Grenville that he himself had brought a message from the King against Wilkes's *North Briton*; was it a greater violation of the privileges of the House of Commons to receive a message from the House of Lords than from the Crown? Grey Cooper[2] spoke well against mobs; Burke warmly against the Lords extorting evidence, and usurping powers. He called Lord Weymouth's letter a *bloody scroll*,[3] and dwelt much on the word *effectual* in the orders to the soldiers. Rigby asked if it would have been wise to order the soldiers to do their duty ineffectually? At past two in the morning the House divided; the courtiers were 239, the minority 135, Grenville and his friends, who were not above ten, being in the latter number. The House then agreed with the Lords and passed the censure.[4]

Soon after the division happened a singular event.

---

[1] This debate is reported in Cavendish, vol. i. pp. 131-8.—L. M.

[2] Secretary of the Treasury.

[3] This expression was not used by Burke, but by Wilkes, who apologised for it as too 'mild and gentle' for the occasion. Cavendish, vol. i. p. 140.—E.

[4] Dr. Blackstone spoke with unusual spirit, and put the case on the right grounds. Serjeant Glynn observed sensibly and fairly, 'Though that letter is not entirely free from all possibility of reprehension, there does not appear to be anything in it to subject the noble writer to Parliamentary censure, but I think it calculated to induce magistrates to exercise a power that ought not to be resorted to but in extreme cases. It does not sufficiently define the occasions upon which it is to be used. Most of the magistrates are uninstructed in the laws of the country, and likely to be misled by the terms of it.'—(Cavendish, vol. i. pp. 139-151.)—L. M.

Some hours before, Humphrey Cotes[1] sent for Sir William
Meredith out of the House, and told him Mr. Allen wanted
to speak with him.   Sir William said he did not know him,
and went back.   This Allen, who had been in the army,
had been deservedly abused in the House by Sir William
for persecuting the condemned chairmen, one of whom
had saved his life.   Sir William afterwards going to the
House, had been met by Allen, who demanded satisfaction.   Sir William said he did not know him ; if he had
injured him he would give him satisfaction next morning,
but would not occasion a disturbance then.   Captain
Walsingham Boyle (who had been concerned with Sir
William in saving the chairmen) hearing of this altercation, complained to the House of the violation of their
privileges by Allen's taking notice of what had passed in
the House.   This occasioned a heat and debate, which
lasted till half an hour after four in the morning, when
Allen was ordered into custody, and to be brought to the
bar the next day with Humphrey Cotes.

Allen absconded for some hours, but surrendered himself in the morning.   He was a handsome young fellow,
and had stolen a marriage with an idiot sister of the
Spanish Charles Townshend ; but he had such a savage
thirst of blood, that he had been broken by a court-
martial at Belleisle, for having forged and sent challenges
to six officers in the names of others.   Cotes was not
called upon by the House, but Allen was carried to their
bar, where he denied the charge,—both he and Cotes
having been so cautious as not to tell Meredith that the
occasion of the challenge was words spoken in the House :
yet Sir William and Captain Walsingham had heard, for
three days, that Allen was lurking about, and intended
to challenge one of them.   The House being satisfied of
the charge, and with the behaviour of the two members,
committed Allen to Newgate.

The same evening, Lord Barrington moved for the
expulsion of Wilkes, for the three libels—of the *North*

---

[1] A noted partisan of Wilkes.

Briton, the *Essay on Woman*, and the Preface to Lord Weymouth's Letter. The House sat again till three in the morning, when the expulsion was voted by 219 to 137. Grenville spoke against it as an accumulative charge, not one of the crimes alone being sufficient to deserve that punishment. Burke spoke admirably on the same side. Lord Granby and Sir Edward Hawke, who had declared so strongly against it, both voted for the expulsion. Conway kept away. Serjeant Glynn gained great fame by the candour of his conduct on the whole proceeding; owning, that as counsel for Wilkes, he had maintained points which he would not assert in the House. Wilkes himself made a very indifferent figure, showing neither parts nor quickness in his speeches or examination of the witnesses.[1]

The same day, Earl Cornwallis[2] kissed hands as Vice-Treasurer of Ireland, to make room for Norton to be Justice in Eyre. This worthless man, though disposed to the Court, as I have said, and originally employed in the

---

[1] Lord Temple wrote an interesting account of this debate to his sister, Lady Chatham, in which he says : ' My brother made what was universally deemed the best speech he ever made, against expulsion.'—(*Chatham Correspondence*, iii. 349-50). This speech was revised and circulated by Grenville himself, and may be read both in Cavendish, i. 158-76, and the *Parliamentary History*, xvi. 546-75. Wilkes was more offended by the unfavourable view taken of his conduct than gratified by the legal arguments in his favour, and his partisan, Almon, published a long and furious reply in the shape of a *Letter to the Right Honourable George Grenville*, etc.—E.

[2] Charles, second Earl Cornwallis. [He was the intimate friend of the Earl of Shelburne. A pleasing portrait is drawn of him by all contemporary writers. If the failure of his American campaigns, where he certainly proved no match for the self-taught commanders, whose ignorance it was the fashion of the day to ridicule, raised a strong presumption against his military talents, he met with great success in India, both as a soldier and an administrator. His conduct in Ireland during the Rebellion likewise does honour to his sagacity and benevolence. He was one of the few statesmen who inculcated the necessity of forbearance and concession in that misgoverned country,— and the coldness with which the Ministers received his remonstrances was the cause of his resignation. The mild dignity of his demeanour faithfully represented the leading traits of his character. He died in India in 1805, in his sixty-seventh year, leaving an only son, on whose decease, without male issue, the Marquisate (conferred on him in August 1792) became extinct.—L. M.]

prosecution of Wilkes, would not support his own principles—at least, his own inclinations—without this immoderate bribe. The Crown, though possessed of so much power by the disposition of honours, offices, and pensions, was sunk to the lowest contempt, and reduced to purchase every man whose vote or service it wanted, and thus was surrounded by none almost but those who had insulted and forced it to buy them. If, on the contrary, the King had tried by good and popular measures to secure the affections of the people, he might have maintained the balance against the parliamentary chiefs : but, having lost the hearts of the nation, his sole resource was the prostitution of honours and money to those who were most obnoxious to himself and the people.

Wilkes was no sooner expelled, than he again presented himself as candidate for the county of Middlesex, and in the *North Briton*, published a very bold address to the freeholders, in which, under the title of *the Administration*, he severely lashed the House of Commons. There was at this time an avowed, though very small republican party, the chiefs of which were Mrs. Macaulay, the historian, her brother Sawbridge, his brother-in-law, Stephenson, a rich merchant,[1] and Thomas Hollis, a gentleman of strict honour and good fortune, a virtuoso, and so bigoted to his principles, that, though a humane and good man, he would scarce converse with any man who did not entirely agree with his opinions. He had no parts, but spent large sums in publishing prints and editions of all the heroes and works on his own side of the question ; but he was formed to adorn a pure republic, not to shine in a depraved monarchy.[2]

---

[1] Mr. Stephenson was the son of Sir William Stephenson, Alderman of the Ward of Bridge Within, and Lord Mayor, 1764-5. I have been told that later in life he met with great losses in trade, which obliged him to make a composition with his creditors, but having subsequently retrieved his circumstances he paid everything in full.—L. M.

[2] Thomas Hollis repudiated the name of republican, and called himself a true Whig. He was unjustly suspected of being an atheist. Lord Chatham called him 'the happiest of beings, by dispensing continually happiness to

Pine.Pinxt.   Jas.Watson.Mezzo.

John Wilkes.

On the 10th, Mr. Seymour[1] moved a question, that condemnation for accumulated libels should not be made a precedent. Lord North proposed to alter the word *accumulated* into *many*, which being adopted, and the favourers of the motion then abandoning it, it was thrown out.[2]

The same day the liverymen of London met, and drew up instructions to their members against the proceedings of the House of Commons. Alderman Beckford attended that meeting, and told them, he should think it his duty to obey his constituents, even in points against his opinion ; and whereas they enjoined an attempt for triennial Parliaments, he wished they were to be annual. He declared too that he never would accept place or pension.

At the India House the Ministers were now successful, and prevailed by 290 voices against 250, to obtain the Company's agreement to pay to the public £410,000 annually, for five years, out of their newly-acquired territories.

Allen might have had his liberty, but refusing to ask pardon of Sir William Meredith, as the House enjoined, was continued in Newgate.

Mr. Grenville, though dipped with them in opposition, had never forgiven Lord Rockingham and his friends for succeeding him in power, and for repealing the Stamp Act, nor had ceased pelting them in pamphlets. Just before the Parliament met, he had written, or assisted in writing, a tract called *the State of the Nation*, in which they had been bitterly treated. Hoping union with him, at least willing to act with him in opposition, they had borne all former provocations. They now at last replied, in a large quarto called *Observations on the State of the*

others.'—(*Chatham Correspondence*, vol. iv. p. 269.) Hollis died suddenly on the 1st January 1774, aged fifty-three. His *Memoirs*, by Archdeacon Francis Blackburne, were privately printed in 1780. (London, 4to, 2 vols.) There is an amusing account of them in Walpole's *Letters*, vol. vii. 346-7.—E.

[1] Henry Seymour, nephew of Edward, eighth Duke of Somerset, and half-brother by the mother to Lord Sandwich, but attached to Grenville. [He was a groom of the Bedchamber, 1761-5, and represented Totnes from 1763 to 1768, Huntingdon, from 1768 to 1774, and Evesham, from 1774 to 1780. He died in 1805.—E.

[2] Cavendish's *Parliamentary Debates*, vol. i. pp. 226-7.—L. M.

Nation. It was drawn up by Edmund Burke, and did more honour to his talents as a writer than as a politician. The book solidly confuted Grenville, exposed him, and exploded his pretensions to skill in finance; but then it made all approach to him impossible, notwithstanding Lord Temple's endeavours to unite them. It almost as explicitly abjured Lord Bute,—a step the party two years after tried as injudiciously to recover, when it was too late. If the work did honour to the author and to his party's principles, yet it showed that that party was composed of impracticable men; and what was worse for their cause, it declared inviolable attachment to the Marquis of Rockingham, a weak, childish, and ignorant man, by no means fit for the head of Administration. Burke had far more shining abilities than solid conduct, and, being dazzled by his own wit and eloquence, expected that those talents would have the same effect on others. His ambition built airy castles, and would not attend to those parts of policy that make no immediate show. One quotation in his book was singularly happy, and in one line drew the portrait of Grenville,—*Vixque tenet lachrymas quia nil lachrymabile cernit.* It was in truth, Grenville's character to weep over woes that he wished to exterminate by rigour.[1]

---

[1] This brilliant composition has so many beauties, and excites throughout such deep interest, that it seems to be almost an abuse of criticism to note its defects. The author, of course, wrote under a strong bias, and for a temporary purpose; but his genius has cast a halo over his opinions and his political associates, which has enlisted posterity on his side.

The passage to which Walpole refers is in reply to some gloomy statements of the decline of our trade.—'What if all he says of the state of this balance were true? . . . If they [custom-house entries] prove us ruined, we were always ruined. Some ravens have always, indeed, croaked out this kind of song. They have a malignant delight in presaging mischief, when they are not employed in doing it. They are miserable and disappointed at every instance of the public prosperity. They overlook us, like the malevolent being of the poet,—

'Tritonida conspicit arcem
Ingeniis, opibusque, et festâ pace virentem,
Vixque tenet lachrymas quia nil lachrymabile cernit."

(Ovid, *Metam.*, vol. ii. pp. 794-6.)

—Burke's *Works*, 1815, vol. ii. pp. 74-5.—L. M.

CHAPTER XI

American Affairs.—Re-election of Wilkes.—His second Expulsion.—Payment of the King's Debts.—Third Election and Expulsion of Wilkes.—Loyal Demonstrations.—Address of the Merchants of London.—Riots.—Luttrell appears as Candidate for Middlesex.—Wilkes again Elected and Expelled.—Luttrell declared duly Returned.—Excitement of the Country.—Meeting of the Freeholders of Middlesex.—Close of the Session.

1769

THE flame Grenville had kindled still blazed in the Colonies. The Assembly of New York declared by vote, that they had an internal legislature of their own, and for that vote their Assembly was dissolved. The English Parliament addressed the King against the refractory behaviour of the colony of Massachusets Bay. He answered, he would give the orders they recommended, as the most effectual method of bringing the authors of the late disorders to condign punishment. The Administration prepared a severe bill of præmunire against the Colonies, and even meditated taking away the charter of Massachusets Bay. The Chancellor was exceedingly alarmed at these authoritative plans, and looked on them as partly levelled at him, who must have contradicted himself ignominiously if he joined in them, or risked the loss of the Seals if he opposed them ; but he prevailed on the Duke of Grafton to overrule the scheme, which had been the work of Lord Hillsborough, and it was laid aside. The Ministers, too, were sufficiently embarrassed with Wilkes.

He was once more re-chosen for Middlesex, February the 16th, without opposition, being proposed by two members, James Townshend and Sawbridge. The next day Lord Strange moved the House that Mr. Wilkes

having been expelled, was and is incapable of sitting in
the *present* Parliament.   This Beckford strongly opposed ;
and Dowdeswell proposed that his crimes should be
specified, as in the case of Sir Robert Walpole.   Grenville
seconded, and moved that mere expulsion should not be
deemed a foundation of incapacity.   When Sir Robert
Walpole was rejected on his re-election, Parliaments were
triennial ; being now septennial, the punishment of Wilkes
would be more than double.   T. Townshend[1] threatened
the House, that the freeholders of Middlesex would *in a
body*, petition the King to dissolve the Parliament.   On a
division for amendment of the question on Dowdeswell's
idea, 102 were for it, 224 against it ; and then the simple
question of expulsion being put, it was carried by 235 to
89.   Wilkes, however, the very next morning persisted in
offering himself again to the county of Middlesex, and
dispersed handbills for that purpose.

The next step of the Court was weak, and betrayed
their timidity.   Not satisfied with the interposition of the
House of Commons in favour of the condemned chairman,
against which no objection could lie, they had recourse
to an expedient, which, however humane, was liable to
censure from the novelty, and did occasion a controversy
in print.   It appeared, that by the negligence of Macquirk's
counsel, no surgeons had been called before the Bench at
his trial, to depose whether Clarke had died of his wounds
or not.   Had he had no counsel, the judges themselves
would have ordered surgeons to give their opinion on
Clarke's death.   On representation of this neglect to the
King, the Chancellor advised his Majesty to refer the consideration to a court of examiners, or surgeons.   Bromfield,
a surgeon, and an apothecary made a report, that in their
opinions, Clarke had not died of his wounds, but from a

---

[1] Cavendish says this threat was uttered by *James* Townsend.   Lord North
called him to order and said,—' every individual who shall be guilty of it, will
commit a breach of privilege, the most culpable, the most punishable, that the
annals of the country can produce.'—(*Parliamentary Debates*, vol. i. p. 229.)
The numbers on Dowdeswell's amendment were 228 to 102—(*Journals of
the House of Commons*, xxxii. 228.)—E.

bad habit of blood, inflamed by strong liquors, after the election. On this Balf was entirely pardoned, Macquirk respited till other favourable circumstances could be examined—and next month he was pardoned too.[1] The grand jury in the meantime found a bill against Sir William Beauchamp Proctor, Tatum, an agent of the Duke of Northumberland, and Broughter, a boxer and yeoman of the guard, for hiring the mob that committed the riot and murder at Brentford—but it came to nothing.

On the 21st a meeting was held at the London Tavern, of the principal gentlemen and merchants of Middlesex in the interest of Wilkes, when three thousand three hundred and forty pounds were subscribed to support him and his cause ; and a committee was appointed to promote the same throughout the Kingdom. The Assembly then formed themselves into a society which they denominated the Supporters of the Bill of Rights. The city of Bath also sent instructions to its members to the same tenor with those of the city of London.

On the 24th was read in the committee of the House of Commons, Sir George Savile's quieting Bill, called the Nullum Tempus, of which an account has been given before. When it had been rejected the last year, there had been a kind of promise that it should be suffered to pass another time ; yet the Ministers, to save as much as possible of prerogative, proposed that the prescription should be granted only for the last sixty years, instead of a current and constant prescription of sixty years against the Crown, as there is between subject and subject. This subterfuge of the Court was, however, rejected by 205 against 124—a wonderful event after the late triumphs of the Administration! Many causes contributed ; honesty probably operated on some, and indignation at the mean evasion attempted. Others who possessed Crown lands

---

[1] John Foot, a surgeon, gave evidence at the trial that Clarke had died of the wounds received at Brentford. The indignation aroused by the pardon of these men was strongly expressed by Burke and Junius. (Cavendish's *Debates*, i. 382 ; Woodfall's *Junius*, i. 446-61.)—E.

preferred the security of their property to present Court favour. The Bedford faction, for some political view, absented themselves, though probably not expecting the Duke of Grafton[1] would receive so total a defeat in a measure to which his own violence had given occasion. In short, that Parliament had some virtues, or some vices, which now and then prevented its being so universally servile as the preceding.[2]

On the 27th the Administration laid before the House the agreement with the East India Company, which after a long debate, in which it was rather discussed than contested, passed without a division, Grenville himself approving it. Lord Clive spoke against it, and gave an account of the bad posture of their affairs in India. He was answered by Governor Johnstone, who imputed those misfortunes to Lord Clive's own conduct, and even reproached him with the murder of the Nabob.[3]

---

[1] The bill was passed by the Lords without opposition, the Duke of Grafton alone saying that he thought it a very bad bill.

[2] The debate is well reported in Cavendish, vol. i. pp. 240-51.—L. M.

[3] Lord Clive endeavoured to prove the agreement to be unjust towards the Company—an opinion in which Mr. Grenville seems to have concurred, but 'four or five hundred thousand pounds is a bait too tempting to be rejected,' and he therefore gave no objection to the motion. Colonel Barré denounced with his usual vigour the constitution of the Company. After referring to the sentiment he had expressed in a former debate, 'that the management of a dominion containing sixteen millions of inhabitants, and producing a revenue of from four to eight millions a year, could not be wisely and safely managed by twenty-four gentlemen in Leadenhall Street,' he proceeded to say, 'The system of the direction, fluctuating as it does from year to year, must be ruinous. Faction, too, that has stolen into almost every public assembly, has found its way among them; at one time making a disadvantageous peace, at another time making one upon more advantageous terms; striking out new wars; not content with the revenues which they already have, but thirsting for more,—it is impossible but India must be a scene of confusion. Instead of this, you might, by the wisdom of your laws and the sagacity of your government, bring millions lying hid in the earth into this country, and at the same time snatch the people of India from the tyranny under which they have been accustomed to live. But instead of this, there is nothing but war from the Carnatic to the Deccan.' Mr. Burke appeared as the advocate of the Company, and defended the annual election of Directors, as a system under which the Company had prospered. 'Men,' he observed, 'continually watched over by their constituents are worked into

The borough of Southwark, and soon after the city of Bristol, sent instructions to their members. To stem the increasing torrent, the Court endeavoured to set on foot counter addresses of loyalty. The first attempt was unsuccessful: a meeting having been summoned in the City to express dissatisfaction at the assemblies in favour of Wilkes, not above thirty persons attended the citation, and they broke up in confusion: but in the county of Essex the Court were more prosperous; the Opponents having met to instruct their members, Rigby and Bamber Gascoyne prevailed on the sheriff and the gentlemen to address the King in high strains of loyalty—an example that was followed in few other places.

Yet under this unfavourable aspect did the Court venture on a measure of great import to themselves threatening much unpopularity, and yet not attended by any uncommon clamour. This was to demand of Parliament the payment of the King's debts. In truth, considering the expenses of the outset of a new reign, of a coronation, of a royal wedding, that the Crown had possessed no jewels,—the late King's having been bequeathed by him to, and re-purchased of, the Duke of Cumberland,—that the King had limited himself to a certain revenue,[1] and considering the numerous branches of the Royal Family, the debt incurred, especially by so young a Sovereign, and amounting to £513,000, could not be thought exorbitant. The Hanoverian revenues, indeed, were now in great part remitted into the Privy Purse; but the nation had nothing to do with that channel of supply, nor could pretend to

vigour. If the Direction was established 'for a number of years, they might form themselves into cabals.'—(Cavendish, vol. i. pp. 251-67.)—L. M.

[1] George III. at his accession accepted a Civil list of fixed amount instead of certain revenues which had been granted to his predecessors. Burke in 1770 estimated the income of the Crown as just under a million, exclusive of the revenues of Hanover and the Bishopric of Osnaburgh. (*Thoughts on the Cause of the Present Discontents.*—Works, 1815, vol. ii. 281.) In Burke's opinion :—' To have exceeded the sum given for the civil list, and to have incurred a debt without special authority of Parliament, was *prima facie* a criminal act.'—(*Ibid.* vol. ii. p. 311.)—E.

ask an account of it. The message of demand was made on the 28th to both Houses. In the Commons, Dowdeswell immediately moved that not only the particulars of the expense might be specified, but that the papers might distinguish under what Administration each debt had been incurred. This was intended to bring out that Lord Rockingham's Administration had been the most frugal. The Ministers pleaded that such minuteness would occasion much delay; and the motion was rejected by 169 to 89.[1] The same fate attended another motion made on March the 1st, by which the Opposition desired that the money might not be voted till the accounts had been examined; but this, as unreasonable, was overruled by 248 to 135.[2]

The next day the Lords entered on the same business. The Lords Temple, Lyttelton, and Suffolk showed the wanton impropriety of not examining the accounts before granting the money. Even Lord Rockingham attempted, though under great perturbation, to open his mouth; and, being very civil and very gentle, he was well heard. The Ministerial advocates, as if imposing a gabel instead of begging a supply for the Crown, behaved with insolence and scorn. Lord Sandwich made a mockery of unanimity, and desired to see who would vote against a measure that was personal to his Majesty. Lord Talbot, talking of the King, and by mistake saying *your Majesties* instead of *your Lordships*, corrected himself; but said he should have used the royal style by design if he had been talking to the mob.

The modesty of the Ministers was not more conspicuous in the other House. On the report from the Committee, Lord North made an able invective against popularity; and avowed that he had voted for every unpopular, and against every popular measure. Rigby went still further

---

[1] See Cavendish, vol. i. pp. 267-78. It is remarkable that Walpole should overlook the violent altercation which occurred in this debate between General Conway and Mr. Burke, in which, as far as can be collected from Cavendish, the latter had the advantage.—L. M.

[2] See Cavendish, vol. i. pp. 278-289.—E.

against instructions to members : asked what place was large enough to hold all that ought to give them ? ' They should meet,' said he, ' in Moorfields, which is the only spot that would give or receive instructions.' He talked of the two pamphlets on the State of the Nation, and declared he gave the preference to Grenville's. It was carried without a division to agree with the Report of the Committee ; which, of course, was in favour of granting the money.[1]   The Lords were as complaisant.   The

---

[1] In these debates on the Civil List very able speeches appear to have been made by Lord North, Mr. Grenville, Mr. Dowdeswell, and Mr. Burke.   An instructive account of them is given by Cavendish, though it is evident that he has failed in his attempt to convey an adequate representation of the brilliant eloquence of Burke.   The rapidity of Burke's utterance, and the late period of the debate in which he spoke, perhaps made this impracticable. He has done more justice to Lord North, whose defence of his political conduct is so illustrative of his general views, and of the course he pursued in Parliament, that I have ventured, notwithstanding its length, to insert it here.

' Those repeated changes of Administration have been the principal cause of the present grievance [the King's debts].   I lament it as much as any man can do. . . . Under an Administration, whose principles I approved, ten years ago I accepted a small office, and was contented with it ; those with whom I served know I never molested them on my own account.   I had formed principles from which I have never deviated,—principles not at all calculated for an ambitious man.   I thought the public had waged a glorious war ; and that that war would be concluded by a necessary peace.   It was never my idea to cry up the peace as the chef-d'œuvre of a great minister. The peace was an advantageous one ; because, in the situation in which the country then stood, it was better to come to such a peace, than to run the risk of another campaign.   If the Ministers had no other choice, they made a good choice ; if the case was otherwise, they made a bad one.   Whether they had or had not, never came to my ears.   I never considered the country so reduced that we could not recover.   A steady manly resistance of the impatience of those who wanted to ease themselves of the burdens left by the war, put the country at length into a situation to meet other wars.   Upon this system I have ever been against popular measures.   I do not dislike popularity ; but for the last seven years I have never given my vote for any one of the popular measures.   I supported the Cyder-tax with a view to the ease of the people, and I afterwards opposed the repeal of the tax—a vote of which I never repented.   In 1765, I was for the American Stamp Act ; the propriety of passing which I took very much upon the authority of the right honourable gentleman ; and when, in the following year, a bill was brought in for the repeal of that act, I directly opposed it ; for I saw the danger of the repeal. And when, again, in the year 1767, it was thought necessary to relieve the people from the pressure of taxation, by lessening the revenue to the extent

Opposition laboured to show that the principal load of the debt had been incurred during Lord Bute's Adminis- tration.   The Duke of Grafton provoking Lord Rocking- ham, the latter replied with spirit unusual to him, and said the Duke had braced his nerves.   The Court-Lords were 60 to 26.

To balance that success Burke endeavoured to revive the clamour on the massacre, as it was called, in St. George's Fields; and moved to inquire into it, and into the part taken by the Lords Weymouth and Barrington— but it was too late.   Sir William Meredith abandoned him, and Grenville discountenanced the motion, which was rejected by 245 to 39.[1]

On the 16th of March came on the third election for Middlesex.   One Charles Dingley,[2] a merchant, had offered himself, in the morning papers, as candidate, and appeared on the hustings at Brentford; but not a single freeholder proposing him, he slunk away, and drove to London as fast as he could.   Townshend and Sawbridge again proposed Wilkes, who was accepted with the greatest shouts of applause.   Yet the House of Commons, the next morning, again declared it a void election; even Grenville allowing it must be so.   Rigby hinted at Townshend and Sawbridge; but said, he would not name them—and though their conduct as members was most indecent and disrespectful to the House, the Ministers did

of half a million, I was against that measure also.   Then appeared on the public stage a strange phenomenon—an individual grown, by the popularity of the times, to be a man of consequence.   I moved the expulsion of Mr. Wilkes.   Every subsequent proceeding against that man I have supported; and I will again vote for his expulsion, if he again attempts to take his seat in this House.   In all my memory, therefore, I do not recollect a single popular measure I ever voted for—no, not even the Nullum Tempus Bill. I was against declaring the law in the case of general warrants.   I state this to prove that I am not an ambitious man.   Men may be popular without being ambitious; but there is rarely an ambitious man who does not try to be popular.'—(Cavendish, vol. i. p. 298.)—L. M.

[1] See Cavendish, vol. i. pp. 307-337, especially the speeches of Lord North, Mr. Burke, and Mr. Grenville.—L. M.

[2] See *supra*, p. 31, note 1, and the *Chatham Correspondence*, vol. iii. pp. 351-2.—E.

not dare to call them to account.[1]   On the contrary, fearing it would occasion louder clamour, should they leave the county without a member, they ordered a fourth writ to be issued, which only drew them into greater perplexity ; timidity and rashness being generally alternate. Burke, expecting that the measure would be to punish the obstinacy of the freeholders by issuing no more writs, had prepared an invective in that view, and vainly attempted to adapt his speech to the contrary sense.   Wedderburne, whose impudence was more dauntless, and who had actually been on the point of concluding a bargain with the Court, but had been disappointed, broke out, with all the rage of patriotism that had missed the wages of profligacy, and said, it was no wonder all respect for the House of Commons was lost, when, in the last Parliament, men had been obliged to follow such low creatures as Dyson and Bradshaw, as often as Mr. Conway and Mr. Charles Townshend had disapproved ministerial measures : 'nay,' added he, 'we all know that this is ordered by *secret influence*'—memorable words, as they fell from one who was a competent witness ; for though they pointed out Lord Bute, Wedderburne had been deep in his confidence, and marked him out now merely because Lord Bute had rather wanted the power than inclination to serve him.[2]

The University of Oxford were the next to display their zeal for the Court, and presented a loyal address ; so did Cambridge, Kent, and the merchants of Bristol. The same was attempted in Surrey, but agreed to by only part of the grand jury.   Liverpool, Lichfield, and Edinburgh followed, and, in general, all the Scotch boroughs,—which did but increase the opposite spirit, and contributed to the mortifications that fell on the Court from such injurious measures.   At a large meeting of the Common Council, previous to one intended at Guildhall,

---

[1] Whately reported to Grenville that he heard the question of the expulsion of Sawbridge and Townshend had been discussed in the Cabinet, and only negatived by a majority of two.—(*Grenville Papers*, iv. 418.)—E.

[2] This debate is reported in Cavendish, vol. i. pp. 345-355.—L. M.

for presenting an address, but twenty-one persons declared
for it, one hundred and forty-one against it; and the
latter voted an address of thanks to Turner,[1] the Lord
Mayor, who had distinguished himself on Wilkes's side.
Shropshire, Leicestershire, and the town of Coventry
joined in the incense to the King; but the latter with a
circumstance peculiarly ridiculous, and which proved how
much the enemies of the Constitution were charmed with
the arbitrary measures of the Court—for the address from
Coventry was drawn by a physician, so rancorously
Jacobite, that at church he always rose from his knees,
when the King was prayed for. The Supporters of the
Bills of Rights advertised against the Coventry address,
which, with the same unconstitutional views, had attacked
that society. Mankind might judge of a cause, in which
King George's and King James's friends were equally interested!—and what interest, but that of despotism, could
they have in common?

The last instance made the Court sick of that fulsome
flattery. The merchants of London, to the number of
six or eight hundred, amongst whom were Dutch, Jews,
and any officious tools that they could assemble, having
signed one of those servile panegyrics, set out in a long
procession of coaches to carry it to St. James's. The mob
accompanied them, hissing and pelting. When they
came to the end of Fleet Street, they found the gates of
Temple Bar shut against them. Another mob was posted
at Gray's Inn Lane. The coaches turned down lanes and
alleys wherever they could, and not a third part arrived
at the palace. Mr. Boehm, Chairman of the East India
Company,[2] concealed the address under the seat of his
coach, which he was forced to quit, and take shelter in a

---

[1] Samuel Turner, of Mincing Lane, Lord Mayor, 1768-9, resigned his
gown as Alderman owing to ill health (10th October 1775), and died on the
23rd February 1777.—E.

[2] Edmund Boehm became a Director of the East India Company in 1784,
but was never Chairman. The names of 'the Merchants Traders and other
principal inhabitants of the City of London,' who signed this address are
given in the London *Gazette* for 25th March 1769 (No. 10924).—E.

coffee-house. In the meantime a hearse, drawn by two black and two white horses and hung with escutcheons representing the deaths of Clarke at Brentford and of Allen in St. George's Fields, appeared in the streets, and was driven to the gates of St. James's, where the attendant mob hissed and insulted all that entered the Court. The Ministers, who had received no intimation of this pageant, remained trembling in the palace ;[1] and all they did was to order the grenadiers to defend the entrance till the magistrates could arrive and read the Riot Act. At last, Earl Talbot took courage, and went down with his white staff, which was soon broken in his hand. He seized one man, and fourteen more of the rioters were made prisoners. The Duke of Northumberland was very ill treated ; and the Duke of Kingston,[2] coming from a visit from Bedford House, was taken for the Duke of Bedford, and was so pelted, that his coach and new wedding liveries were covered with mud. It was half an hour past four ere the address could be carried to St. James's ; and then was not presented by the Chairman, who was not in a condition to appear. At night, a proclamation was issued against riots. Ten of the rioters were discharged : the grand jury

---

[1] Yet it had been mentioned that very morning in the newspapers as intended.

[2] Evelyn Pierpoint, the last Duke of Kingston, K.G. He was then just married to the famous Miss Chudleigh—a marriage afterwards disallowed by the House of Lords. [The Duke was the only son of Lord Newark, only son of the first Duke of Kingston. His father died at the early age of twenty-one, and he had the misfortune to be brought up by his grandfather, a haughty, selfish, licentious man, who appears to have been equally a tyrant in his family and out of it. Thus he became bashful and dull, and displayed few if any of the talents which had characterised his race, and were so evident in his aunts, Lady Mary Wortley Montagu and Lady Mar. He raised a regiment in 1745, which is often mentioned in the history of that campaign as Kingston's light horse, and, what was not then common with Peers, he served with it. He died at Bath in September 1773. The 'Duchess' survived him till 1788, when she died at Paris, aged sixty-eight. —L. M. Elizabeth Chudleigh had been privately married on 4th August 1744 to the Hon. Augustus John Hervey, afterwards third Earl of Bristol (see *supra*, vol. ii. p. 124, note 2), and on 8th March 1769 went through the ceremony of marriage with the Duke of Kingston. She was convicted of bigamy in April 1776.—E.]

threw out the bills against the other five.   Such was the consequence of an unpopular Court, at once affecting popularity, and affecting to despise it !

Had they been content with sillily assuming a share in the affections of the people, which they did not possess, no great mischief had been done.   By provoking their resentment in the same breath, they had well nigh driven the people into rebellion ; and, by making the House of Commons the instrument of their irregularities, they effected a contempt for Parliaments, which, perhaps, did not displease the machinators.   Liberty stood in an alarming position : her buckler, the Parliament, was in the hands of the enemy, and she was reduced to beg that enemy to break that buckler—an alternative of almost equal danger, whether granted or refused.   It required a man of the firmest virtue, or a ruffian of dauntless pro-stitution, to undertake the office of opposing Wilkes in the decisive contest for the county of Middlesex.   There was a young officer, called Colonel Lutterell, whose father, Lord Irnham, was devoted to Lord Bute.   They were descended of a good Irish family, who had been attached to and had betrayed King James the Second ; and the morals and character of both father and son, especially of the former, were in no good estimation.   The father had parts, wit, and boldness : [1] the son affected to be a bravo, too, but supported it ill.   The son was pitched upon by the junto for candidate for Middlesex ; and Lord Holland and his sons openly espoused him.   This last circumstance, and the zeal of the Scots, crowned his unpopularity ; and lest it should not, Wilkes gave out that Lutterell was to be rewarded with a daughter of Lord Bute.   One of the race, not long after, attained a far more elevated match.

So desperate did Lutterell's cause appear, that great bets were made on his life ; and at Lloyd's coffee-house, it was insured for a month.   A third candidate soon appeared, one Captain Roache, another duelling Irishman,

---

[1] Lord Irnham, on a family quarrel, afterwards challenged his son to fight.   [See more of the family, *supra*, p. 145, note 4.—E.]

supposed to be selected by Wilkes, as a proper antagonist to Lutterell.

The struggle now became very serious. The House of Commons party—at least in the approaching violence—affected the tone of legality, and ordered the sheriffs to call on the magistrates to attend and keep the peace at Brentford. On the other hand, a new indictment was preferred at Hickes's Hall[1] against Macquirk, the chairman, for the murder of a constable; but the grand jury would not find the bill; yet the next month a new bill was found against him, and he was forced to abscond. The Treasury offered a reward of £500 for discovering the person who, at the procession of the merchants, had, with a hammer, broke the chariot of one Ross, an aged merchant, and wounded him in several places. The celebrated and unknown writer Junius threw his firebrands about, among so many combustibles, but aimed them chiefly at the head of the Duke of Grafton.[2]

But though the Court affected to proceed according to law, its votaries acted as if a martial campaign was opened. An advertisement on Lutterell's side called on *gentlemen* to accompany and defend him, and not to suffer the mob to govern. Captain Roache, at the same time, advertised that he acted in concert with Wilkes; and told Lutterell, that if there should any disorder arise, he should ask no questions but of him. Lutterell replied, that he would not fight till after the election. The Duke of Northumberland fearing for his own popularity, gave out that he had influenced no votes on either side.

On the 12th, Colonel Lutterell proceeded to Brentford with a much smaller troop of gentlemen than he had expected; and the mob having assembled before his door,

---

[1] The Sessions House of the County of Middlesex, St. John's Street, Clerkenwell. It was built in 1612 at the cost of Sir Baptist Hickes, and was the scene of the trial of the regicides, and of William Lord Russell. It was pulled down in 1782, and a new building, still in use, was built on Clerkenwell Green.—E.

[2] The date of the first letter published by Junius is the 21st of January.—L. M.

that little band of heroes stole away to the election by
breaking down the wall of the garden behind Lord
Irnham's house. This prevented their rendezvous at
Holland House, where a great breakfast had been prepared for them.   Stephen Fox,[1] Lord Holland's son,
proposed Lutterell, as Mr. Townshend did Wilkes.
Townshend desired the people to behave with temper and
decency; told 'them, that was no time to be unruly: if
they should be denied justice, then would be the moment
to defend themselves by the sword. For Wilkes were
given 1143 votes; for Lutterell, 296 ; for Serjeant Whitaker, who had thrust himself into the contest,[2] only 5 ; for
Captain Roache, not one—but he was hissed, laughed at,
and forced to retire, it being suspected that the Court had
bought him.

While this business was in agitation, the House of
Commons voted the militia perpetual, on a division of 84
to 79.   Beckford and Barré abused the Rockingham
party ; and each faction avoided taking part with Wilkes
and the Supporters of the Bill of Rights—a disunion that
made the Court amends for the errors of their own conduct.

Wilkes being returned by so great a majority, was again
rejected by the House: and the Ministers avowed that
they intended, according to precedent, to substitute
Lutterell on the poll, as being the legal candidate who
had had the greatest number of voices ; and the sheriffs
were ordered to attend next day on purpose. General
Conway strongly supported that intention, for the dignity
of Parliament. He had studied the case laboriously, and
persuaded himself that it was founded on the law of Parliament ; yet neither he nor its warmest advocates could
produce a parallel case, all the precedents quoted for
establishing the second person on the poll having happened

---

[1] Elder brother of Charles Fox, and M.P. for Salisbury. He succeeded
his father as second Baron Holland in July 1774, and died on the 26th
November following, aged twenty-nine.—E.

[2] William Whitaker, King's Serjeant, gained sufficient notoriety by his
antagonism to Wilkes, to be ridiculed in Foote's *Lame Lover* (1770), under
the name of Serjeant Circuit. He died on the 17th October 1777.—E.

only where the rejected person had been incapacitated by
Act of Parliament, as minors, etc.; whereas Wilkes lay
under no legal incapacity, but had been declared incapable
by a vote of one House only, which does not constitute a
law. Had Conway, Sir Edward Hawke, and Lord Granby
been firm to their first resolution, the Court would not
have ventured on such obnoxious and alarming precedents.
It was not less prejudicial, that Lord Chatham, though so
long announced by Lord Temple, did not appear during
that whole session; whether still temporising with the
Court, or that his intellects were yet too disordered, had
he stood forth the champion of Wilkes, at that crisis, it
might have shaken the predominance of the Court.
Norton himself was irresolute; shuffled at the consultations
held at Lord North's, and though bought to be on his own
side, could not be steady to it. The House again endeavoured to avoid mention of Townshend and Sawbridge;
but Edmondson,[1] a foolish Scot, insisted on having the
list read of those who had proposed Wilkes—yet no
notice ensued—though Townshend, to force out the name
of Lord Holland's son, asked who had proposed Lutterell?

The next day, though Saturday, the House sat, and the
debate lasted till two o'clock on Sunday morning, when it
was carried to admit Lutterell by only 197 voices to 143—
so little was the Court sure of their majority on so violent
a measure! Some of their friends quitted them. Harley,
the Lord Mayor, fearing for his personal safety in the
City, was permitted by the Duke of Grafton to vote
against the vote: and several Tory members for counties
absented themselves not to offend their constituents,—
evidence how little addresses had spoken the real sense of
the counties. Burke and James Townshend were severe
against the measure; Serjeant Glynn and Grenville[2]

---

[1] Archibald Edmonstone of Duntreath, Stirlingshire, represented the county
of Dumbarton 1761-80, and again 1790-6. From 1780 to 1790 he sat for the
Ayr burghs. In May 1774 he was created a Baronet, and died on the 20th
July 1807, aged eighty-nine.—E.

[2] Mr. Grenville spoke twice in this debate. Early on Saturday he was
called up by an observation of Mr. Onslow that Alderman Beckford was not

temperate, and the latter much applauded. Beckford, on
the military procession of the gentlemen, said it put him
in mind of Muley Ishmael, King of Morocco, who, when
he meditated a murder, put on his yellow sash. When
gentlemen in lace appeared, it announced a massacre: and
he compared the times to those of Rehoboam, who, rejecting the advice of his father's counsellors, followed that of
the young men, by which he lost ten tribes, and reigned
over the two little ones (Scotland). Much complaint was
made of the arbitrary doctrines suggested by the writers
on the side of the Court. Norton, Lord North, and the
Attorney-General De Grey spoke firmly for Lutterell.
Stephen Fox indecently and indiscreetly said, Wilkes had
been chosen only *by the scum of the earth*[1]—an expression
often retorted on his family, his grandfather's birth being of
the lowest obscurity. Young Payne, in another pompous
oration, abused the Supporters of the Bill of Rights,
protesting, on his honour, that his speech was not premeditated; but, forgetting part, he inadvertently pulled it
out of his pocket in writing! Charles Fox, with infinite
superiority in parts, was not inferior to his brother in

at liberty to reason against a resolution of the House of Commons. 'Sir,'
said he, in a tone exceedingly animated, 'the man who will contend that a
resolution of the House of Commons is the law of the land, is a most violent
enemy of his country, be he who or what he will. The law of the land, an
Act of Parliament, is to be the guide of every man in the kingdom. No
power—not an order of the House of Commons can set that aside, can
change, diminish, or augment it. I do say, and I will maintain that ground
—let any gentleman call me to order—that the law of the land, an Act of
Parliament, cannot be altered, enforced, augmented, or changed by a vote of
either House of Parliament. That, I say, is the law of this country.'
Immediately after this speech Mr. Grenville spat blood.—(Cavendish, vol. i.
pp. 370-1.)

At a later period of the evening Mr. Grenville entered fully into the
questions of the House, and discussed with great ability the celebrated cases
of Ashby *v.* White, and Rex *v.* Lord Banbury, where in the former instance
the decision of the House of Commons, and in the latter of the House of
Lords, had not been recognised by the courts of law.—L. M.

[1] This expression was attributed by mistake to Charles Fox in Cavendish's
account of this debate (vol. i. pp. vii, 377, 378). Sir Stephen Fox, the
first Lord Holland's father, is said to have been a choir boy in Salisbury
Cathedral.—E.

insolence.[1] Lutterell, the preceding night, had been assaulted by persons unknown, as he quitted the House ; and, for some months, did not dare to appear in the streets, or scarce quit his lodging. He was hissed out of one of the theatres ; and going afterwards to Dublin, and attending the debates of the House of Commons there, heard himself named with very opprobrious terms, which he resenting, the member answered with a firmness that Lutterell declined encountering.

As the colonies were not less disposed to mutiny than the capital, Governor Pownal, as a step to a repeal of the American duties, which had produced but two hundred and seventy pounds, moved to appoint a Committee to consider the state of America. Conway, who knew it was intended to repeal the new duties the next year, and who, for the sake of peace, wished to give that prospect to the colonies, moved that only [then] those duties should be considered : but Lord North, whether from firmness, pride, or jealousy of Conway, objected strongly, and said, it was below the dignity of the House to hold out any such hopes ; and though the confusion increased so fast that the stocks fell, from apprehensions of a rebellion, the obstinacy of the Ministers would not palliate any part of the disorders. Conway would not increase the flame by dividing the House, and the motion was rejected.[2] The session was no sooner at an end, than the Ministers gave assurances of repealing the taxes.

Happily for peace, the Opposition was divided. Wilkes and his friends inclined to riots and tumult. Sawbridge, and the more real patriots, encouraged by Lord Rockingham, were for proceeding more legally and temperately. Yet the aspect was so gloomy, that the town was surrounded by troops, and no officers suffered to be absent without leave.

[1] The debate is reported in Cavendish, vol. i. pp. 366-86.—L. M.

[2] An account of the debate is given in Cavendish, i. 391-401. Conway's proposal was to 'agree to take the Act into our consideration next session.' The decision to retain the tea duty, when the other taxes were abolished, was only carried in the Cabinet by the casting vote of Lord North.—E.

The Court of Aldermen, in the meantime, heard the opinion of counsel, on the eligibility of Wilkes for alderman. De Grey and Dunning, Attorney and Solicitor-Generals, Yorke, and the Serjeants Glynn and Lee, pronounced in his favour; but Norton, the Recorder and Common-Serjeant,[1] dissenting, ten aldermen to six rejected him.[2]

The supporters of the Bill of Rights were more propitious, and agreed to pay as far as five thousand pounds of his debts, but compromised with his creditors at five shillings in the pound; yet promising to pay more, if the collection to be made round England in the summer should answer,—a fund that produced nothing.

On the 27th, a very numerous meeting of the freeholders of Middlesex was held at Mile-end, when they were informed that the meeting had been so long deferred on account of the number of articles to be inserted in the petition which it was proposed to present to the King against the Administration. It was then read, unanimously approved, signed by as many as could sign, that night, and ordered to be left at the proper places for other subscriptions; and to be presented to his Majesty by Serjeant Glynn, Sawbridge, Townshend, and several more—Sawbridge desiring that nobody would attend the delivery, that they might not be misrepresented as riotous and rebellious.

Two days after, being the last day for receiving petitions, and the session on the point of concluding, Sir George Savile, in a very thin house, presented a petition, signed by a few freeholders, against Lutterell, and desired to have the consideration postponed to the next session, or to have a call of the House, with orders sent to the sheriffs of

---

[1] Thomas Nugent held the post of Common-Serjeant from 1758 until his death on 18th May 1790.—E.

[2] The Court of Aldermen did not dare to enforce this decision. On his release in April 1770, Wilkes writes to his daughter: 'I was sworn into office without any opposition; and all the aldermen present took me by the hand, and wished me joy, with great *apparent* cordiality.'—(Almon's *Memoirs of Wilkes*, 1805, iv. 25.)—E.

counties to inform the members of the intended business ;
but that proposal was rejected, and the petition was
allotted a hearing on the following Monday, by 94 of the
Court party to 49. It was accordingly heard on May the
8th. Serjeant Whitaker, one of the late candidates, and
Graham, an esteemed Scotch lawyer,[1] were counsel for
Lutterell ; Serjeant Adair [2] and Mr. Lee [3] for the petitioners. Dr. Blackstone, who argued for the incapacity
and expulsion of Wilkes, was severely confuted out of his
own Commentaries on the Law ; [4] and George Grenville

[1] Afterwards the Right Hon. Sir Robert Graham, one of the Barons of the
Exchequer. He died in 1836, at the great age of ninety-one. He believed
himself to belong to the Montrose family. It is more certain that he was the
son of a schoolmaster at Dalston. His personal accomplishments and
amiability made him a general favourite throughout life, which perhaps
prevented his attaining any considerable reputation as a lawyer.—L. M.

[2] James Adair, well known at this time both as sound lawyer and as a strong
partisan of Wilkes. He became a Serjeant-at-law on the 28th April 1774
and a King's Serjeant in 1782. He succeeded Glynn as Recorder in 1779,
and was appointed Chief Justice of Chester in 1797. He sat for Cockermouth
from 1775 to 1780, and for Higham Ferrers from 1793 until his death on 21st
July 1798. Adair was for some years in close political connection with Fox,
but separated from him on the outbreak of the French Revolution.—E.

[3] John Lee, or, as he was usually termed, 'honest Jack Lee,' was a sound
lawyer, and for many years had the lead on the Northern Circuit, where his
practice was very considerable. He excelled, Lord Eldon has recorded, in
cross-examination.—(Twiss's *Life of Lord Eldon*, vol. i. pp. 107-8.) A brief
blunt way of expressing himself, much originality, and frequent sallies of a
wit, which, though not of an elevated character, was very amusing, gave him
a short-lived celebrity. He was Solicitor-General from April to July 1782
and from April to November 1783. In the great debate of the 17th February
1783, on Lord Shelburne's Peace, he took a prominent and not very judicious
part. He succeeded Wallace as Attorney-General in the November following,
and held that office till the Duke of Portland was dismissed. He died at
Staindrop, in the county of Durham, in August 1793, leaving, it was said, a
great estate.—L. M.

[4] Mr. Grenville cited from Blackstone's *Commentaries* (first edition, vol. i.
pp. 169-170), the passage enumerating the nine cases of disqualification (of
which cases expulsion was not one), and ending—' but subject to these restrictions and disqualifications, every subject of the realm is eligible of common
right.' In the editions, *subsequent to Wilkes's* case, the sentence goes on,
' though there are instances wherein persons, in particular circumstances, have
forfeited that common right and been declared ineligible *for that Parliament*
by a vote of the House of Commons, or *for ever* by an Act of the Legislature.'
This difference in the two editions led to the favourite toast at political

as roughly handled by Norton. Charles Fox, not yet twenty-one, answered Burke with great quickness and parts, but with confidence equally premature. The House sat till half an hour past two in the morning, when Lutterell's seat was confirmed by 221 against 152.

As the house was now to rise, and Captain Allen would, of course, be discharged, it was apprehended that he would challenge Meredith and Walsingham; to prevent which, the House enjoined them both to accept no challenge from him, but to lay before a justice of peace the information that had been given to the House of his conduct, that he might be bound over to his good behaviour. Captain Walsingham said, he would certainly obey their commands, but hoped they did not expect, if Allen should attack him in the street, that he would not defend himself. Allen was discharged; abused Walsingham the next day in the papers, and then sank into obscurity.

Wedderburne, who had been brought into Parliament by Sir Laurence Dundas, the rich commissary, but, on being disappointed of a bargain with the Court, had voted on the opposite side, now vacated his seat, to leave Sir Laurence at liberty to choose a more compliant, or less interested member.

The turbulent aspect of the times, and the perilous position into which the Court had brought itself by the violent intrusion of Lutterell, naturally pointed out coalition to their several enemies. Accordingly, the Marquis of Rockingham and George Grenville, at the head of their respective factions, dined together at the Thatched House Tavern, St. James's Street, and agreed to support the cause of Opposition in their several counties during the summer; but the tempers of the leaders were too dissimilar, their object too much the same, and the resentment of Grenville for past offences too implacable to admit of cordial union.

---

meetings of 'The first edition of Doctor Blackstone's *Commentaries.*' Mr. Grenville's speech is given by Cavendish, vol. i. pp. 430-1, where, however, it is not so severe or powerful as the accounts of it in Walpole and Junius (*Letters*, xviii., xix.) would lead one to expect.—L. M.

The same day the King put an end to the session. He was much insulted in his passage to the House of Lords, and heard still worse aspersions on his mother.

On the 24th of May, the petition of the freeholders of Middlesex was presented to the King by Serjeant Glynn and six others. Another from Boston was carried by Colonel Barré.

CHAPTER XII

1769

I MUST now turn to foreign affairs, or events connected with them.

In the conclave, the Jesuitic party, alarmed at the demand made by the Bourbon Crowns of suppression of the Jesuits, had fixed on Cardinal Chigi for Pope—but miscarried. The French and Spanish Ambassadors told that faction, that had they elected him, they alone would have enjoyed him; insinuating that he would not have been acknowledged by the allied Crowns. Cardinal Bernis was despatched to Rome, with orders to put a negative on any candidate but Cardinal Ganganelli; and succeeding, was named Ambassador to the new pontiff.[1]

---

[1] The Cardinal was drawn from the obscurity in which he had lived since his disgrace in 1758 for the purpose of this mission. He continued Ambassador at Rome until his death, in 1794, in his eightieth year. A memoir of him, by the Abbé Feletz, of the French Academy, forms one of the best-written articles in the Biographie Universelle. It would be more valuable if it were less of an éloge. The Cardinal judged wisely in opposing the Austrian alliance, but, like other French statesmen, he took care to make his opposition subservient to his interest. Indeed, there is little either in his moral or political conduct to deserve commendation until he was securely settled at Rome. He owed his elevation entirely to Madame de Pompadour,

He was a Roman monk of the lowest extraction, and had exercised all the affected virtues of his order with a perseverance worthy of the ambition of Sixtus Quintus. But though his success was adequate, the times demanded talents of another complexion ; and though Ganganelli's address was as well suited to retrieve the affairs of the Church as some of his ablest predecessors had been to build up its greatness, yet no abilities could reconcile the blackest and most revengeful set of men to their own destruction ; and though Ganganelli endeavoured by temporizing and delays to ward off the blow that would deprive the Papal throne of its most trusty satellites, yet the two Crowns at last forced from him the fatal Bull that abolished the order and exposed the Pope to the vengeance of the Jesuits, who became his assassins, when, in spite of himself, he had been obliged to discard them as his champions.[1]

The ball at Court on the King's birth-night was disturbed by a quarrel for place between the Russian and French Ambassadors. France yields the precedence to nobody but to the Emperor of Germany ; and the Comte du Châtelet, their Minister here, had received positive orders not to give place to the Russian. Du Châtelet was enough disposed to assume any airs of superiority : at Vienna, on a former embassy, he had embroiled his court with the Imperial by wrong-headed insolence. He was warm, captious, and personally brave. Count Czernichew was magnificent and ostentatious, but profuse

whose favour he had earned by betraying to her the King's intrigue with Madame de Choiseul—a secret with which that lady had imprudently intrusted him.—(See more of him in the *Mémoires de Duclos* (1864), vol. ii. pp. 259-331 ; Lacretelle's *Histoire de France*, vol. iii. p. 161.)—L. M.

[1] The disapprobation with which Ganganelli was known to regard the policy of the Jesuits procured him the support of France and Austria, and consequently his election. It was not, however, until the year 1773 that he issued the brief for the extinction of the order. The troubles in which this step involved him shortened his life. His advanced age, for he was sixty-four years old, the cares of Government, and his sedentary, studious habits, were held insufficient causes for his death, without adding it to the catalogue of the crimes of the Jesuits ; and volumes were written to support and to repel the charge.—L. M.

of civilities and attentions, and no ways quarrelsome. He was sitting next to Count Seilern, the Imperial Ambassador. Du Châtelet came behind, and crowded himself in between them, taking place above Czernichew. This occasioned much pushing and struggling, and the Russian told the Frenchman he was very impertinent, and then quitted the bench. As they left the room when the ball was finished, Count Czernichew's coach drawing up, he offered to set Du Châtelet at home, which was accepted ; but, being entered, Du Châtelet proposed that they should decide the quarrel with their swords ; and they endeavoured to go into St. James's Park, but the gates were shut. It was said that Du Châtelet made apologies for his behaviour, and declared that he had meant no personal rudeness. On the other hand, he was allowed to have shown most spirit throughout the dispute ; yet he was not without much anxiety how his conduct would be regarded at home, where it was rather wished to soften the Court of Russia, now beginning to triumph over the Turks. But Du Châtelet had two powerful mediators—the eagerness of the Duc de Choiseul to humble the Czarina, and his inclination for Madame du Châtelet, not only the favourite of his all-powerful sister, the Duchess de Grammont, but her secret rival with him. Madame du Châtelet was a handsome and very sensible woman, but of an indolence beyond example. The Duc de Choiseul liked her, and she was far from averse to him, yet had resisted his love and that liberality and power which had thrown every other French woman he had a mind to into his arms. Du Châtelet, indeed, had chosen not to leave her exposed to too great temptation ; and, notwithstanding her extreme indifference, which here only served to give offence, had obliged her to attend him on his embassy.[1] Count Czernichew was recalled, with

---

[1] The Count du Châtelet, afterwards Duc, has been mentioned with respect by the French historians of the day, and his name is associated with more important transactions than this miserable affair. The King's esteem raised him to the command of the guards on the death of the Duc de Biron. In common with other enlightened men attached to the Court, he supported

apparent dissatisfaction.[1]   He was not fortunate in his embassies : he had been nominated to that of China, but the Chinese monarch forbade his approach, declaring he would have no alliance with a murderess.   Du Châtelet's intemperance in the King's presence was very ill taken here, where his forwardness, and his wife's disgusting coldness, had raised no prejudice in their favour.   The King took every opportunity to distinguish the Russian by the most marked civilities; and it was proposed to signify the royal displeasure by acquainting the foreign Ministers *that there was no rank in the box allotted to them at the balls at Court; and that his Majesty gave that notice from having been extremely offended at what had passed.* Lord Hertford, as Lord Chamberlain, was to give the notice; but fearing it was too strongly worded not to give great disgust in France, he refused to make the notification, unless authorized by the Privy Council.   On this the message was reconsidered, and the latter part was changed for the words *to prevent disagreeable altercations for the future,*—a medium still liable to ridicule; for how could a ball at Court be a private ball, when everybody was taken out to dance by the Lord Chamberlain according to their rank?   It was, in effect, depriving the foreign ministers alone of rank on those occasions.[2]

the reforms best calculated to ameliorate the condition of the people. His popularity caused him to be fixed on as a successor to Brienne in the Presidentship of the Council,—a dangerous honour, which he wisely declined. He was, however, one of the early victims of the Reign of Terror, and after a fruitless attempt to commit suicide, perished by the guillotine on the 13th of December 1793. His wife soon followed him to the scaffold.—L. M.

[1] It was believed that he had acted under secret instructions from the Empress; although, in conformity with the practice of the Russian Court, he was left to bear the blame of failure. On his return to St. Petersburg he was placed at the head of the marine department, and held that post during several years, with a very poor reputation. He escaped dismissal only because Catherine made it a principle to change as seldom as possible either her Ministers or Ambassadors.—(Tooke's *Life of Catherine the Second,* vol. i. p. 304; vol. ii. p. 46.)—L. M.

[2] Circulars were addressed by Lord Rochford to the British Ministers at foreign Courts with an account of this transaction.—(See letter to Sir A. Mitchell, in Ellis's *Original Letters,* 2nd series, vol. iv. pp. 519-21.)—L. M.

This squabble, and almost every other business of more importance, was forgotten in the stormy scene that succeeded the rising of Parliament. Wilkes on his part, Lord Shelburne and Beckford on theirs, laboured incessantly during the whole summer to spread the flame of dissatisfaction on the violent measure of forcing Lutterell into Parliament; and though it caught not universally, the spirit of remonstrating and petitioning made such progress in several counties and boroughs, as alarmed the Court, and still more the sober part of mankind; who, though disapproving the conduct of the Administration, were apprehensive of such tumults, if not risings, as might, by not being strong enough to correct, throw additional power into the hands of the Crown—a prospect that, perhaps, lessened the panic of the Court, otherwise sufficiently apt to tremble. The supporters of the Bill of Rights circulated a letter, recommending subscriptions for Wilkes; but found men more willing to sign remonstrances than to contribute their money. Townshend and Sawbridge were chosen Aldermen of London and Sheriffs of Middlesex.

The same day, the livery of London determined to petition the King on grievances; and on the 5th of July their petition was delivered to him by the Lord Mayor, Beckford, and three more, but was received with the utmost coldness and neglect.

Two days after, the Court was surprised with a more unexpected phenomenon. Lord Chatham appeared at the King's levee when it was thought he would never produce himself again, or was not fit to be produced in public. He was perfectly well, and had grown fat. The Duke of Grafton had just time to apprise the King of this mysterious visit. The King was very gracious, and whispered him to come into the closet after the levee, which he did, and stayed there twenty minutes. Much silence was observed on what passed; though by degrees it was affirmed that the conversation was only general and indifferent. Yet hints were dropped that the King, sounding Lord Chatham on the Middlesex election, the opinion he gave was not favourable to his Majesty's wishes.[1] The active part taken by Lord Shelburne, Beckford, and Calcraft, made this greatly probable ; and his Lordship's subsequent conduct corroborated the idea. Still was Lord Chatham very desirous of recovering his power ; and it was not his style to be harsh in the closet.[2] It was remarked, too, that, not to embitter his reception, he had come when Lord Temple[3] was detained at Stowe, by entertaining there several of the foreign ministers. Lord Chatham lingered affectedly, in the outward room, after his audience, as if to display the recovery of his health and understanding, To the Duke of Grafton and the Bedfords he was awkward and cool ; embraced Lord Granby and General Harvey[4] (a personal military favourite of the King), and was very civil to Lord Hertford and Mr. Conway. In the evening he returned to Hayes.

Whatever were the motives of his re-appearance the

[1] A minute of Lord Chatham's representations to the King is given in the Duke of Grafton's *Memoirs*, as if on his Majesty's authority. It confirms the statement in the text, with the addition, however, of Lord Chatham having assured the King that in his state of health office could no longer be even desirable to him.—L. M. [This minute is printed at length in Lord Mahon's *History of England*, 1851, vol. v. App. pp. xxxii.-iv. Chatham's own account of his reception by the King will be found in the *Grenville Papers*, vol. iv. pp. 426-7.—E.]

[2] Being asked soon afterwards, by Sir W. Meredith, if he was likely to come in, he replied, ' Good God ! I !—with whom, and for whom ? ' There would have been great sense in this answer, if he had not often shown that he was indifferent *with whom*, and nobody could tell *for* whom he had ever come in : though his enemies would say, *only for himself* ; and Britain ought to say *for her* in his successful Administration.

[3] Lord Temple, too, as if not without hopes, had shifted off to September the meeting in Buckinghamshire for determining whether that county should petition or not ; and he might hope that the popular clamour would drive the Court to have recourse to Lord Chatham and him.

[4] Major-General Edward Harvey, Adjutant-General of the Forces since 1763, had served with distinction in the Seven Years' War. He was M.P. for Gatton, 1761-8, and for Harwich, 1768-78. He became a Lieutenant-General on 26th May 1772, and was appointed Governor of Portsmouth in 1773. He died on 27th March 1778.—E.

prospect certainly favoured him, whether he had a mind
to present himself as a mediator to the fears of the Court,
or as a Captain-General to the Opposition.   His creatures
governed the City: Lord Granby, influenced by Calcraft,
and dreading the loss of popularity, talked of resigning.
The Chancellor was disgusted with Grafton, whose
marriage had hurt him at Court.   Ireland, by the absurd
conduct of Lord Townshend, was in confusion; and the
Bedfords were pressing to send Lord Sandwich thither,
which would have increased the ill-humour.   And though
the Ministers had thoughts of giving satisfaction to the
Colonies, yet, having refused to give that assurance in
Parliament, the Americans would no longer trust them.
The Virginians had voted the right of taxation to be in
themselves, and resolved on a petition against our sending
for the criminals to be tried in England,—a violent
measure, dictated by rashness, and, almost as soon as
announced, dropped by timidity.   Great divisions reigned
in the East India Company, in which Lord Clive and Sir
Laurence Dundas were contending to engross sole power,
the Company having more places to bestow than the First
Lord of the Treasury; the exorbitant wealth of our empire
going hand-in-hand with the advance of prerogative; in
the views of most of our patriots.   Wilkes, in the meantime, whatever were his views, had honesty enough not to
smother his private resentments; and, at this very moment,
published an envenomed pamphlet against Lord Chatham.
It was unjustly silent on his merits and services, but touched
with truth the defective parts of his character.

A former friend of Wilkes, who had abandoned him,
was more cruelly, because more iniquitously, treated.
Among the rabble of Wilkes's agents was one Horne,
parson of Brentford.   He was son of the poulterer to the
Princess of Wales; but, whether from principle, vanity, or
want of more decent means to attempt distinguishing
himself, he had attached himself to that demagogue; and,
with slender parts, had become his scribe in composing
scurrilities for the newspapers, and his factor at all popular

meetings.[1] In other respects his morals were not reproached; though, as came out afterwards, he had, to
please Wilkes, ridiculed his Lords the Bishops, and, to
please himself, indulged in more foppery than became his
profession. He now infamously aspersed Mr. Onslow,[2]
one of the Lords of the Treasury, as having accepted
£1000 to procure a place for a person in the West Indies,
—a transaction which was proved to have been a gross
imposition on the person who paid the bribe, and in which
Mr. Onslow had in no shape been concerned, till the
defrauded person applied to him for redress. Horne
impudently avowed the printed charge to be his; for
which Onslow prosecuted, and cast him in damages at the
assizes in Surrey.[3]

Some damp, too, was thrown on the zeal of the Opposition, by the refusal of Essex, Hertfordshire, Norfolk,
Lincolnshire, and Kent, to join in the popular petitions.
The city of Bristol, on the other hand, determined to
petition, and voted their contempt to their member, Lord
Clare: but the most grievous outrage fell on the Duke of
Bedford. He was Lord-Lieutenant of Devonshire, had a
great estate in the county, and exercised most signal charity
there. In order to prevent a petition of the county, he
went down thither; but while he was at prayers in the
Cathedral of Exeter, a tumultuous mob assembled, pour-
ing out execrations on him; and had not the bishop
conducted him by a private passage to the palace, his life
had been in danger. At Honiton, the fury of the people

---

[1] If these Memoirs had been written at a later period, Walpole would have
mentioned Horne Tooke's talents with more respect. He was, however, at
this time little known, except for his quarrel with Wilkes, when, as Lord
Brougham justly observes, 'he was clearly in the right; . . . but he was the
object of general and fierce popular indignation, for daring to combat the
worthless idol of the mob.'—(*Historical Sketches*, vol. ii. p. 119.)—L. M.

[2] See *supra*, p. 127, note 4.—E.

[3] The trial took place at Kingston on 6th April 1770, when Onslow was
non-suited. The case was re-heard at Guildford in the following August, and
Onslow obtained damages for £400, but judgment was subsequently arrested
by the Court of Common Pleas on purely technical grounds.—(Woodfall's
Junius, vol. i. pp. 186-196, and Wilson's *Reports*, vol. iii. pp. 177-188.)—E.

rose to such a height, that they pelted him with stones, and set bull-dogs at him.[1]

In the meantime, Lord Bute returned privately to England from the waters of Barege, which, it was given out, had perfectly restored his health : but the temper of the times not favouring his timidity, or the latter renewing his disorder, he, in a short time, retired to Italy.[2] The Court of France, however, not being the dupe of his pretended loss of credit, gave him the same guard, at his lodgings at Barege, as attended the Comtesse de la Marche,[3] a Princess of the blood ; and his vanity was so weak as to accept this safe homage.

His faithful devotee, Lord Holland, was scarce less obnoxious to the City. The contemptuous flippancy of his sons, and his own [4] indiscreet interference in behalf of Lutterell, had brought him again on the stage, which he pretended to have quitted. The multiplicity and difficulty of his accounts as Paymaster during the war had prevented their being liquidated. The Barons of the Exchequer had called on him to make them up. He had obtained from the Crown a delay of process, pleading the impediments he received from the proper officers in Germany. This was, probably, true. It is also probable,

---

[1] The Duke gives some account, in his plain, simple style, of these brutal outrages in his Journal.—(Cavendish, vol. i. p. 621.) He appears to have had a narrow escape of being murdered at Honiton. It is pleasing to find in his entry of the following day a picture presenting a striking contrast to this disgraceful tumult :—'I went in the morning to Barwick Place, where my ancestors last lived, in Dorsetshire. It is a fine farm, but a dismal place. From thence I went by the sea-side through Kingston Russell farm, to Mr. Hardy, my tenant's house, where I dined. This is an exceedingly fine farm, and has the finest ewe leasows I ever saw in my life. After a very good farmer-like dinner, and a hearty welcome, I set out for Blandford.'—L. M.

[2] Bute does not appear to have had any interview with the King during this visit to England. See the *Grenville Papers*, vol. iv. p. 434.—E.

[3] Louis François Joseph, Comte de la Marche, son of Prince Louis François de Bourbon-Conty, married on the 27th February 1759, Fortunée Marie, Princesse de Modène.—E.

[4] He had, moreover, at his seat at Kingsgate, in the Isle of Thanet, erected a pillar to the honour of Alderman Harley, the most unpopular of all the City's magistrates.

R.Brompton.pinx.

The Earl of Chatham.

that he was not impatient to be disburthened of such large sums,[1] on which he made considerable interest. The petition from Middlesex had made this one of their charges, in their bill of grievances, and described Lord Holland as *the defaulter for unaccounted millions.*[2] Touched to the quick at this imputation, he wrote a civil letter to the Lord Mayor, complaining of the aspersion, and referring him for the falsehood of the accusation to Alderman Beckford, whom Lord Holland said he had satisfied of the injustice of it. The Mayor returned only a card, to say he was not answerable for the contents of the petition; yet he had harangued on it, as well as presented it. Beckford advertised that Lord Holland had sent him his defence, but that it had *not* satisfied him. Lord Holland then published a justification in the papers. Indeed, the violence of the petition was much blamed; and, as if conscious of it, the authors had neither ventured to sign or date it.

Whatever had been Lord Chatham's views in going to Court, it appeared that now, at least, his part was taken. A reconciliation was made between him and Mr. Grenville, which, though never cordial, served at least to alarm the Bedfords, who, according to their laudable practice, made immediate overtures to the three brothers,[3] offering to be content to save Lord Gower, Rigby, and one or two

---

[1] These accounts were not settled at Lord Holland's death, and his family profited of the interest of £400,000 still remaining in his hands. Lord North was very earnest to have the account made up, and yet it was not finally closed in the middle of the year 1777, which shows the intricacy and difficulty of terminating such accounts.

[2] Walpole is not quite accurate in the text. The petition was from the Livery of the City of London, and it described Lord Holland as 'the public defaulter of unaccounted millions' (Woodfall's *Junius*, vol. i. pp. 175*-186). The delay in making up the accounts was neither illegal nor unusual, though it probably enriched Lord Holland to the extent of £250,000.—E.

[3] Lord Chatham, Lord Temple, and Mr. Grenville. A petition from Ailesbury being soon after agreed on, the members of the meeting drank a health to the union of the three brothers. How little union there really was amongst them appeared afterwards, for Mr. Grenville had before his death made his peace with the Court without any consideration of Lord Chatham, and so did Lord Temple in like manner in 1777. All the latter part of

more of their friends at most : in which number they were careful *not* to stipulate for their ally, the Duke of Grafton. These overtures, though renewed at different times, were rejected. As if to condemn themselves more, they published a severe pamphlet against the political conduct of Lord Chatham.

Wiltshire and Worcestershire then agreed on a petition, and one from Surrey was presented. But the capital stroke was struck by the electors of Westminster, who petitioned the King *to dissolve the Parliament,*—a step not only absurd, but of most dangerous precedent. To require him to dissolve an assembly so obsequious, and of whom they complained for humouring his vengeance, was on the face of it ridiculous and void of all probability of success. A refusal, indeed, they might wish to receive, as it would but inflame their grievance : but on pretence of violated liberty to seek for redress from the Throne, the aggressor against the bulwark of liberty, however then betrayed to the Crown, was as noxious a measure as could have been devised. What King but might obtain some servile addresses against the most incorruptible House of Commons? Was prerogative the champion to resort to in defence of injured freedom ? The invitation sent to the Danes by our shortsighted and ignorant ancestors, and the expedient of calling over the heir of the Crown of France by the barons in the reign of King John, were scarce more big with folly and indiscretion. What could triumphant rebellion have demanded more of a King than to dissolve one Parliament and expose himself to a new election amidst enraged subjects ? It was the act of a rash multitude—yet did not want abettors, who ought to have acted on sounder and soberer principles. Was this, alas ! a moment to fill the nation with tumult and disorder ? Was the constitution so gone (and

---

Lord Temple's life was one continued scene of quarrels and reconciliations with his family and friends, according as his passions or restless ambition dictated. [See the MS. Memoirs of the Duke of Grafton, Appendix, on the subject of these petitions.—L. M.]

nobody thinks worse than I do of the provocation given
by the Court in the case of Lutterell) that anarchy was
the sole engine left that could restore it ? Could Lord
Chatham, or Lord Temple, or Grenville (of whom the
former had lost their popularity, and the latter never had
any) hope to

'Ride in the whirlwind, and direct the storm ?'[1]

No—Wilkes and every turbulent agitator in the several
counties would have risen on the froth of a cauldron
composed of such pernicious ingredients. The intrusion
of Lutterell was not an evil adequate to such remedies.
True patriots will bear with some ills, and temporize till
a fitter opportunity. Nor would the remedy have been
remote, would the plaintiffs have had virtue to wait and
avail themselves of it. Would the people resist corruption,
and elect none but men of virtue and principle, the election
of another Parliament would furnish redress. Corrupt
members must be the consequence of corrupt constituents.
The people had not virtue, nor their leaders patience to
profit of, or wait for, so constitutional a remedy.

Lord Shelburne attacked the Duke of Bedford in his
own town of Bedford, and carried a mayor against him.
The celebrated Junius published an infamous attack on
the same Duke, on the insult he had received in Devonshire, by justifying which the writer gave a riot the air of
premeditated assassination.[2] Sir William Draper, a brave
officer, attached to the Duke and Lord Granby, who had
been abused by the same author, but not of sound
intellects, published, with his name, a challenge to the
dark satirist,[3] which the latter answered with parts, and
without any manly spirit. About the same time, one
Dr. Musgrave, who had hawked about to Lord Chatham
and other discontented great men, and to some Ministers,

---

[1] 'Rides in the whirlwind, and directs the storm.'—Addison's *Campaign.*—E.
[2] Letter to the Duke of Bedford, 19th September 1769. Twenty-third
Letter.—L. M.
[3] Sir William Draper's Letter to Junius, 7th October 1769. Junius's
Twenty-sixth Letter.—L. M.

and been rejected by all, an offer of a discovery which he pretended to have made, that the late peace had been bought by France of the Princess Dowager, Lord Bute, and Lord Holland, now published this wild accusation, and cited the Chevalier D'Eon as one of his evidences. The latter, whose head had been turned by the vanity of being an under instrument in concluding that peace, flatly disavowed him; and though in the following winter he had his charge laid before Parliament, it was grounded on such paltry information, picked up in a French coffee-house, that faction itself could not countenance him; and the man and his accusation being voted infamous, were heard of no more.[1]

The young Emperor of Germany, Joseph the Second, now began to make himself noticed. Though behaving with perfect deference to, and appearing to live in cordial amity with, his mother, the Empress-queen, he discovered symptoms of not intending to waste his reign in inactivity. He gave great attention to the army; and, as a model of royal wisdom to be studied, had an interview with the King of Prussia; at which visit many passions must have been smothered on either side.

The Turks having met the Russian army in those vast plains that divide their empires, now recovered their superiority by the advantage of their cavalry, better suited to desultory war: but they had scarce stemmed the torrent of invasion, before the Czarina struck Europe with wonder and respect by a measure at once great, daring,

---

[1] Samuel Musgrave was born at Washfield, Devonshire, on 29th September 1732, and was educated at Oxford, where he obtained the Radcliffe travelling fellowship, and graduated M.D. in 1775. He held the post of physician to the Devon and Exeter hospital from 1766 to 1768, and in August 1769 published the *Address to the Gentlemen, Clergy, and Freeholders of the County of Devon*, containing the charges, which were brought before the House of Commons (*Parliamentary History*, xvi. 765-85). He died in Hart Street, Bloomsbury, on 5th July 1780, aged forty-seven, in great poverty. Though unsuccessful as a physician Musgrave was an accomplished Greek scholar. His notes on Euripides were purchased by the University of Oxford, and were incorporated in the edition which was issued from the Oxford Press in 1778.—E.

and desperate. She notified her intention of sending a fleet to attack Constantinople itself. The idea was said to be her own, and she persisted against the advice of her Ministers. The length of the voyage, its dangers, and the almost hopeless prospect of success, were lost in the grandeur of the project. I was then at Paris : the French ministry were confounded, and despatched couriers by land to rouse the Ottoman Monarch : French engineers followed to assist him in fortifying the approach to his capital, which lay, as he thought, securely surrounded by endless tracts of sea and land. The Duke of Choiseul, who had sown those seeds of wide-spread desolation, was confounded at seeing himself excelled in a nobler style. But few days before this intelligence reached him, he had had the vain levity, as I was supping with him at his own house, to send for the last Paris Gazette, which he had dictated himself, to prove the late victory of the Turks, and read it to the company. His invasion of Corsica, and the savage cruelties that were exercised there after the conquest, were puny consolations to his meddling am-bition—yet was all the military glory that decorated his administration. The first advantages gained there by the French had been solemnized in a ridiculous manner by ostentatious inscriptions, that were soon followed by defeats; but hosts continually poured in on the abandoned islanders ; and the deficiency of military skill in Pascal Paoli, the Dictator of the aspiring Republic, and even his want of valour, as the French themselves asserted, reduced Corsica beneath their yoke. Paoli, who aspired to power, not to the fame of virtue, distinguished between his country and his hopes, and not having fallen like Leoni-das, did not despair like Cato. He made his escape and arrived in England, where his character had been so ad-vantageously exaggerated by Mr. Boswell's enthusiastic and entertaining account of him,[1] that the Opposition were ready to receive and incorporate him in the list of popular

---

[1] James Boswell's *Account of Corsica, the Journal of a Tour to that Island ; and Memoirs of Pascal Paoli* appeared in 1768.—E.

tribunes.   The Court artfully intercepted the project;
and deeming patriots of all nations equally corruptible,
bestowed a pension of £1000 a year on the un-heroic
fugitive.   Themistocles accepted the gold of Xerxes, and
excused himself from receiving a visit from Mrs. Macaulay,
who had given him printed advice for settling a republic.
I saw him soon after his arrival, dangling at Court.   He
was a man of decent deportment, vacant of all melancholy
reflection, with as much ease as suited a prudence that
seemed the utmost effort of a wary understanding, and so
void of anything remarkable in his aspect, that being
asked if I knew who it was, I judged him a Scottish officer
(for he was sandy-complexioned and in regimentals) who
was cautiously awaiting the moment of promotion.   All
his heroism consisted in bearing with composure the
accounts of his friends being tortured and butchered, while
he was sunk into a pensioner of that very Court that had
proclaimed his valiant countrymen and associates rebels.[1]

Not so passive the English.   The weavers mutinied
against their masters, and many were killed by the guards.
The Livery of London rejected Sir Henry Banks, a senior

[1] This does not agree with the authenticated accounts of the war in
Corsica.   So far from it, Paoli at first succeeded in repelling the attacks of
the French, notwithstanding their superiority of numbers.   They were
worsted in an engagement near Loreto, with great loss, several companies
having been drowned in the Golo in the attempt to make their escape.   On
the 29th of October the corps sent to attack Murato received a signal defeat,
their commander being among the slain.—(Sismondi's *Histoire de France*,
vol. xxix. p. 380.)   The overwhelming force brought over by the Count de
Vaux early in 1769 soon dispersed the Corsican levies, and rendered all
further resistance on the part of Paoli perfectly vain.   Paoli was much respected in England by men of all parties.   At the commencement of the
Revolution he was invited to France, and after an enthusiastic reception by
the National Assembly, placed in the command of Corsica, with the rank of
Lieutenant-General of the Island.   The troubles that followed led him to
offer the Crown to England in 1793; but the English rule proved unfortunate
both to the Corsicans and to himself.   He soon returned to England, and
died in the neighbourhood of London on 5th February 1807, in his eighty-
first year.   He left a considerable fortune, part of which eventually fell under
the administration of the Court of Chancery, and the Lord Chancellor issued
a commission to Corsica to ascertain his heirs.—See more of him in Capefigue's
Diplomates Européens, pp. 123-133.—L.M.

Alderman, for Lord Mayor; and Beckford and Trecothick being returned by them to the Court of Aldermen, and the former having the majority was elected a second time. He excused himself on pretence of age, which was but turned of sixty, and infirmities which he had not. He was pressed again to accept, and peremptorily refused the office; but the Sheriffs, with a train of coaches, entreating him, at the request of the Livery, not to deny himself to their wishes, he at last yielded. The Livery then inquired what answer had been returned to their petition? The Aldermen, to soften them, replied, that none had been given, but his Majesty would undoubtedly consider of the most constitutional means of redressing their grievances. They next called for Lord Holland's letter to the Lord Mayor, who produced it; adding, that he did not know how Lord Holland, as a gentleman, could account for publishing his (the Mayor's) letter—as if it was justifiable to tax that lord in a public manner, without process or proofs, of embezzling millions; and unjustifiable in him, in his own defence, to print the Lord Mayor's evasion, I might almost say disavowal, of the charge! Sinking under the aspersion and loads of abuse, Lord Holland retired to France on pretence of conducting thither his wife's sister, Lady Cecilia Lenox, who was dying, and died there, of a consumption. The City, as if he had fled from the charge, instructed their Members to endeavour a parliamentary inquiry into his conduct, and to impeach him if matter were found— but it came to nothing; and their silence cleared him.

The Marquis of Rockingham and the Cavendishes had kept aloof from the factious meetings of the rest of the Opposition, and given no countenance to the spirit of petitioning, which had now gained Hereford, Newcastle, and the counties of Gloucester and Cornwall. The Duke of Richmond, who was in France, where I was too, told me with satisfaction that his friends had resisted an example so inconsistent with the principles of liberty as appealing to the Crown against the House of Commons. Their resistance, however, was not stubborn enough to hold out against popularity, and the arts of a man who meant nothing less than to assert the constitution, and who made use of the grievance complained of to force the Crown to employ him, lucratively to himself, in every attack it meditated against the constitution. This was Alexander Wedderburne, whose name will be read with horror when this transaction is remembered, and compared with a change of conduct as sudden as the former, and as diametrically opposite to this parenthesis of effected zeal for liberty, and attended by the share he bore in lighting up a civil war, the view of which was to enslave America. Edmund Burke, too, had perhaps some influence in seducing the Whig lords into adoption of the popular measure. Not content with Lord Rockingham's feeble politics, and hoping better from the union of the three brothers, he concerted with them the petition for Buckinghamshire; and he, Grenville, and Wedderburne drew another for Yorkshire, the ablest of all those performances; and the Marquis, the Cavendishes, and the worthy Sir George Savile, promoted that and another from Derbyshire. A patriot remonstrance composed by an Irishman born a papist, and by a Scottish creature of Lord Bute, was deservedly ridiculed.

The ministers, who should have met the storm early, and who by calling the Parliament might have intercepted many petitions, sought to keep off the discussion there, and would not let it meet till after Christmas. The Duke of Grafton, who had been honoured with the Garter, and elected Chancellor of the University of Cambridge, could not bear the thoughts of business. He diverted himself in the country, coming to town but once a week or once a fortnight, to sign papers[1] at the Treasury; and as seldom to the King. I could but reflect how different had

[1] According to the Duke's own account in his *Memoirs* he was at this time on uneasy terms with his colleagues, of whose general policy he disapproved, and by whom he was generally outvoted in the Cabinet. Nothing but the absence of an adequate excuse for resignation kept him in office. It may be observed, also, that his marriage (to Miss Elizabeth Wrottesley), which took place on the 24th of June, had been followed by his installation at Cambridge, where his presence was indispensable. See the Duke of Bedford's Private Journal, Cavendish's *Parliamentary Debates*, vol. i. p. 619.—L. M.

been the application of Sir Robert Walpole, my father, who, without relaxation but for two fortnights in the year, found it difficult enough to govern the kingdom and keep Opposition at bay, though secure of the King, secure of peace with France by meeting as pacific dispositions in Cardinal Fleury, void of alarms from Ireland and America, that were as quiet as his own county of Norfolk, and called on for no attention to a new empire that had now accrued to us at the eastern boundary of the world. The consequences were such as might be expected. Walpole maintained the equilibrium; under Grafton everything fell into confusion. Were any representations made to him, he threatened to resign, affirming that he only retained his power, because his quitting at that crisis would produce a dissolution of Parliament, from which he foresaw the worst consequences. The only step he took was to advise with the Chancellor, who told him surlily, that his Grace had consulted him but twice last session, and then had acted directly contrary to his advice. He was as blunt with the King, who telling him he hoped there was no truth in what he saw in the papers that his Lordship had thoughts of resigning the Seals, he replied, There was universal discontent amongst the people. Yet Hussey, the Chancellor's friend, was warm against the petitions, and said, if anybody moved in Parliament, as Lord Chatham threatened to do, for a dissolution of Parliament, he would vote for sending that person to the Tower. Sir Walter Blacket told his constituents, at Newcastle, that he would cut off his hand rather than sign a petition to the King to interfere with a resolution of the House of Commons. In fact, the lower people alone, whom it was easy to lead, gave in to petitions. The gentry in general discouraged, yet dared not openly oppose them, either fearing for their future elections, or dreading the abuse that was cast on all who opposed the popular cry. Sawbridge and Calcraft obtained at Maidstone a petition from the county of Kent, though all the magistrates shrunk from it, two gentlemen only appearing

there, and they dissenting. Sawbridge told the mob the
King had abused his prerogative by pardoning murderers.
Another demagogue was less successful—Mr. Thomas
Pitt,[1] Grenville's creature, having harangued the County
of Cornwall in favour of a petition, was severely reproached
with having sold his own borough of Old Sarum to a
Scotch placeman ; and for meaning less a redress of
grievances than an opportunity of selling it again by a
new general election.   Townshend, no less hot than
Sawbridge, abused in open court the courts of justice ;
and at a trial of some weavers for destroying looms, being
desired by the judge to quiet a riot without doors, returned
and denied there being any tumult.   He and Sawbridge
repairing to Spitalfields, the late principal scene of
uproar, Sir Robert Darling, a justice, told them there had
been no mob till their arrival ; and if they would not
retire, he would commit them, which they were forced to
do ; but being ordered to attend the execution of two
condemned cutters, they refused, because the spot was not
specified in the sentence—a sacrifice to the mob that
scandalized the merchants, who had suffered by the late
outrages, and were exposed to daily injuries.   The criminals, however, were at last hanged ; but the sheriffs
fearing to be insulted by the populace, and to avoid being
reduced to call in the military, went guarded by a crowd
of constables, and were obliged to have the convicts
hanged precipitately.   Yet the mob pelted the sheriffs,
cut down the gallows, carried it with one of the bodies to
the house of the prosecutor, and destroyed his looms.   A
justice of peace sent for guards from the Tower, while
Sawbridge pleaded to the rioters that he had done every-

---

[1] Mr. Thomas Pitt, nephew of Lord Chatham, was on some occasions a
man of probity and generosity.   He gave five thousand pounds a-piece to his
two sisters, left destitute by their father ; and himself marrying Miss Wilkin-
son, whose elder sister had disobliged their father by marrying against his
consent, both Mr. Pitt and his wife would not conclude their marriage without
disclaiming all advantage to the prejudice of the elder sister. [See vol. i.
p. 270, note.   His nominees were William Gerard Hamilton, and John Craufurd, Chamberlain for the County of Fife.—L. M.]

thing in his power to save the criminals—a proof that his objection to the spot of execution had been solely an evasion offered to popularity. The sheriffs were as negligent of their duty on being required to suppress the tumults on Wilkes's[1] birthday, when many windows were broken for not being illuminated.

It was not so valuable a triumph as he expected, when, on November the 10th, Wilkes carried his long-protracted cause against Lord Halifax. The damages were laid at £20,000 : the jury gave him £4000. One of the books of the Treasury was produced, in which had been entered a promise by the now zealous patriot, Mr. Grenville, that Lord Halifax should be indemnified, if cast in the suit.[2] The jury having disappointed the expectations of the populace by so moderate a fine, were hissed, and forced to escape by a back way.

The graver citizens, who do not relish liberty at the risk of their property, grew alarmed at these wild proceedings, and began to wish again for the decorous ascendance of moneyed men. The first stand they made was in Broad Street Ward, where they elected one Rossiter Alderman against Bull, a man set up by the Supporters of the Bill of Rights. Soon afterwards, attempts being made to introduce new Common Councilmen into several wards, the richer citizens exerted themselves to disappoint, and did disappoint, many of the turbulent candidates.

The scene in Ireland was not less alarming than the ill humour in England. An augmentation of the forces was designed there. Lord Townshend, afraid of a remnant of popularity, forbore to announce it in his speech at opening the session. It was even omitted in the estimates of the army ; the Ministers there not having then acquainted themselves with what the charge would amount to. The Opposition moved, and carried by 13, two questions for

[1] He was on that day aged forty-five, the date of his famous number and device. [Wilkes was born on 17th October 1727. He was consequently forty-two on 17th October 1769.—E.]

[2] The knowledge of this fact is said to have been the reason why the jury did not give higher damages.—L. M.

addressing the Lord-Lieutenant to know the reason of the omission. The augmentation, however, was carried by 170 to 50. In all other questions, the Viceroy was defeated, particularly in one very important to the Sovereignty of England. It is usual, on calling a new Parliament, to assign as the cause some bill sent over by the Privy Council. The English Government always take care it should be a money bill. This bill, now returned to them from England, the House of Commons in Ireland rejected. The blow struck at the whole constitution of Ireland, as regulated in subservience to England by Poyning's Act. The same innovation had been made in the reign of King William. Lord Sidney, then Deputy of Ireland, immediately, without waiting for directions from England, prorogued their Parliament, after making a strong protest against the rejection. He kept it prorogued till April, however inconvenient to the Government; the King in the meantime having nothing but his hereditary revenue. The punishment, however, fell more heavy on the Opposition by the odium it drew on them from the public creditors and the pensioners of the Court, who all remained unpaid during the suspension of Parliament. The Duke of Leinster,[1] a weak man, who aspired to be Lord-Lieutenant; Lord Shannon, son of the late Speaker, who wished to be one of the Lords Justices, and was very artful; and the present Speaker Ponsonby,[2] who coveted Lord Clanbrazil's place[3] for two lives, were at the bottom

---

[1] James Fitzgerald, Earl of Kildare, first Duke of Leinster. [An amiable nobleman, always zealous to promote the welfare of his country. He died in 1773.—L. M.]

[2] In the money-bills, the Irish Parliament had endeavoured to lay a tax on English beer, but it was rejected by a few voices; the Speaker, fearing to lose his place of £4000 a year at the head of the revenue, should they provoke England too far. They made an alteration, however, in their own gauging, which some here thought equivalent to a tax on our beer, and the Council were inclined to reject that alteration, yet, desirous of getting the money-bills passed, and the Attorney-General declaring that it was no violation of Poyning's Act, the alteration was suffered to remain, and the money-bills were sent back uncorrected.

[3] Of King's Remembrancer. It was a little before this time that Calcraft, ignoble as his birth and rise were, aspired, by the Duke of Grafton's favour,

of the new intrigues of the Opposition. The Duke of Grafton, the Chancellor Camden, and the English Council advised immediate prorogation ; but Lord Hertford, better acquainted with Ireland, where his estate lay, and which kingdom he had governed, besought them to wait till the money-bills, which are always transmitted hither before Christmas, should arrive. This was sound advice ; for, though the rash order was given, the money-bills, which were actually passed and on the road, did arrive before Lord Townshend could receive the command for prorogation, which, when he executed it, was no longer an impediment to the collection of the revenue.

In the beginning of December, the English Privy Council sat on the dissolution of the Parliament so much demanded. All were unanimous against it, yet the Chancellor peremptorily condemned the introduction of Lutterell. Mr. Conway, by my advice, proposed a popular declaration in the King's Speech against unusual exertion of prerogative. Most of the Council approved the idea ; and, at Mr. Conway's request, I drew words for that purpose ; but he had not weight enough with the Duke of Grafton to get them admitted, or the King had too much influence over his Grace not to overrule so unpalatable a condescension.

A momentary triumph the Duke obtained over the popular party. Vaughan, a sanctified leader of the Bill of Rights, offered him £5000 for the reversion of a place in America. The Duke, who should only have exposed the man, prosecuted him : yet Vaughan had much to plead in his excuse. Great debts were owing to him in the colony, of which the place in question was the Register, who resided in England, whence it was difficult to get his debts, which amounted to £80,000 registered ; and therefore, he had tried to purchase the place, which had been often sold, for his son.[1] The Duke's over affectation of virtue drew on him from Junius a detection, in which his active

---

to the title of Earl of Ormond. George Selwyn said, ' Calcraft might have pretensions to that title, as no doubt he must have had many *Butlers* in his family.'

[1] Junius's account of the prosecution (Letter xxxiii is fair.)—making the usual

aversion to corruption did not appear quite so pure as his passive. It was proved that he had bestowed on Colonel Burgoyne a place, which the latter was to sell to reimburse himself for the expenses of his election at Preston. Some other papers from the same hand fell cruelly on Burgoyne.

As the Session approached, Lord Chatham engaged with new warmth in promoting petitions. He asked Mr. Cholmondeley,[1] Member for Cheshire, why his country had not petitioned? and told him he himself would move for dissolution of the Parliament; and, if not able to stand on his legs, 'I will speak,' said he, as he lay on his couch, 'in this horizontal posture.' Calcraft was not less zealous, and more active. He and Sir Joseph Mawbey obtained a petition from the county of Essex, though neither High Sheriff, the Members, nor one gentleman of the county would attend the meeting, at the head of which they were forced to set Sir Robert Bernard, Knight for Huntingdonshire.

In the City, attempts were made to save three more condemned cutters of looms, and hand-bills were dispersed inviting the weavers to assemble on the morrow in Moorfields, in order to petition the King for a pardon; but Beckford, the new Lord Mayor, and the Sheriff Sawbridge went thither and persuaded them to disperse; and the cutters were hanged without disturbance.

These many essays towards an insurrection were crowned by the unparalleled remonstrance of Junius to the King,[2] the most daring insult ever offered to a prince but in times of open rebellion, and aggravated by the many truths it contained. Nothing could exceed the singularity of this satire, but the impossibility of discovering the author. Three men were especially suspected, Wilkes, Edmund Burke, and William Gerard

deductions.—See also Rex *v.* Vaughan (Burrow's *Reports*, vol. iv. p. 2494)—by which it seems that the motion for the criminal information was made by Mr. Dunning.—'An Appeal to the Public on Behalf of Samuel Vaughan, Esq.,' London, 1770, 8vo, states some mitigating circumstances.—L. M.

[1] Of Valeroyal. [Thomas Cholmondeley of Vale Royal sat for Cheshire from April 1756 to March 1768. He was not in Parliament at this date.—E.]

[2] Letter xxxv. See Woodfall's *Junius*, 1814, vol. ii. pp. 62-89.—E.

Hamilton. The desperate hardiness of the author in attacking men so great, so powerful, and some so brave, was reconcileable only to the situation of Wilkes; but the masterly talents that appeared in those writings were deemed superior to his abilities: yet in many of Junius's letters an inequality was observed; and even in this remonstrance different hands seemed to have been employed. The laborious flow of style, and fertility of matter, made Burke believed the real Junius: yet he had not only constantly and solemnly denied any hand in those performances, but was not a man addicted to bitterness; nor could any one account for such indiscriminate attacks on men of such various descriptions and professions. Hamilton was most generally suspected. He, too, denied it—but his truth was not renowned. The quick intelligence of facts, and the researches into the arcana of every office, were far more uncommon than the invectives; and men wondered how any one possessed of such talents, could have the forbearance to write in a manner so desperate as to prevent his ever receiving personal applause for his writings: the venom was too black not to disgrace even his ashes.[1]

A *North Briton*, of very inferior or no merit, followed this remonstrance,[2] and spared the two royal brothers no more than Junius had palliated the errors of the King. The Duke of Cumberland, a weak and debauched boy, was censured for an intrigue with a lady of rank, which became of public notoriety, and will be mentioned hereafter. The Duke of Gloucester, a virtuous, discreet, and unexceptionable Prince, had involved himself in a more serious affair; of which, as I can, I must give a more particular account than was known to others.

Maria Walpole, second natural daughter of my brother, Sir Edward, and one of the most beautiful of women, had

---

[1] The evidence of Sir Philip Francis being the author of Junius has been observed by an eminent lawyer who took no part in the controversy, to be such as would be held conclusive by a jury on a question of fact.—L. M.

[2] The *North Briton* for December 30, 1769.—E.

been married, solely by my means, to James, late Earl of
Waldegrave, Governor to the King and Duke of York, an
excellent man, but as old again as she was, and of no
agreeable figure.   Her passions were ambition and expense : she accepted his hand with pleasure, and by an
effort less common, proved a meritorious wife.   When
after her year of widowhood she appeared again in the
full lustre of her beauty, she was courted by the Duke of
Portland ; but the young Duke of Gloucester, who had
gazed on her with desire during her husband's life, now
openly showing himself her admirer, she slighted the
subject, and aspired to the brother of the Crown.   Her
obligations to me, and my fondness for her, authorized
me to interpose my advice, which was kindly but un-
willingly received.   I did not desist ; but pointing out the
improbabilities of marriage, the little likelihood of the
King's consent, and the chance of being sent to Hanover
separated from her children,[1] on whom she doated, the
last reason alone prevailed on the fond mother, and she
yielded to copy a letter I wrote for her to the Duke of
Gloucester, in which she renounced his acquaintance in
the no new terms of not being of rank to be his wife, and
too considerable to be his mistress.   A short fortnight
baffled all my prudence.   The Prince renewed his visits
with more assiduity after that little interval, and Lady
Waldegrave received him without disguise.   My part was
soon taken.   I had done my duty—a second attempt had
been hopeless folly.   Though often pressed to sup with
her, when I knew the Duke was to be there, I steadily
refused, and never once mentioned his name to her afterwards, though as their union grew more serious, she
affectedly named him to me, called him *the Duke*, and
related to me private anecdotes of the royal family, which
she could have received but from him.   It was in vain ;
I studiously avoided him.   She brought him to see my
house, but I happened not to be at home ; he came again,

---

[1] By Earl Waldegrave she had three daughters,—the Ladies Laura, Maria,
and Horatia.

alone: I left the house. He then desisted, for I never
stayed for his court, which followed the Princess Dowager's,
but retired as soon as she had spoken to me. This, as
may be supposed, cooled my niece's affection for me; but
being determined not to have the air of being convenient
to her from flattery, if she was not married, and having
no authority to ask her the question on which she had
refused to satisfy her father, I preferred my honour to her
favour, and left her to her own conduct. Indeed my own
father's obligations to the royal family forbade me to endeavour to place a natural daughter of our house so near
the Throne. To my brother the Duke was profuse of
civilities, which I pressed him to decline; and even
advised him not to see his daughter, unless she would
own her marriage, which might oblige the Duke, in vindication of her character, to avow her for his wife. Married,
I had no doubt they were. Both the Duke and she were
remarkably religious; and neither of them dissolute
enough to live, as they did at last, with all the liberties of
marriage. The King and Queen denied their legal union,
yet the respect with which they treated her spoke the
contrary; and the homage which all men and all women
paid her by a fortune singular to her, assured the opinion
of her virtue, and made it believed that the King, privy to
their secret, had exacted a promise of their not divulging
it. By degrees her situation became still less problematic;
and both the Duke and she affectedly took all occasions
of intimating it by a formal declaration. At first she had
houses, or lodgings, in the palaces nearest to his residence;
and the latter were furnished from the royal wardrobe
without limitation. She changed her liveries to a compound of the royal—was covered with jewels—the Duke's
gentlemen and equerries handed her to her chair in public
—his equipages were despatched for her—his sister, the
Queen of Denmark, sent her presents by him, and she
quitted all assemblies at nine at night, saying, 'You know
I must go.' At St. Leonard's Hill, in Windsor Forest,
near his own lodge at Cranbourn, he built her a palace,

and lay there every night : his picture and Lord Waldegrave's she showed in her bedchamber.   These were not
the symptoms of a dissoluble connection !   Once they
both seemed, in 1766, to be impatient of ascertaining her
rank.   She had obtained lodgings in the most inner court
of the palace at Hampton, and demanded permission of
Lord Hertford, Lord Chamberlain, for her coach to drive
into it, an honour peculiar to the royal family.   He, feeling
the delicacy of the proposal, which would have amounted
to a declaration, unless a like permission had been
indulged to other countesses residing there, delayed
mentioning it to the King, to whom he knew the request
would be unwelcome.   Lady Waldegrave sent to the
Chamberlain's office to know if it was granted.   Lord
Hertford then was obliged to speak.   The King peremptorily refused, saying, he would not break through old
orders.   Afraid of shocking her, Lord Hertford begged I
would acquaint Lady Waldegrave.   I flatly refused to
meddle in the business.   In the meantime the Dukes of
Gloucester and Cumberland went to Hampton Court.
The former asked Ely, of the Chamberlain's office, if the
request was granted ; and being told Lord Hertford was
to ask it of his Majesty, the Duke, losing his usual temper,
said passionately, 'Lord Hertford might have done it
without speaking to the King (which would have been
rash indeed !)—but that not only Lady Waldegrave's
coach should drive in, but that she herself should go up
the Queen's staircase.'   This being reported to Lord
Hertford, he again pressed me to interpose ; but I again
refused : but, lest the Duke should resent it, I advised
him to write to my niece : but she threw up her lodgings,
when she could not carry the point she had aimed at.
She obtained, however, about a year after, a sort of
equivocal acknowledgment of what she was.   The Duke
of Gloucester gave a ball to the King and Queen, to which
nobody, without exception, but certain of their servants
and their husbands, and wives, and children, were admitted : yet Lady Waldegrave and her eldest daughter

appeared there.   She could have no pretension to be
present, being attached by no post to either King or
Queen ; and it spoke itself, that the Duke could not have
proposed to introduce his mistress[1] to an entertainment
dedicated to the Queen.   The Princess Dowager (and she
was then believed to be the principal obstacle to the
publicity of the marriage) alone treated Lady Waldegrave
with coldness[2] — another presumption of their being
married.   His declining health often carried the Duke
abroad.   The Great Duke, with whom he contracted a
friendship, told Lady Hamilton, wife of our Minister at
Naples, that the Duke had owned his marriage to him.
It was this union that was censured in the *North Briton*,
as threatening a revival of the feuds of the two roses, by a
Prince of the blood marrying a subject.

[1] The King and Queen certainly intended it should be supposed Lady
Waldegrave was the Duke's mistress.   The world interpreted it in a contrary
sense in compliment to the Queen's virtue, who on that occasion wished her
virtue had been thought more accommodating.

[2] Walpole is mistaken here.   The King was at least as much opposed to
the Duke of Gloucester's marriage as the Princess Dowager.   As late as in
1775 his sentiments remained unaltered, and in granting the Duke permission
to travel on the Continent, he positively declined to make a provision for his
Royal Highness's family.   In a letter to Lord North, 16th January 1775, the
King says—'I cannot deny that on the subject of the Duke of Gloucester my
heart is wounded.   I have ever loved him more with the fondness one bears
to a child than to a brother.'   'A highly disgraceful step,' etc., —'his wife,
whom I can never think of placing in a situation to answer her extreme pride
and vanity. . . . Should any accident happen to the Duke, I shall certainly
take care of his children.'—(*Correspondence of George III. with Lord North*,
1867, vol. i. p. 222.)

Eventually the King acted with great generosity towards the Duchess and
her son and daughter by the Duke.   Their conduct was so irreproachable that
the marriage could no longer have been a subject of regret to him.—L. M.

END OF VOL. III.

Crown 3, 11
Politics 11, 13, 14, 27

Ideology p12 of Jesuits 24
13 expulsion 8

Party 16

Catk 35

Church 34

biblio 6